Apostle
to the Wilderness

Apostle to the Wilderness

Bishop John Medley and the Evolution of the Anglican Church

Barry L. Craig

Madison • Teaneck
Fairleigh Dickinson University Press

Associated University Presses
2010 Eastpark Boulevard
Cranbury, NJ 08512

The paper used in this publication meets the requirements of the American National Standard for Permanence of Paper for Printed Library Materials Z39.48-1984.

Library of Congress Cataloging-in-Publication Data

Craig, Barry L., 1960–
Apostle to the wilderness : Bishop John Medley and the evolution of the Anglican Church / Barry L. Craig.
p. cm.
Includes bibliographical references and index.
ISBN 0-8386-4085-0 (alk. paper)
1. Medley, John, 1804–1892. 2. Church of England—Canada—Bishops—Biography. 3. Anglican Communion—Canada—Bishops—Biography. I. Title.
BX5620.M4C73 2005
283′.092—dc22 2005010165

PRINTED IN THE UNITED STATES OF AMERICA

to
Hazen and Eileen Craig

Contents

Preface

BISHOP JOHN MEDLEY WAS A PIVOTAL FIGURE IN VICTORIAN CANADIAN church and society, especially in eastern Canada. Unlike many English bishops, Medley's subsequent fame is incommensurate with his importance and accomplishments. His own diocese, of which Medley was the founding bishop, has never undertaken to collect his papers, books, or other relevant material. Despite his leading role in the development of a pluralistic Canadian society, there is no scholarly biographical treatment of Medley's life and thought. Although he was the most theologically significant thinker ever to wear a mitre in the Canadian Anglican Church, Medley has received next to no attention from that institution.

Recent historiographical developments in the study of the Church of England have caused us to reconsider much of the ecclesiastical history of the nineteenth century. The great events and movements of that century largely created the modern Anglican Communion. While the nineteenth-century church in England has received close examination and has been immeasurably illuminated by these recent studies, the Church of England, outside of Great Britain, has been largely ignored. Given that the overwhelming majority of modern Anglicans live outside Great Britain, this neglect is significant.

This book aims to address the two deficiencies identified above. First, the life of a prominent, yet overlooked Victorian churchman will be studied. By closely studying John Medley's writings and his role as bishop, I will reveal, as clearly as possible, his intellectual development and the character of his theology. I will argue that Medley was important in his own right and also as a lens through which to gain a better understanding of one aspect of the Victorian Church. This latter goal will hopefully open the door to redressing the comparative neglect under which the Victorian colonial church has languished in contemporary scholarship. In addition, I have intended to apply some of the revisionist conclusions reached by scholars such as Peter Nockles, Nigel Yates, Frances Knight, and Arthur Burns toward a rethinking of the nineteenth-century church in eastern Canada.

The idea for this research was suggested to me by the Reverend

Doctor David Mercer, who subsequently assisted me in countless ways. I would also like to acknowledge my thesis adviser at the University of Wales, Lampeter, Dr. Frances Knight. This book developed from my doctoral dissertation and Dr. Knight was invaluable from beginning to end, offering insights, pointing out errors, and encouraging me to improve the work. It is consequently a far better work than it would have been, as a result of her time, attention, and insight. As external examiners of the dissertation, Dr. Sheridan Gilley and Dr. Nigel Yates offered many helpful suggestions and valid criticisms that sharpened my focus.

I have been helped by the comments and suggestions of many other scholars and friends. Among them, I thank: Dr. David Bell, Dr. William Christian, Fr. Lawrence Crumb, Dr. Peter Erb, Dr. Gregg Finley, the Venerable Lyman Harding, the Reverend Doctor Ross Hebb, the Reverend Doctor Ranall Ingalls, Mr. Harvey Malmberg, Dr. Peter Nockles, the Right Reverend Geoffrey Rowell, and Mr. Eric Swannick.

I have also been assisted by the staff of various institutions including the Provincial Archives of New Brunswick (especially Ms. Twila Buttimer), Pusey House (especially Fr. William Davage, Fr. Phillip Ursell, and Fr. Peter MacNab), Rhodes House (especially Ms. Lisa Farelly), the Bodleian Library, Lambeth Palace Library, the British Library, the National Archives of Canada, the Harriett Irving Library at UNB, the University of King's College Library (especially Ms. Patricia Chalmers), the Atlantic School of Theology library (especially Mr. Michael Bramah) and the archives of the Anglican Church of Canada. I must offer particular thanks to my colleagues at St. Thomas University in Fredericton who have encouraged me, offered suggestions and direction, and helped to minimize errors in the text, especially Dr. Christine Cornell and Dr. Patrick Malcolmson. For assistance in preparing the final manuscript I am indebted to Ms. Debbie Hudson, Mr. Ted Jones, Ms. Mary Craig and Mr. Stuart Forestell. I would also like to thank Ms. Christine Retz and the staff of Associated University Presses for their guidance and patience.

Finally, this book would simply never have seen the light of day without the encouragement, support, and love of Sara, Patrick, Mary, and Catherine.

Abbreviations

Bodleian Library	BodL
British Library	BL
Lambeth Palace Library	LPL
National Archives of Canada	NAC
Provincial Archives of New Brunswick	PANB
Pusey House Archives	PH
Rhodes House	RH
University of King's College	UKC
Canadian Journal of Theology	*CJT*
Dictionary of National Biography	*DNB*
Journal of the Canadian Church Historical Society	*JCCHS*
Oxford Dictionary of the Christian Church	*ODCC*
United Society for the Propagation of the Gospel	SPG

Apostle
to the Wilderness

The Most Reverend John Medley, First Bishop of Fredericton and Metropolitan of Canada. (This picture is published with the permission of the Dean and Chapter of Christ Church Cathedral.)

Introduction

WRITING IN THE LATE NINETEENTH CENTURY, TOM MOZLEY GLOWingly described the Oxford of his youth. The towering figures that he had rubbed shoulders with there were eulogized in generous terms:

> There can seldom have occurred in the history of the world such an example of many men of high qualities and considerable promise bringing their respective powers and opportunities to a religious cause, not clearly defined and offering no earthly inducement whatever. . . . All were to retrace their steps to an age of which they knew nothing, except that it was in every respect the very contrary of that we live in. As far as any hope of comfort, luxury or splendour was concerned, it was march to the North Pole, the Equator, or nowhere at all. That a dozen men with golden futures should abandon them for such an enterprise would be something; but hundreds did so, and if I name a few, many of my readers could easily double or quadruple the list.[1]

Mozley, brother-in-law of John Henry Newman, thus characterized this rare generation who appeared together on the nineteenth-century English ecclesiastical scene. He went on to list what he took to be the best and the brightest of these "men with golden futures": Copeland, Williams, the Wilberforces, Oakeley, and Ward, all of whom later became famous or notorious. Included among them was "(John) Medley," first bishop of Fredericton.[2] With his characteristic inaccuracy,[3] Mozley translated Medley from Fredericton to Newfoundland, but his point was valid. John Medley was considered by his peers as a notable figure during a significant period of church reform.

Allowing for some hyperbole on Mozley's part, this was nevertheless a remarkable period in the English Church. The universities were at the zenith of their power in church and society. Ecclesiastical scholarship was at a height not seen since the seventeenth-century Caroline period, if then. Leaders of notable charisma arose, both clerical and lay. At the center of all of this was that movement of reform, renewal, and controversy that arose at Oxford University.

As arguably the most influential development within the Church of England since the Reformation, the Oxford Movement has been the focus of a mountain of scholarship over the past century and a half. The revival of primitive and medieval sacramental forms, renewed emphasis on the historic episcopate, and an insistence on the independence of the church from the state were all prominent positions advocated by the movement, and each, among other theological assertions, became subject for spirited and sometimes divisive debate in the Victorian Church.

The members of this movement, often referred to as the Tractarians (named after the series of controversial tracts on theological subjects that they authored) have been similarly the objects of much critical attention.[4] Much study has been devoted to the Tractarian understanding of episcopacy and authority in general. John Medley, the first bishop who was closely associated with the Tractarians, has not received a serious theological examination to this date. Medley was no grey ecclesiastical bureaucrat. Instead, he was a Victorian "Renaissance man." Diocesan bishop for nearly half a century, he was also an amateur architect and patron of the Gothic Revival movement, a composer of hymns, anthems, and other choral music, a translator of the church fathers, a translator of Scripture, and a liturgist.

Historiography

Although there are a number of secondary works on Medley, mostly of short length or narrow focus, Medley has not received a great deal of critical study in the century since his death. To date, there has been only one complete biographical study of his life, and that was produced over a century ago. The *Life of Medley,*[5] by his protégé and friend, the Reverend William Q. Ketchum, was written in the spirit of nineteenth-century hagiography. It lacks critical distance from its subject and fails to recognize Medley's early connections to the leaders of the Oxford Movement.[6] If one is familiar with the controversies of the period and those of Medley's own diocese, one is able to infer something about Medley's involvement in those various disputes from reading Ketchum's biography. There is little direct material that would enlighten us concerning Medley's position on many of the great theological, liturgical, and political questions that swirled around him throughout his long life.

Two decades after Ketchum's biography a shorter account of Medley's life was written by W. O. Raymond. This essay was included in Bertal Heeney's *Leaders of the Canadian Church.*[7] This revealed little new material about Medley, save for a few amusing anecdotes. For the most part it relied on the earlier published biography. In addition to these biographical works, background color about Medley and the Fredericton of his day has been provided by the letters of Juliana Ewing.[8]

The study of Bishop Medley then lay more or less dormant for more than forty years until it was reinvigorated by Eugene Fairweather. Professor Fairweather, who had earlier published what was to become a standard collection of Tractarian texts,[9] wrote a series of three articles for the *Canadian Journal of Theology* that brought to the forefront again some of Medley's stature in, and contributions to, the Victorian Church.[10] The first of these articles established John Medley's image for the succeeding generations of scholars. Entitled "A Tractarian Patriarch: John Medley of Fredericton," it sought to remedy the relative lack of scholarly interest in the man whom Fairweather called "the first Tractarian bishop."[11] Although George Selwyn of New Zealand (1841) and Edward Feild of Newfoundland (1844) were consecrated prior to Medley, Fairweather rightly argued that neither of these estimable figures was as closely connected personally with the Tractarians.[12] So closely did Fairweather identify Medley with the Tractarian movement that he was able to say, "When Medley speaks on moral issues we might as well be listening to Pusey or Newman or Keble."[13] Fairweather went on to outline the substantial character of Medley's place in relation to the Tractarian movement. In two subsequent articles, Fairweather demonstrated, respectively, the connection between Medley and Gladstone, and Medley's courage in defense of the persecuted Ritualists.[14]

One would have wished that Fairweather's valuable contributions had opened the floodgates for a torrent of Medley scholarship, but sadly, that was not the case. Lyman Harding prepared a paper for the annual meeting of the Canadian Church Historical Society in 1966 that was subsequently published.[15] Harding distilled the biography of Ketchum and offered further analysis of Medley's life in the light of Fairweather's work and numerous recent historical studies of the Victorian period and its great figures. In the same year, D. S. Richardson completed a thesis at Yale University on the architectural significance of Christ Church Cathedral, Medley's greatest monument.[16] In the mid-1970s Christopher Headon completed a doctoral dissertation for McGill University entitled "The Influence of the Oxford Movement Upon the Church of England in Eastern and Central Canada, 1840–1900."[17] This work and subsequent articles by Headon[18] further argued for Medley's place in relation to the Tractarian movement of the nineteenth cenury. In 1983 and 1984 brief histories were locally produced on Christ Church Cathedral and Christ Chuch Parish Church, Fredericton, which cast light on Medley's contribution to local church architecture.[19] The former of these two works, by Robert Watson, was later illustrated and published in a small booklet.[20] In addition to studies of architecture, which thus involved study of Bishop Medley, there had also been some attention paid to Medley's musical interests. Notably, a thesis by Tim Cooper demonstrated the extent of Medley's contribution to church music.[21] There have also been some less extensive studies touching on Medley's musical contributions.[22]

At the end of the 1980s Medley was again given prominence in a substantial scholarly treatment. Gregg Finley's doctoral dissertation, "New Brunswick's Gothic Revival: John Medley and the Aesthetics of Anglican Worship,"[23] focused on Medley's relation to that great phenomenon that was the Gothic Revival in art and architecture. Finley's subsequent book, *On Earth as it is in Heaven,* illustrated by Lynn Wigginton, brought Medley into the consciousness of many ordinary Canadian readers.[24] In addition, Finley has written three articles further exploring Medley's contribution to architecture.[25] Medley has also been briefly covered in several general church histories.[26] But the secondary literature on Medley, including books, theses, and articles still only adds up to about two dozen titles.

In comparison to many of his peers John Medley has thus received comparatively little scholarly attention.[27] Yet, Medley was a well-connected man. He came from a family of some means, studied at Oxford, and later made acquaintance with many of the young men who would be star players on the Victorian ecclesiastical and political stages. For example, he was on close personal terms with Edward Bouverie Pusey, one of the three great figures of the Oxford Movement.[28] They counseled one another in their respective griefs as they both endured tragedies in their personal lives. John Keble, the second of the triumvirate, was also counted as a close friend of Medley's.[29] Finally, John Henry Newman, that figure who towered over the Church of England even long after he had seceded to Rome, was also acquainted with Medley, although less intimately than were Pusey and Keble.[30]

If Medley knew only these three men, that would surely be enough to ensure his worthiness as an object of historical inquiry. But Medley was also associated with a host of greater and lesser figures in the Victorian Church, either because of his acquaintance with them at Oxford[31] through his incumbencies in Exeter,[32] or though his subsequent career as bishop of Fredericton.[33] Outside of directly ecclesiastical circles Medley was more than a mere acquaintance of the great Victorian reformer and later prime minister W. E. Gladstone.[34] Medley, who had received Gladstone's support in his early years, had in turn supported Gladstone in some of his political travails, and when in England was a guest of the prime minister at his home. Even here Medley encountered a colorful cast of Victorian celebrities that included John Ruskin, the tremendously influential art critic and writer.[35]

There was more to Medley's stature than who he knew. He was also respected for *what* he knew. Gladstone was said to have remarked that no wiser head wore a miter in all the English Church.[36] Medley was a respected scholar in his own right. Before becoming bishop and accepting all the consequences that the necessary demands of that office had on his literary work, Medley had shown considerable academic promise. He had published a substantial essay on the apostolic succession,[37] sufficiently well argued that Keble planned to edit and present it as one of the *Tracts for the Times.*[38] In addition, he was also part of another great Tractarian scholarly enterprise, *The Library of the Fathers,* and was considered, before his elevation to the episcopate, for the editorship of part of the *Library of Anglo-Catholic Theology.*[39] He had also published an article on what was to become a great passion of his, church architecture.[40] Medley founded and was a member of the influential Exeter Diocesan Architectural Society[41] and was also connected with the more widely known Cambridge Camden Society (later the Ecclesiological Society).[42] Well read on architecture and other ecclesiological matters, he was well known in those circles that had as their aim the restoration of Gothic forms in church architecture. He had written a widely read small book on *The Advantages of Open Seats,* an important practical topic for many ecclesiologists and Tractarians.[43] He was also a celebrated preacher,[44] having published many of his sermons at the behest of various congregations.[45] Finally, he was a composer of choral tunes and texts.

By the time that Medley returned to England as an old man for the Lambeth conferences in 1878 and 1888 he was generally venerated for his wisdom and devotion.[46] Great missionary, teacher, builder, preacher—all of these were labels that could be applied to Medley without dispute. Yet somehow his fame was not all that it could have been. After his death Mr. Justice Coleridge speculated that it was Medley's single-minded dedication to his diocese that prevented him from gaining greater honor. Perhaps if Medley had returned to England, following the example of Selwyn and other colonial bishops, he would have achieved greater fame.[47] But early on in his episcopate Medley had made it clear that he intended to stay by his post as long as God directed.

So, for a life that touched so many of the great events and figures of a very turbulent era, one incomplete biography and a handful of short articles does not seem to be very satisfying. If that were all we knew of John Medley, we would be missing a great deal. It is in the light of this relative paucity of scholarly examination of John Medley that this present work is conceived. There has not as yet been any detailed treatment of Medley's theological thought. To be sure, his theology was a prominent part of Fairweather's treatment in his "Tractarian Patriarch" article, as well as being briefly sketched in Headon's thesis. Medley's general theological outlook is broadly described by Finley. Yet no one has, to this point, produced a thorough examination of Medley's theology.

At first sight one is tempted to simply say, "He was a Tractarian and so presumably held those views promoted by the Oxford Movement." But there is a problem with this generally accepted categorization. While accurate to a degree, there was in Medley what one can see as an inconsistency, but perhaps this was actually a subtlety, which makes such easy categorization problematic. Medley certainly held positions that were classic examples of Tractarian teaching. Yet, he also communicated other ideas that at least some of his Tractarian brethren would have sharply repudiated.

Medley's own position is related to a much larger question about that philosophical revolution, of which the Oxford Movement was one small consequence. The great eighteenth-century movement that we call the Enlightenment and the various reactions to it, of which the Romantic movement was the most widely known, are central to our understanding of the theological position of the Tractarians and Bishop Medley.[48] This work intends, in part, to address Medley's place in the philosophical and theological context of the era.

Our view of Medley must also be reappraised in the light of Peter Nockles's magisterial work *The Oxford Movement in Context*,[49] which has forced us to reassess many notions about the place of the Tractarians and their relation to the wider church. Nockles successfully rehabilitates our image of the older High Church tradition. While the Tractarians tended to denigrate the earlier High Churchmen as "high and dry," Nockles has exposed the error in this assessment. In light of this recent work, there is some argument to be made whether or not Medley was "a Tractarian Patriarch" at all. Perhaps he was part of that more conservative (and in some ways more authentically Anglican) tradition that is called High Church.

To understand Medley then, we must first understand him in his proper intellectual context. This involves a consideration of his relationship to Tractarianism and Romanticism. It has been suggested that the Tractarians were in some measure irrational or antirational.[50] This is to be understood as part of the overall Romantic reaction to the rationalism associated with the Enlightenment. E. B. Pusey, one of the founders of the Oxford Movement, was quite clear in his condemnation of rationalism.[51] J. H. Newman and other Tractarians were equally critical of the limits of reason in religious matters.[52] Was the return to nature, feeling, emotion, symbol, and art that we find in the Oxford Movement an expression of a balanced response to the Enlightenment? Or was it just as limited in its emphasis, only in the opposite direction?[53]

Secondary to this question is the question of the degree of Medley's sympathy for Romanticism and other aspects of anti-Enlightenment thought. Finley has argued persuasively for Medley's connection to the Romantic movement.[54] The entire Gothic Revival program is quite clearly an expression of Romanticism.[55] Here again in Medley we encounter a certain ambiguity that resists pigeonholing. Medley's personal austerity, like that of Pusey, set him apart from the more florid expressions of Tractarian piety and aesthetic thought. Although there are scarcely any direct philosophical references in Medley's writings, his position toward reason is not simply antithetical. In fact, he often appears as a defender of reason against excessive feeling on the one hand, and abstract authority on the other. Similarities and differences between Medley and what might be taken to be normative Tractarian positions are revealed when we consider the following particular areas: the place of reason, architecture, the sacraments, and the relations of church and state.

The Place of Reason

We continue to wish for the discovery of a lost cache of Medley letters dealing with a host of topics, such as the relation of reason to revelation. Barring that happy circumstance, we are left with a more difficult task. We must construct his position based upon references scattered throughout his sermons and other published works. From these sources, it is clear that Medley was far from a simple antirationalist. However, he was no philosopher. Not many of the first generation of the Oxford Movement showed much interest in philosophy, apart from Newman. Even with Newman, his interest in philosophy was chiefly to show the limitations of Enlightenment rationalism.[56]

Medley spoke several times of the virtue of reason and the danger of simple abandonment to feeling. But he also safeguarded the prerogatives of revelation and deprecated the form of investigation that was commonly called "rationalism." What rationalism meant to the Tractarians is a central question. It certainly included all forms of scientific and metaphysical speculation that disregarded the claims of faith. It also included the work of those religious thinkers who did not readily accept the supernatural element in Christianity. From Pusey's early writings on German rationalism, we know that, in his opinion, the "rationalists" included many of the leading Lutheran theologians of the day.

Medley the Architect

Medley's architectural interests have received a relatively large degree of scholarly attention, as we have seen, and we need not till again already cultivated ground. Some consideration of the place of Medley's architectural interests in the context of his wider theological understanding is of value. For example, an examination of aspects of Medley's ideas on church architecture provides elements of a more complete description of his place within the Victorian theological spectrum. We are also able to see if Medley's architectural and aesthetic views are part of a coherent personal theological position. Given the importance that he placed on church building throughout his episcopate, it would be impossible to avoid his architectural interests in any comprehensive account of his intellectual position.

The Sacraments

At first glance, Medley's sacramental theology appears to represent Tractarian thought. However, his greater sympathy for the Reformation set him apart from most of the leading Tractarians. In regard to the Reformation, Medley exhibited the same critical stance as his Tractarian colleagues. Cranmer and the other great reformers were not without fault in his estimation. The continental reformers, especially Calvin, met with the full force of Medley's scorn. All of this was in keeping with that Tractarian position that found moderate expression in Medley and Keble and more extreme voice in Newman and Froude.[57] Because the Tractarians saw the Church of England as being of apostolic foundation, the Reformation was not central to its history. Important as it was, it did as much harm as good.

Here Medley departed from the normative Tractarian view. His appreciation of the English Reformation was greater than that generally associated with his colleagues. For Medley, the Book of Common Prayer was absolute, as it was for most Tractarians in the early days of the movement. Medley went so far as to say that the Prayer Book and the Bible were the only two books to which he could subscribe to every phrase without reservation.[58] While we ought not to confuse the Tractarians with the later Ritualists, it is clear that some of the Tractarians, if not most, sought a form of liturgy that was "more ancient" than that of the Book of Common Prayer.[59] Medley never supported this position. Although he could defend the Ritualists in his old age,[60] he never supported Prayer Book revision. The richer expressions of revived ceremonial were never part of Medley's own churchmanship.

Governing Medley's sacramental theology was his sense that the natural world could be a vehicle for divine grace. As in architecture and music, in the sacraments human beings were able to participate in making God present to the world. The outward forms of religion were thus more than mere accidents. They were solemn receptacles for the divine. There is throughout Medley's work an attempt to balance the natural world on the one hand and the divine order on the other. His sacramental theology is a clear example of this effort.

Church and State

Another lens through which to view Medley's understanding of the relationship between the natural and the divine is his position on the relationship of the church to the state. For him, the church was a divine society, not of human invention. While he abhorred the Erastianism with which the older High Church party was often charged, he came to his explicit support of disestablishment by stages.[61] Initially, it was grounded upon quite pragmatic reasons. If the colonial church received virtually no real benefit from the Crown, why continue the pretense of calling it an "established church?" It was dishonest and led both Churchmen and Dissenters to suppose that Anglicans received more favours than they in fact did. This mere observation of the reality of the colonial situation gave way to a more strident call for separation of church and state both in England and Canada as the years of his episcopate passed. We can find the roots of his liberal position with regard to establishment in the first work that he ever published, on the apostolic succession. Here he articulated a view of the church as a sacred and spiritual body—the Body of Christ—over which no civil authority could be considered as true head. While this was a standard Tractarian view, Medley went on to develop a more positive account of the church in society than was held by Keble, for example. Medley was no republican; he spoke fondly of the Queen. But, he was also clear that the Episcopal Church in the breakaway United States of America was as much the spiritual heir of the early church as was the Church of England itself. Medley would go so far as to see the American Church as enjoying advantages over the mother church.[62]

The Complexities of Medley's Thought

John Medley was intimately connected with both the Oxford and Gothic Revival movements, and is associated with the Ritualists. Part of the task of this work will be to separate these and other strands in Medley's thought and practice. It may be the case that Medley was an atypical representative of Tractarianism and the Gothic Revival. On the other hand, it may be that we need to expand our understanding of the intellectual territory occupied by those movements' respective adherents.

I intend to demonstrate the core of Medley's theological position. His published works, as well as those other records available to us, allow us to form a fairly clear picture of his views on several important matters. As relatively little biographical material is available, we must proceed to form our judgments based upon his opinions, taken at face value in most cases. We will assume that the works that we do have, taken together and carefully studied, provide an accurate picture of his views on the matters that they explicitly address.

There are several themes to which Medley repeatedly returned in sermons, charges, and other writings over the years. Among them were the place of human reason and its relation to revelation and tradition, the sacramental life of the Christian, and the relation of the church to the state and other secular institutions. It will be argued that these disparate themes are related and that Medley's theological thought has a certain unity. This unity is not entirely a tidy one. In fact, part of the interest in studying Medley is the extent to which his thought fails to conform neatly to established party or other ecclesiastical norms. In particular, we will see that his relationship to Tractarianism was far from simple.

Medley's Tractarianism was not as simple as it has always been portrayed. His theology was also more dynamic than has been previously recognized. There was a consistent core to his thought that remained despite the many adaptations of his earlier positions. His rigorous avoidance of party politics and labels pointed to a vision of the church that he believed could transcend the particular doctrinal, ecclesiological, and liturgical struggles of the nineteenth century.

Sources

Those who have studied Medley and have sought to write on him have all encountered the same initial obstacle. Most of Medley's personal letters have been lost. How this happened is unknown. But Gregg Finley, Lyman Harding, and the *Dictionary of Canadian Biography* all repeat the story that Mrs. Medley destroyed his papers, letters and all, presumably to prevent his successor, H. T. Kingdon, from having access to them. This notion presumably arose from the fact of the well-known antipathy between Margaret Medley and Kingdon.[63] This appears not to have been the case. Archival research indicates that far from wanting her husband's papers shielded from public scrutiny, Margaret Medley desired to have them used by scholars.[64] In fact, she was critical of Ketchum's biography, precisely because it failed to make use of those letters and documents that would have further illuminated, for example, Medley's participation in the Oxford Movement.[65] There is some evidence to indicate that the letters and papers may have passed to Medley's son, Edward.[66] However, research has so far failed to uncover them.[67]

It is consequently necessary to locate letters that Medley wrote by guessing who his correspondents may have been, then hoping that the letters have survived. Thus far, a few dozen of Medley's letters have been unearthed, beyond the half dozen that have been previously published. We have, therefore, a small portion of Medley's private correspondence, his published books and articles, a number of his sermons and his charges to the diocesan clergy made at three-year intervals throughout his episcopate. There are also records of his appearances at successive Lambeth Conferences and a full and extensive series of reports and miscellaneous letters to the SPG. Finally, we have the *Annals of the Diocese of Fredericton,* a handwritten journal, detailing Medley's day-to-day activities as bishop. In comparison with the collected works of some other Victorian notables there is not a vast amount available to us. Nevertheless, what we do have is enough to reconstruct John Medley's position on several crucial theological points.

1

Medley's Life—The Early Years

MOST BIOGRAPHICAL INFORMATION ON JOHN MEDLEY IS DEPENDENT upon W. Q. Ketchum's earnest, but often sketchy and occasionally inaccurate biography. Ketchum's work is particularly lamentable for the dearth of information on Medley's childhood, education, early friendships, experiences at Oxford, and generally all that pertains to his life prior to his consecration as bishop of Fredericton. It also fails to record the nature of Medley's continued relations with friends in England following his arrival in Canada. There is no mention of continued correspondence with Pusey, Keble, Williams, Liddon, Church, Coleridge, or any of the host of other important associations that we know he had.[1] Finally, Ketchum's work sheds little light on those controversies that dogged Medley's reform efforts in his new diocese. There are elliptical references to minor opposition, but little to suggest the turbulence caused by the arrival of this bishop, suspected of being a "Puseyite," in a profoundly Low Church province. Given Ketchum's long personal association with Medley and Mrs. Medley's cooperation with the project, the defects in his biography are even more regrettable. In the absence of sufficient primary documents, most subsequent work on Medley has relied on this flawed record to construct a scholarly picture of his life.

Before beginning an analysis of Medley's theology it is necessary to draw a picture of Medley the man. Beyond Ketchum, there are other sources that allow us to form a more adequate, if still incomplete, picture of his life. The outlines of Medley's life are briefly given here to enable the reader to understand better the specific areas of his thought that will be examined below.

EARLY YEARS

John Medley was born on December 19, 1804. His baptismal certificate records his parents as George and Henrietta Medley.[2] He was baptized at St. George's, Hanover Square, London. This church, at which George Frederick Handel used to worship, was a spiritual home for a virtual who's who of notable eighteenth- and nineteenth-century Englishmen. Its wardens included such names as Shaftesbury and, interestingly in light of Medley's future connections, the Honorable Phillip Pusey, father of E. B. Pusey.[3] Medley's parents' address was given by Ketchum as Grosvenor Place, London.[4] This too is an interesting coincidence, inasmuch as the Pusey family's London home was at 35 Grosvenor Square.[5] His father, evidently a man of some means, judging from their address and Medley's later liberality, died when John was a child. His mother Henrietta, whose family background is not known to us, raised him alone, with the specific notion of training him for the ministry.[6] He began to memorize the Psalter from the age of four. He began the study of Latin at age six, Greek at age ten, and Hebrew at twelve. He had private tutors and then was educated first at "Rev J. Sawyer's school," followed by "school in Bristol, Bewdley and Chobham."[7] About the age of fourteen, he sent his mother a sermon he had composed, with the hope that in years to come he would be delivering real sermons.[8]

Little else is known about Medley's family circumstances. However, many years later he was to suggest that his upbringing had been in an Evangelical household. In a letter to the lieutenant governor of New Brunswick in 1860, Medley referred to the Bible Society.[9] He wrote that he "was brought up (as one may say) to the Bible Society, but, with others, was led to see [the errors of that position]."[10] The Bible Society to which Medley referred was the British and Foreign Bible Society. In New Brunswick, as elsewhere, it represented the Evangelical party within the Church of England as well as Dissenters without.[11] The particular position to which Medley objected in the letter was the Bible Society's practice of distributing the Scriptures apart from the Book of Common Prayer. To circulate the Scriptures "without Church Teaching" was not warranted by the New Testament itself, in Medley's view.[12]

At nineteen he entered Oxford, becoming a student at Wadham College. This was a college notable for its Evangelical leanings.[13] It had also been the college of Christopher Wren, whose architectural interest, if not his taste, Medley later shared.[14] Medley graduated with honors in 1826.[15] Among his examiners at Oxford was C. T. Longley, later Archbishop of Canterbury.[16] Medley received his master's degree in 1830.[17]

We know that Medley was taught by Charles Lloyd, among others.[18] Lloyd's influence on individual Tractarians has been well documented.[19] A High Churchman, Lloyd's students included Newman,

Froude, and Pusey.[20] We do not have a record of the event or process by which Medley made the transition from "Bible Society" Evangelical to High Churchman, but his attendance at Lloyd's lectures was surely a landmark along the way.[21]

During Medley's time at Wadham, Newman and Isaac Williams were students at Trinity, Pusey a student at Christ Church, and Hurrell Froude at Oriel. All of them were within four years of the same age. At the same time, Keble was a tutor, while J. T. Coleridge had just left Oxford. W. E. Gladstone and Charles Marriott would follow a few years later. In later years Medley maintained close friendships with most of these men. It appears that he met many of them only after they had left Oxford. Part of this may be due to Medley belonging to Wadham, while most of the Tractarians were at Trinity, Oriel, or Christ Church. It may also be the case that Medley, still an Evangelical, had not yet embraced the peculiar ethos that was to animate the other members of the Oxford Movement.

In a letter to Pusey dated May 1841 Medley spoke of his wife's recent death and mentioned that the first manifestation of her illness occurred when Pusey "first came down to Salterton" and that this was their "first meeting."[22] By this account Pusey and Medley met, not at Oxford, but many years later. Yet it was some time prior to 1841, since Pusey wrote to Newman in 1839 that he had been down to Exeter to preach for Medley.[23] Newman was not introduced to Medley until December 14, 1839.[24] Keble and Medley evidently did not meet until at least 1835. Keble wrote to Newman in January of that year: "G. Cornish writes me word that his friend and curate Medley has been converting a whole host of Clerical unbelievers to the doctrine of the Apostolical Succession . . . they desired him to put it in a Tract: which he is doing, and I am to revise the same."[25] This seems to imply that Keble did not as yet have a personal relationship with Medley although, as with Pusey and Newman, this was to change later.

The "Cornish" to whom Keble referred was George James Cornish, the vicar of Kenwyn, Cornwall.[26] He was born at Ottery St. Mary and was a close friend of J. T. Coleridge and John Keble.[27] Cornish was a poet, and Keble had included some of his verse in *The Christian Year.*[28] It was perhaps through his association with Cornish that Medley met those people who had a profound effect on the course of his life. Medley later collaborated with another member of the Cornish family, George Kestell Cornish, on his work for the *Library of the Fathers.*[29]

Medley was married in 1826 to Christiana Bacon, daughter of the sculptor, John Bacon Jr. The marriage was performed at Salcombe

Regis, Devon, where G. J. Cornish was curate.[30] This early marriage to a notable family supports the suggestion that Medley had significant private means. Medley was ordained deacon in 1828 and priest the following year. He began his ecclesiastical career serving as curate at Southleigh, Truro for three years and then as incumbent of St. John's, Truro from 1831 to 1838. At this time Truro was part of the Archdeaconry of Cornwall, still in the diocese of Exeter. It was during this latter period that Medley was described by Keble as Cornish's curate. In 1838, Medley was appointed vicar of St. Thomas's, Exeter.

During his time at Exeter, Medley would have certainly been exposed to ample High Church influences. James Duke Coleridge, brother to J. T. Coleridge, was prebendary of Exeter and had been vicar of Kenwyn prior to Cornish.[31] The bishop was Henry Phillpotts, the High Church warhorse, who had been appointed in 1830. The influence of Phillpotts on the young Medley is difficult to assess. However, the parallels in their mature theological positions are too significant to dismiss its effect simply.[32]

While at St. Thomas's, Medley served as a prebend of Exeter Cathedral, although there is some confusion over the dates.[33] At this time he would have been in contact with S. S. Wesley, the cathedral organist, who influenced Medley's musical tastes in years to come.[34] During these years Medley acquired a reputation as an accomplished preacher. No less a judge than E. B. Pusey wrote to J. H. Newman, commending Medley in this regard.[35]

Fellow Partners in Affliction

It was with Pusey, of all the Tractarian leaders, that Medley had the closest relationship, according to the evidence we possess. This friendship between Medley and Pusey is revealed in a series of letters between them, of which we have only those ones written by Medley.[36] At the heart of their correspondence and relationship was an intimate sharing of the sorrow produced by their respective personal tragedies.

The first letter that we have is one written in 1840. Medley had written to Pusey asking for advice:

> I have to preach a Visitation Sermon for the Archdeacon and have chosen the subject of the Church fallen, i.e. the Church Catholic in her several branches by division and our own branch more particularly, in several points to be named, with some hopes of our rising again. What I want is some accurate information on the state of the Greek Russo, Greek Syrian and Abyssinian Churches, and I do not know precisely where to lay my

hand on it—Could you or Newman merely name the books where it is to be found? Or are there none?

I also want your advice on a scheme which I have projected whether wisely or otherwise time may show, for establishing a kind of Baptismal Temperance Society, avoiding the Manichaeism of it, and merely renewing the baptismal pledge: but connecting it also with a Friendly Society, the members of which should meet twice a year after going to Church, and enjoying any recreational amusement, as music etc. The rules are not drawn up, but I want to know if you see anything objectionable in the principle. I think we leave the poor too much to themselves and do not attempt to refine and Christianize their amusements.

At the time of this writing, Medley was evidently on cordial terms with Pusey (and perhaps Newman), while seemingly also in general agreement with the Tractarians' aims. The letter went on to raise a pastoral issue with Pusey about a woman who had become a Socinian.[37] In describing how he had dealt with this matter, Medley explained that the woman "wished to read anything I might put into her hands especially some parts of the Oxford tracts. I recommended parts of Vol. I." When this recommendation is combined with Medley's proposed subject for the visitation sermon on the "hopes of our rising again," it appears that Medley was comfortably in the Tractarian camp.

The next letter in the series, dated December 21, 1840, was of quite a different nature. These letters are worth noting inasmuch as they shed light both on the intimate friendship between Pusey and Medley and on that peculiarly Romantic form of melancholy that Pusey possessed in large measure and that Medley for a time shared. The occasion of the letter was the death of Medley's wife, Christiana. At this time Medley was curate of St. Thomas's, Exeter. Pusey's wife had died the previous year, a loss that had devastated him.[38] Medley wrote,

My dear Dr. Pusey,
The outside of this letter will convey to your mind what has happened. I do not say that your prayers have not been answered. Probably like mine they have and in the best way; but you know what a bitter trial it is to pass through. Yet I can see much very much merry indeed—one thing is, that she was spared that extreme suffering which usually falls to the lot of persons in her complaint and I can never thank our Heavenly father enough that her mind was truly "left in perfect peace." You might [have seen] enough of her to see how lowly and gentle a spirit she was and her tranquillity was extraordinary. On the Wednesday before her death she received the Holy Communion and repeated all the responses in a clear audible voice most correctly, with an expression of the most lowly reverence and yet unfeigned joy on her countenance. She was collected to the

> Lord and on Friday evening fell asleep without one sigh or struggle. Think of me and pray for me on Thursday evening next. One thing I must mention, my dear Dr. Pusey, which has after given me considerable pain . . . my foolish obtuseness—in asking you about that passage of S. Chrysostom in my study. It was, I am persuaded, intended to be an index to God's will respecting me but I was blind to it. I pray now to sanctify the trial and deliver me above all things from that horrid apathy and selfish worldliness which is worse than the deepest strokes and which one often sees afterwards—The children are thankfully in very good health. I am, my dear Dr. Pusey your fellow partner in affliction, J. Medley[39]

Unfortunately, we have no record of the particular circumstances by which Pusey and the Medleys first became acquainted, nor of the subsequent particulars of their relationship. Christiana Medley died on a Friday evening and Medley's letter to Pusey is dated just two days later. That Medley had taken the time to write to Pusey so soon after his wife's death perhaps indicates the closeness of their relationship.

The next letter that we have underlines Medley's continued struggle after his wife's death as well as Pusey's concern for his friend. Dated five months later, Medley was still locked in the deepest mourning. Pusey had evidently been one of those endeavoring to comfort him. "I have had many letters from kind friends but yours has, I think (though the saddest of all) given me the most solid comfort, and not least from our being yoked together in suffering. Life is, as you say, cut in two and there is nothing more to fix one's heart upon."[40] The sorrow experienced by Medley at this point was extreme in its effects as he recounted to Pusey, the "kind of horror" that overcame him upon first awakening each morning. He blamed himself for being too caught up in worldly affairs and attending too little to the interior life. This charge is little supported by what we know of Medley's rather earnest character and devout habits.[41] Like Pusey,[42] Medley saw his wife's illness as a "visitation" from God, one for which his own sins were at least partially the cause.[43] This "kind of horror" that Medley described remained with him long after his wife's death and corresponds to the intense grief experienced by Pusey the year before.[44] These two austere Christian men, closely involved in a significant and tightly focused theological movement, experienced parallel suffering within the span of little more than a year. It is perhaps little wonder that they should have been drawn together by their trials.[45]

Their correspondence continued through 1841. Medley sent Pusey a sermon[46] and added comments, further revealing his state of mind. He confessed that nothing in life any longer seemed to hold interest for him. By now, Medley had become concerned that his daughter, too, might be taken by death. His letters to Pusey are grief-filled, without any trace of relief.[47] Medley's pastoral responsibilities prevented him from the sort of withdrawal from society that was Pusey's response to grief. The intense sorrow conveyed by these letters would only deepen in the coming months.

A few weeks later Medley responded to a letter Pusey had evidently written, recommending a young man for one of the training schools that Medley oversaw. He began his letter with the bluntness that was to be his trademark, telling Pusey that "I scarcely think such a youth as you describe would suit our Training School, or yet would do him the good you could wish."[48] Medley was keenly interested in public education, both in England and later in New Brunswick. He had been appointed as an inspector by the Exeter Diocesan Board of Education and as a consequence had made a tour of the schools in the diocese.[49] Among the more notable recommendations in his reports was that greater emphasis should be placed on the teaching of music. He also advocated lessening the use of corporal punishment, and significantly, the introduction of literature beyond the Bible in National and Sunday Schools. We will see that he advocated the reading of a wide range of secular subjects to the clergy who would later be under his charge.

Having answered Pusey's question Medley returned to the subject that was ever on his mind. The letter goes on to describe the chapel of ease that he was building (with his own funds) in his parish as well as the monument to his wife that he was erecting in his own church. Christiana's father, the celebrated sculptor John Bacon, had produced the effigy himself.[50] Even here, while describing some work that ought to give him pleasure, Medley was wracked with guilt that he may be "giving honour to the creature which is due to the Creator,"

> [for] my heart tells me how much better I loved her than I confess I have as yet loved the only adorable object of our love. Submission must be our true happiness: yet when the bitter remembrance comes back day by day and hour by hour and when one has none to whom one can perfectly unloosen oneself it is difficult to be happy. . . . I discern much more on earth [that] even amidst the most brutal separations there is the consciousness of mutual love: the same hours of prayer and certain agreed upon thoughts and feelings, but what these feel or think of us who are out of the body is such a mystery that one is forced almost to look away from it. Do you understand the words of the revelation literally that "souls" or disembodied spirits make use of the medium of language? Whenever you have a few moments you cannot tell how much comfort a letter from you will give to your obliged and affectionate, John Medley.[51]

While he acknowledged the duty to "submit" to the divine will, Medley was so tormented by the "bitter remembrance" that this task was exceedingly difficult to discharge. For Medley his love for Christiana was greater than that for God—a remarkably intimate admission. His longing for his late wife prompted him to hope that there was some possibility of "spiritual" communication with the departed.

Pusey certainly responded with kindness to Medley's vulnerable state as another letter from Medley to Pusey three days later indicates. "I had just returned from a sad pilgrimage to the Church where I was married that day 14 years since when your kind note lay on my table. It was a great comfort to me, for I was half disposed to fear about publishing the sermon, but I have heard that it has been a comfort to one under similar sorrow to ours. . . . If we may but get to paradise we shall soon rejoice together and how great a joy that will be."[52] If anything, Medley's melancholy seemed to deepen with time. In January of the following year he again wrote to Pusey. The occasion was the election for the Poetry Professorship at Oxford.[53] He would have voted for Williams, he told Pusey, but in fact he had taken his name "from the books" years previously.[54] The deep depression continued to haunt him, he related. In making pastoral visits to the homes of the dying, he often wished to trade places with them, so that he might leave this life of sorrow. He worried too that the departed forget those who remain on earth.

> There again a strange thought troubles me that spirits no longer remember those who are in our condition and that amidst the blaze of celestial glory I may be forgotten. Yet this is perhaps all earthly. The text you mention "God will bring with him" seems more like individuality than any other and so gives me a little comfort—that generalizing sort of notion of being swallowed up in the love of God without recognition is I confess very grating to me. One can realize communion without carnal notions, but without recognition of character I cannot. There is a notion some people entertain of the departed watching over us. But Scripture does not I think countenance it, but rather it is the angels' part to do so. I wish I could see it, but the text is silent. Perhaps you never felt these feelings but you may have done so or if not you can and do for your friend. When the first stroke came I seemed all confidence in God, now I find resignation more difficult and my burden more heavy. I often think on the words "look not on the morrow." But who can help it?[55]

No generalized notion of eternal salvation or even union with God was able to counteract his fear of the loss of a personal bond with Christiana. He was also engaged in a battle between his sense of duty toward his children and his emotions that would call him to death. The latter was "a desire [that] comes over me like a strange dream."

By 1843, Medley no longer addressed his letters "My dear Dr.

Pusey," but "My dear friend." He wrote to offer his personal support for Pusey as well as his theological approval of the notorious sermon that had just caused Pusey's condemnation by the university.[56] Pusey had evidently sent Medley a copy, about which Medley declared that he "cannot understand why it was condemned," inasmuch as it seemed to him to be thoroughly scriptural and in accord with the catechism. Medley, of course, was not alone in his defense of Pusey. Public protests and letters were published by Mr. Justice Coleridge and Gladstone, among many others.[57] Medley, in his letter to Pusey, defended Pusey's doctrine. Others, perhaps uneasy with certain expressions that seemed to suggest the doctrine of transubstantiation, were more inclined to defend Pusey on the basis that the university had pursued a flawed and unjust process.[58]

The last letter that we have between the two friends was once again concerned with personal matters. In 1843 Medley's eldest daughter, Emma, died.[59] On April 22, 1844, Pusey lost his beloved daughter, Lucy. Medley wrote soon after to express his sympathy.[60] Whether his own depression had lifted or he was, by an effort of will, repressing his melancholy in order to offer comfort and hope to Pusey, Medley's tone is subtly different than in earlier letters.

> My dear friend,
> A sacred sorrow again binds us together: for I have only just learned of the loss of your eldest child. Another safely landed on the heaven shore (for we cannot be presumptuous in so saying) is in reality a sure cause for thankfulness and even joy. How many sufferings are spared which we have felt. How many an hour of anxiety spared. The race is won by one who has just started from the goal. I have heard with great sorrow that this fresh stroke has weakened your bodily strength. I trust when change is possible you will seek it. If it be in the direction of the North of Devon, I shall be able I hope to see you and may minister to your comfort. But you are continuously remembered by your unworthy yet affectionate friend,
> John Medley

Unfortunately we can only guess as to the continued course of Medley's state of mind, as there are no further letters between Medley and Pusey available. It is a question of some interest as to why a relationship so intense in nature should apparently be so suddenly severed. From this date onward there is no further record of correspondence or personal contact between John Medley and E. B. Pusey.[61]

The year 1844 marked the end of the first part of Medley's life. It was in the autumn of that year that he was approached about becoming bishop of Fredericton.[62] In 1845 he was consecrated bishop and left England. In the same year occurred the single most momentous event of the Oxford Movement—Newman's conversion to the Roman Catholic Church. Following these events and possibly other factors unknown to us there were substantial changes in Medley's positions on several points.

Preparations for a Bishop in New Brunswick

While Medley was still a student at Oxford, movement had begun in the British North American colony of New Brunswick to secure a resident bishop.[63] The Church of England had a presence in North America from shortly after the first English settlement in Virginia in 1607.[64] However, although under the supervision of the bishop of London, the colonial church would lack its own episcopate for nearly two centuries. This would later be considered by many High Churchmen as one of the factors contributing to the American revolution and the subsequent loss of that jewel of the English imperial crown.[65]

Several historical and demographic factors affected the Church of England's relationship to the civil government of New Brunswick and Canada. Originally populated by various tribes of aboriginal people, the first Europeans to explore the country were Vikings who arrived sometime at the end of the first millennium. They established no permanent colony. John Cabot reached Newfoundland in 1497 and claimed it for England. Jacques Cartier explored Quebec at the end of the sixteenth century and Samuel de Champlain did the same in Nova Scotia and New Brunswick at the beginning of the seventeenth century. All three territories were claimed for France.[66]

Nova Scotia and New Brunswick were linked together for the first two centuries following European arrival. Settled by the French, immigrants from England, Scotland, and Ireland only arrived later in the seventeenth century. The territories passed back and forth from French to English hands until the Treaty of Utrecht in 1713, which brought peace and English rule to most of Nova Scotia, while France continued to control the rest of it along with all of New Brunswick. The settlers in Nova Scotia and New Brunswick were chiefly French Roman Catholics. However, under English authority, SPG missionaries were sent out to the small English enclaves in Nova Scotia. The resumption of fighting between France and England saw the rest of Nova Scotia, New Brunswick, and eventually the rest of what was then Canada pass finally into British hands. As yet there were no English settlements in New Brunswick except for a French border fort that had earlier been captured.[67] British policy toward the French majority in New Brunswick was often heavy-handed and cruel. The low point came with the expulsion of several thousand French (Acadian) settlers in the mid-eighteenth century. Suspected of being allies of France, they were violently uprooted from their homes and land and dispersed elsewhere, many being sent to faraway Louisiana.

Prior to the American Revolution, New Brunswick was populated by a mix of French Roman Catholics and smaller numbers of New Englanders, who had gained farmlands after the Seven Years' War.[68] Significant English settlements in New Brunswick were not established until after the American Revolution, when the "Loyalists" arrived. These settlers, who had remained loyal to England during the revolution, sought shelter from persecution in neighboring British colonies. Beginning in late 1782 the first of eventually several thousand Loyalists arrived in New Brunswick from America. Some left to return to the United States after surveying the austere conditions of their new home, but most remained and with them began the real progress, however halting at first, of the Church of England in New Brunswick.[69]

It was not until after the Revolution that Samuel Seabury was consecrated at Aberdeen, Scotland on November 14, 1784. The following year he became the first Anglican bishop of the United States of America—indeed, the first Anglican bishop outside of Great Britain and Ireland. Nova Scotia had been granted a legislature in 1758. This assembly established the Church of England in the colony, granting freedom of worship to all protestant Dissenters.[70]

Thomas Chandler was the first nominee as bishop of Nova Scotia. As Chandler was unable to assume his office because of poor health, Charles Inglis was installed in the position. Inglis had been rector of Trinity Church, New York, during the revolutionary years, but had left with other Loyalists in 1783. In 1787 he was appointed bishop of Nova Scotia and consecrated at Lambeth Palace on August 12. He had jurisdiction over all of Upper and Lower Canada, New Brunswick, Prince Edward Island, Bermuda, and Newfoundland—that is, the whole of British North America. Thus a single bishop had the entire responsibility of a territory vastly larger than the whole of Great Britain. As a result of this, Inglis was only able to visit New Brunswick seven times in the almost thirty-year length of his episcopate.[71]

The Loyalist clergy themselves have generally been thought to have been a decidedly Low Church group. It has been the tendency to assume that they brought with them a spiritual ethos that owed much to New England Congregationalism. For example, Lyman Harding suggests that the Loyalist refugees were "frankly Erastian."[72] Medley himself did not shrink from offering similar criticisms of those who had prepared the ecclesiastical ground in New Brunswick. In later years he was fairly scathing in his account of Loyalist religion.[73]

It is likely that this picture of the Loyalist Anglicans was at least unfair, if not downright false. There is compelling evidence to support the view that many hardworking, devout clergy who adhered to the same High Church principles that Medley advocated had been at work for decades prior to his arrival in the province. Recent research has pointed to a High Church tradition in the American refugees that has generally been overlooked in the past.[74] If we examine those clergy residing in the diocese prior to Medley's arrival, at least some of them were of a sufficient caliber to earn even his praise in later years. It was, after all, their initiatives, expressed through the Diocesan Church Society, that resulted in the call, and eventual establishment of an independent diocese in New Brunswick, with John Medley as its first bishop.

Throughout this period, petitions had been made by prominent New Brunswickers for their own resident bishop.[75] Because of the distances involved, bishops from Nova Scotia only visited New Brunswick sporadically.[76] The Saint John *Courier* noted in 1824 that it had been twenty years since a bishop had last visited New Brunswick.[77] It was not until 1844 that the repeated requests were granted and John Medley was appointed the first bishop of Fredericton. Although the Church of England was nominally established in New Brunswick, in practice its status was very far from that of the church in the home country.[78]

Nominated as Bishop

John Medley was nominated as bishop of Fredericton in the autumn of 1844. As to how this came about, he proclaimed ignorance of the matter, even late in his life.[79] Harding speculates that since Coleridge and Gladstone were treasurers of the Colonial Bishoprics Fund, they might have exerted their influence.[80] Ruth Teale suggests that Pusey was responsible for the nomination, though no concrete evidence to support this claim has yet surfaced.[81] Little is known of Medley's family background that would indicate any political ties that would have been part of the consideration. He had served as vicar of St. Thomas's, Exeter from 1838 until 1845 and was thus under Bishop Henry Phillpotts, whose support of his prebend is noted in Archbishop Howley's letter offering the bishopric to Medley.[82] The archbishop of Canterbury wrote Medley on October 31, 1844, formally offering him the newly created Diocese of New Brunswick.[83] Ketchum printed the letter, which reads in part:

> It has been determined to separate the Province of New Brunswick from the Bishopric of Nova Scotia, of which it now forms part, and to erect it into an independent Bishopric. It is most desirable that this important station should be filled by a clergyman well qualified by learning and ability, by temper and judgement, by piety and soundness of doctrine, to discharge its arduous duties.
>
> I have been informed by competent judges that you possess these qualifications in no ordinary degree, and their report has been fully confirmed by the answer of the Bishop of Exeter to my inquiries. I therefore request your permission to mention your name to Lord Stanley as Bishop.
>
> The office is not to be coveted on account of its emoluments. The income will be about nine hundred a year, or perhaps a little more; but the style of living in the country is not expensive. That which will recommend it to you will be the consideration of the benefit which the Church and the cause of religion in general will derive from the superintendence of a zealous and judicious Bishop, which in the present state of the colony is much needed. There are few situations in which a good man could be more useful.[84]

The archbishop was certainly accurate in stating that the diocese was not to be coveted for its emoluments. A few years later, an income of £2000 was considered by most as inadequate for a new English diocese and Medley was to survive on less than half of that.[85] The archbishop's suggestion that the cost of living was less in Canada was misleading. Books, and many other items were significantly harder to obtain, and thus more expensive than in England. In addition, in Medley's case, a substantial part of his income was used toward church construction and renovation, as well as the establishment of his own residence.

A letter from J. T. Coleridge to John Keble, dated November 10, 1844, informed Keble that Medley had been offered the missionary diocese. Coleridge encouraged Keble to advise him on the matter: "Medley too I suppose will be with you when you receive this and you will have to advise him on his weighty question. If the climate or the hardships to which a missionary Bishop may be exposed should be thought by medical men too severe for his constitution it is due to the Church to decline the office; but one ought to be well assured of this lest he should be found to have been looking backwards with the hand once on the plough. I am told that the climate though cold is very fine: dry and healthy and very favourable to pulmonary tendencies."[86] Keble responded the next day, "I earnestly hope he will accept the bishopric and I think he will if the doctors do not forbid him. I wish you would all get healthier and stronger."[87] Coleridge and Keble had earlier corresponded on the dire need in the colonies for good clergy.[88] They had also decided to aid the recently formed Colonial Bishoprics Fund[89] with proceeds from the *Christian Year* and from Keble's edition of Hooker's *Works*.[90] Keble later wrote to ensure that his donation, specifically directed toward Medley's work in his new diocese, remain anonymous.[91] Medley did not take long to make his decision. We have a letter from Phillpotts to Medley dated November 26 acknowledging the resignation of his position as incumbent and prebend in the Diocese of Exeter.[92]

Prior to Medley's nomination as bishop of Fredericton, he had suffered a number of personal tragedies that may well have influenced his decision to accept the colonial bishopric. In 1839, his second son, Thomas Fisher Medley, died.[93] In 1841, his wife had died from consumption. Much of the care of the household fell to Medley's eldest daughter Emma. Alas, in 1843 she died of scarlet fever.[94] This required Medley's mother to close her own home and move to Exeter to care for the remaining five children. In September of 1844, Medley and a party of others, including his mother, traveled to Oldridge by carriage to visit the newly restored church that the Medleys had funded. Years later, Medley's curate recounted the story: "The Vicar [Medley] drove a hired pair of horses, with Preb. Cornish and his sister, the Hon. Mrs. Shore, in the carriage. On the return journey the pole-strap was not pulled tight enough and on the Whitstone hill it [let go]. One horse began to kick, and then both bolted. The Vicar kept the carriage straight but at the brook turn at the bottom of the hill the carriage broke in two. Mrs. Medley was killed instantly, and the Vicar and Mrs. Shore were thought to be. Prebendary Cornish was thrown out but turned a somersault and landed unhurt on his feet. After some days the Vicar and Mrs. Shore recovered consciousness."[95] Fulford claimed that it was while Medley was unconscious that he received the offer to become bishop of Fredericton.[96] Either this was an unofficial notification, or Fulford's memory was incorrect, as we know the letter from Archbishop Howley to Medley was dated October 31.[97]

Medley was consecrated on May 4, 1845 in Lambeth Palace by the archbishop of Canterbury (Howley), assisted by the bishops of London (Blomfield), Lincoln (Kaye),[98] Rochester (Murray), Hereford (Musgrave), and Lichfield (Lonsdale). The timing was fortuitous for Medley, coming just before the storm caused by Newman's conversion to Roman Catholicism five months later. His association with the key Tractarians surely would have proved a greater obstacle to his nomination thereafter.

Medley in Episcopal Context

John Medley was not the only High Churchman or Tractarian on the Episcopal bench in the mid-nineteenth century. In fact, as Nigel Yates points out, High Churchmen of one stripe or another were strongly represented among the Anglican episcopate through most of the nineteenth century.[99] As Yates and Peter Nockles have made clear, this nineteenth-century episcopal High Churchmanship continued a tradition that had a long pedigree in the Church of England. Immediately prior to the Tractarians, such bishops as Richard Mant, of Killaloe and Kilfenora (then later Down and Connor and Dromore), had held to not only doctrinal High Churchmanship but had possessed some appreciation for architecture and ritual.[100]

Medley's own former diocesan, Henry Phillpotts, was a lifelong committed High Churchman. Suspected of Tractarian affiliations, he was, at the very least, supportive of many of the same principles as the Tractarians. Generally remembered most often now for his feisty if not pugnacious manner, Phillpotts was also, as Arthur Burns makes clear, committed to diocesan reform.[101] It was Phillpotts who appointed Medley prebendary of Exeter and he seemed to have had a genuine regard for his departing priest. Unfortunately no correspondence between Medley and Phillpotts has yet been discovered.

To apply a simple ecclesiastical label to Phillpotts is a complicated thing. Norman Sykes, in the foreword to G. C. B. Davies's biography of Phillpotts, suggests that "he was a champion of the principles of the Tractarian revival."[102] This view is echoed by Desmond Bowen.[103] This is to be contrasted with the view that, "although a High Churchman, he had no sympathy with the Oxford Movement."[104] It might be more accurate to describe him as "an old fashioned High Churchman."[105] But even this label is perhaps too tidy for a person of Phillpotts's somewhat less than restrained temperament. While a supporter of some goals that were coterminus with those of the Tractarians, his old Tory reliance on the power of the state to control dissent could not have been further from Tractarian ideals. Peter Nockles demonstrates that Phillpotts was one figure who exhibited the distinction between the High Church and the Tractarian position.[106] Arthur Burns further explicates Nockles's judgment of Phillpotts as a High Churchman. He goes on to rehabilitate Phillpotts as a High Churchman who, despite his Tory inclinations, proved to be an effective diocesan reformer.[107] One might say that Phillpotts began and ended as a High Churchman, despite some convergence with Tractarian positions in his middle years. Phillpotts and Medley concurred on some issues and diverged sharply on others.

In addition to Phillpotts, other English High Church bishops included Samuel Wilberforce of Oxford, Christopher Wordsworth of Lincoln and the bishop of New Zealand, G. A. Selwyn, who was later translated to Lichfield. While we have no correspondence between Medley and any of these English bishops,[108] Medley did make mention of Wordsworth's death in his 1886 charge. Listing those who had directly aided the diocese, Medley added: "Among our numerous benefactors of this kind must be especially enshrined in our remembrance the honoured name of the late venerable Bishop of Lincoln, whose deep and extensive knowledge of the Holy Scriptures and of the works of the primitive fathers, and whose unswerving loyalty to the Church is a safe guide to studious clergy; whilst his unsparing liberality has enabled us to enjoy the benefit of his labours at one-half the price which we should otherwise have paid."[109] This last remark was substantiated by the presence of many of the bishop of Lincoln's theological works in Medley's own library as well as in the various deanery libraries that he established.[110] This was the case with Wilberforce also, as the Fredericton diocesan and deanery libraries were well stocked with his writings. Medley was personally acquainted with Selwyn, having hosted him in Fredericton in 1874 when Selwyn preached at the cathedral.[111] Wordsworth, Wilberforce, and Selwyn were, like Medley, bishops who had close contacts with the Tractarians, yet developed positions that were quite distinct, in many respects, from those of the Oxford Movement. Along with the numerous moderate High Church bishops in the mid-nineteenth-century Church of England, there were others who were closer to an explicitly Tractarian position. These would include Walter Ker Hamilton of Salisbury, the first Tractarian to be appointed to an English diocese.[112]

One comparison of interest might be made between John Medley and A. P. Forbes of Brechin. While the situations in Britain and the colonies were so vastly different as to make comparisons between British and Canadian bishops and dioceses problematic, it is interesting to place Medley beside another High Church bishop who was a rough contemporary. Consecrated in 1847, just two years after Medley, Forbes enjoyed a nearly thirty-year episcopate. Moreover, he was so strongly associated with the Tractarian bishops as to be awarded the title "The First Tractarian Bishop."[113]

Between Medley and Forbes there are some obvious similarities. Both were born into prosperous families and went on to develop friendships with the most prominent churchmen of the age. In particular, they were close personal friends of E. B. Pusey. They were both, in some measure, scholars.[114] Both became bishops at the relatively young age of forty and owed at least some debt in this regard to the assistance of William Gladstone.[115] Both received some degree of notoriety for their Tractarian connections. Both bishops were early pioneers in the attempt to apply the new Tractarian principles to the administration of an actual diocese. Both, in different ways, were engaged in the translation of the English Church into a different milieu. Both evidenced a genuine concern for the poor and working class in their pastoral ministry.[116] Added to these were a host of common interests—in architecture, liturgy, and church government, to name a few.

A. P. Forbes achieved greater and more widespread fame than did Medley. The simple fact that he was a bishop in Great Britain, rather than in far off colonial North America, was certainly a factor in this. However, Forbes was also more actively involved in some of the great controversies of the day than was his colonial peer. While Medley was extremely cautious, with regard to public pronouncements on controversial issues, Forbes's position on the eucharistic presence, for example, provoked one of the great doctrinal battles of the mid-Victorian period.[117] While there is evidence, as Rowan Strong shows, that the length and bitterness of this battle was to some degree caused by Forbes's own intransigence, it might also be suggested that remarks made by Forbes in the hothouse of the Victorian British church could easily have gone unnoticed if uttered in New Brunswick or Newfoundland. As a consequence, it was in many ways easier to be about the business of a bishop, even a Tractarian bishop, in the colonies than in the mother country. In addition, Medley was always clear that the avoidance of controversy and party disputes was essential to the success of his pastoral mission.

It might also be observed that Forbes exhibited a degree of extremism that was altogether lacking in Medley. Forbes's flirtations with Rome, either in the form of schemes for reunion or as a result of personal dissatisfaction with the Church of England, would have been wholly foreign to Medley. The desire for a clear dogmatic authority that was so strong in Forbes,[118] and many other Tractarians, was something that in Medley, if present at all, was certainly muted. Medley seemed more easily able to reconcile himself with a democratic age, supporting lay representation in synod. This measure was strongly opposed by Forbes.[119] Some of these differences may be explained by their different contexts. Maintenance of the church and state *status quo* was far less tenable for Medley, on the border of the United States, than it was for Forbes even in Scotland. Alternatively, it may be that Medley was the more prudent choice of bishop for a colonial situation in North America because of his greater appreciation for toleration. While no less doctrinally orthodox than Forbes, Medley certainly appeared to have had a more limited, and thus perhaps more realistic, view of the prospects of rigid dogmatic uniformity in any church existing in an increasingly pluralistic modern society.

While Forbes and Hamilton would have differed on particular points, and they would both have gone considerably further than their moderate High Church brethren, there was agreement on many common High Church positions. The real presence, baptismal regeneration, and the historic episcopate would have been accepted by these and most other High Churchmen of the day. Medley would have been in broad agreement with all of these positions.

Departure from England

Before Medley departed for Canada, a public meeting to bid him farewell was held at Exeter on May 13, 1845, with Phillpotts presiding. Among those who made addresses on the occasion was William Hart Coleridge, nephew of Samuel Taylor Coleridge and himself a former missionary bishop to Barbados. After presenting Medley with a substantial donation toward the erection of the cathedral that he had announced his intention to build, Coleridge made clear that Medley was to carry the Tractarian and ecclesiological plans forward in his mission diocese: "It will be a primary object of your solicitude, not only under the Divine blessing, to feed the flock committed to your charge with the wholesome doctrine of the Gospel, and duly to administer the discipline of the English Church, but to exhibit also, before the eyes of your people—to their hearts and to their understandings—the scriptural ritual of that Church, in all the fullness and impressiveness of a faithful outward observance."[120] Phillpotts spoke next and expressed his mixed emotions on this occasion. He regretted losing "one of the most valuable and exemplary of [his] clergy," yet recognized that Medley had been "called to a larger and nobler field of labour."[121] He then went on to stress another plank of the High Church position (i.e., the importance of episcopacy), saying that at last the missionaries of the church are to be accompanied by "the superintendence of the high officer of the Church, whom Christ Himself has appointed, to be over her in His name."[122]

In responding to these and the other addresses made, Medley betrayed none of the nervousness that a young bishop (just forty years old) might well feel on the eve of his departure for an unknown missionary field. Scarcely acknowledging the personal praise directed toward him, Medley thanked those present for their gift toward the new cathedral. He then affirmed Phillpotts's point that the sending of missionary bishops to the colonies was a sign of life, where previously there had been coldness in the extremities of the church. He was free of any fantasies about the new frontier. Instead, he explained to his audience how the colonial church situation differed from that of England, taking the opportunity to criticize the government for its unwillingness to further the church there. Medley then went on to say that the government treated denominations in the colonies according to "the numerical principle." In New Brunswick of course, the Church of England was a minority. Yet, the new bishop believed that this governmental indifference was not without its benefits. He thought it could have a positive effect on the bishop in that "It leads him then, not to look for his connection to the state, so much as to the spiritual power and authority given him by the Lord Jesus."[123] This again recalled the notion of a "primitive bishop," a powerful image for the Tractarians and a truly revolutionary one with regard to church-state relations.

It was, in many respects, a remarkable speech for such an occasion. Rather than the polite platitudes that a departing missionary might make after receiving a generous donation, Medley chose to launch a quite pointed attack upon establishment. There were two elements present that would contend for many years in Medley's thought. There was a pragmatic spirit that caused him to face the political realities of the day. Whether establishment was good or bad, the point was that it was not actually in effect in the colonies, so it was pointless to pretend that it existed. Set against this practical inclination was the noble ideal of the pure Church of Christ, "in all its fullness and glory," existing "far above men," indifferent to "the smiles of princes." The contrast between the hard-nosed practical spirit and the Tractarian idealism is quite striking.

Having grown up in a prosperous and devout home, and prepared from childhood for the ministry, Medley had surely become all that his mother would have wished. Educated at Evangelical Wadham college, Medley later came into contact with the most dynamic High Church figures of the Victorian era. Through his scholarly abilities and interest in ecclesiology, he became highly regarded by the Tractarians, although the depth of his agreement with Tractarian doctrine remains to be examined. Nominated as bishop to a missionary diocese, Medley was given the chance to put into practice the theories of ecclesiology, episcopacy, and diocesan reform that he had been exposed to in England. Because of the peculiar circumstances of the colonial church, he had a remarkable degree of latitude in carrying out his designs.

2

John Fredericton—Missionary to the Wilderness

The Church of England in the Canadian Context

From the outset the position of the Church of England in Canada had never been strong in reality, although on paper it possessed many privileges. For example, in New Brunswick and Nova Scotia, although the church was nominally established, there was no legal provision for the collection of church rates, nor any other means of support for a parochial system.[1] In many places, such as Quebec and New Brunswick, members of the Church of England were a minority with respect to a French Roman Catholic majority. While some bishops, such as Mountain in Quebec and Strachan in Ontario, attempted to assert the privileges of the Church of England, they were largely unsuccessful.[2] Other denominations made strong claims to be afforded equal treatment and had the political power to support those arguments.

The Canadian Church was poor and disorganized in comparison with its English equivalent. Without strong government support and any organized parochial system or institutions such as universities and seminaries, it was only a shadowy image of the English Church. While some missionary bishops quickly realized and accepted this difference, others fought instead to reproduce the English system on Canadian soil.

John Medley was not the only Canadian High Church missionary bishop. In fact, of the bishops who occupied the neighboring dioceses of Nova Scotia, Quebec, and Ontario (as well as Newfoundland, which was not yet a part of Canada) in Medley's lifetime, most were High Church, if not avowedly Tractarian, in character. In many cases they were connected to and sponsored by the same group of influential churchmen to whom Medley owed his position. The story of High Churchmanship and Tractarianism in nineteenth-century Eastern Canada has been ably told by Christopher Headon.[3]

One of the earliest High Church bishops in Canada was Jacob Mountain of Quebec,[4] who owed his position to the patronage of George Pretyman-Tomline, the bishop of Lincoln and later of Winchester.[5] Mountain strongly defended the value of establishment despite the overwhelming French Catholic character of Quebec society. Jacob Mountain's son, George Jehoshaphat Mountain, became bishop of Montreal and later bishop of the whole diocese of Quebec.[6] George Mountain exhibited a more marked High Church emphasis than the moderate position of his father. The younger Mountain often promoted "the ordinances and constitution of [the] apostolic Church."[7] He combined an evangelical piety with a High Church doctrinal emphasis.[8] Yet, even the younger Mountain shunned advanced ritualist practices and went out of his way to avoid public religious controversy.[9]

One of those bishops to whom Medley might be most closely compared would be Edward Feild of Newfoundland.[10] Born in 1801, Feild attended the same grammar school (Bewdley) as Medley, and went on, briefly, to study at Medley's old college, Wadham.[11] While at Oxford, Feild made the transition from Evangelical to High Churchman.[12] One of the precipitating factors in this conversion was the influence of Charles Lloyd, whose lectures Feild attended.[13] In these details, Feild paralleled Medley's own course. Like Medley, Feild was an advocate of the Gothic Revival and upon ordination set about to impress ecclesiological principles upon the churches in his care. He removed galleries and added "free and unappropriated seats."[14]

Consecrated bishop in 1844, just a year before Medley, Feild was sent to the remote and rocky colony of Newfoundland, off Canada's eastern coast. If New Brunswick was bleak and isolated, Newfoundland was even more so. In Newfoundland, Feild actively promoted High Church principles. In this connection he differed from Medley when it came to approach and style. Feild was less patient and far more aggressive in dealing with Low Churchmen and Evangelicals. Where Medley sought consensus and preached toleration, Feild stressed obedience and doctrinal uniformity. For example, he declared his absolute opposition to the Gorham judgment (as had Medley, albeit in more measured tones), then went on to warn that anyone who did not teach an orthodox doctrine of baptismal regeneration would be driven from his diocese. As a consequence of this uncompromising approach, Frederick Jones observed that in the process of building a diocese Feild was also "antagonizing Roman Catholics, dividing Anglicans, alienating Methodists, arousing anti-Tractarian sentiment, [and] splitting Protestant unity."[15] In his zeal to protect church rights and privileges in the area of education he thus managed to simultaneously offend both dissenters and Roman Catholics.

While Feild shared Medley's determination to end reliance on the SPG grants, he was zealous in claiming what other denominations felt to be excessive shares of government education funds. This financial emphasis led him into areas of controversy that Medley would certainly have avoided. For example, Feild refused the sacraments to those who were unwilling to pay into a church dues system that he had conceived.[16] In contrast Medley generally avoided such warnings or threats. Nor did he endeavor to coerce uniformity on even such important matters as baptismal regeneration. In short, while undoubtedly dedicated and energetic, Feild lacked a degree of prudence that Medley possessed, often pursuing what he took to be church principles in damaging ways.

Another neighboring High Churchman, similarly dedicated, also faced his share of challenges and controversy. Hibbert Binney of Nova Scotia had been consecrated in 1851. He had succeeded the High Churchman, John Inglis, son of Charles Inglis, the first bishop of Nova Scotia. Although Binney was born in Nova Scotia, his family had moved back to England when he was a small child. Raised an Evangelical, Binney came into contact with the Tractarians while a student at Oxford, where he is believed to have known E. B. Pusey.[17] He was also a correspondent of Gladstone's, writing to him in 1881 to oppose the Deceased Wife's Sister bill.[18]

As in New Brunswick, in Nova Scotia there was a strong Evangelical body who were deeply vigilant for any signs of Tractarianism in their midst. Like Medley, Binney publicly denounced party spirit and allied himself with no party.[19] In his first charge to the diocese of Nova Scotia, Binney spoke in words that, as we shall see, could have been Medley's own: "Finally let me exhort and entreat you to shun all party spirit. I am truly thankful that this Diocese has continued so free from this evil, and that though there are, as there ever must be, differences of opinion amongst you, there has never been any positive division into parties one against another. Party spirit is destructive of genuine piety. Every party will run into extremes, and wherever this spirit prevails true Christian charity will be blighted, will drop and die."[20] Despite this care for avoiding factional disputes, Binney still promoted a distinctively High Church account of episcopacy, and sought to renew church architecture in his diocese along Gothic lines.[21] He fought for the use of the surplice in preaching and credence tables in sanctuaries.[22] Nevertheless he is reported to have responded censoriously when one of his clergy in a sermon referred to his use of "Confession."[23] Despite Evangelical accusations to the contrary, the evidence suggests that Binney was cautious and conservative in his application of High Church principles.

In addition to Mountain, Feild, and Binney, most of the other eastern Canadian bishops exhibited High Church or Tractarian sympathies. For example, John Strachan, the first bishop of Toronto (1839–67), was an old High Churchman who had been influenced by Bishop Hobart of New York.[24] Francis Fulford, bishop of Montreal (1850–68) was a friend of J. H. Newman until the latter's secession to Rome. As bishop, Fulford stayed with Bishop Wilberforce and dined with Gladstone and Phillpotts when in England.[25] John Travers Lewis, the first bishop of Ontario (1862–1901), was a moderate High Churchman who tolerated, if not actually encouraged, ritualist parishes in his diocese and counted bishops Selwyn and Wilberforce among his friends.[26] Thus, Medley was not alone in advocating High Church positions in Canada.

Stepping into Controversy

When John Medley left for Canada, he took all five of his surviving children with him.[27] His daughter Christiana Elizabeth Medley subsequently returned to England, marrying Henry Lancaster.[28] His son John Bacon Medley returned to England and became a priest. Charles Steinkofft Medley served as a rector in the Diocese of Fredericton until his death. Spencer Manley Medley served as captain in the Royal Navy, retiring finally to New Zealand, where he married Mary Taylor.[29] Finally, Edward Shuttleworth Medley became a priest, serving under his father in the diocese of Fredericton, before returning to England to take up appointments there.

Some sense of the difficulty of Medley's task in his new diocese must be gained. To begin with, the diocese was immense by English standards. Nearly thirty thousand square miles, New Brunswick was more than half of the size of England. Compared to the mother country, it was a primitive land and adherents of the Church of England were few in number. Although the colony numbered approximately 200,000 persons by midcentury, Anglicans were a minority. In 1861, the largest religious denomination was Roman Catholic, which accounted for 34 percent of the population.[30] Anglicans numbered 17 percent of churchgoers, just 25 percent of the Protestant population. They were outnumbered by Baptists and nearly matched by Presbyterians. There were also significant numbers of Methodists and Congregationalists. The number of Anglicans in the province remained relatively constant through the remainder of the nineteenth century, with Roman Catholics increasing their share of the overall population.[31]

New Brunswick was not particularly strong economically. The port city of Saint John was the principle center, with a population of thirty thousand.[32] It led the provincial economy, which was heavily involved in shipbuilding and timber exporting. Apart from Fredericton, most other towns, such as Chatham, were located along the long coastlines, where these same industries could flourish. Outside of the main centers, most inhabitants of the province lived in relative poverty, eking out a living through subsistence farming or logging. Farmers received little support or encouragement from the local government, whose members were largely representatives of the timber trade and directed their attentions to its enrichment.[33]

When Medley arrived he found the province in dire economic straits and the situation was to become worse during his early years. The economy had always been almost wholly dependent upon the timber trade and was thus subject to external pressures beyond its control. With the imperial government's movement toward free trade in the 1840s, tariffs that had protected New Brunswick's principle industry vanished, leaving the province in severe difficulty. The resulting depression produced, as Scott See succinctly describes it, "high unemployment, bankruptcy, out-migration, legislative indebtedness and abysmal provincial credit."[34] The decade of the 1840s was one of crushing economic hardship.

It was in the midst of this severe economic crisis that New Brunswick began to receive large numbers of Irish immigrants. While Irish immigration had been a fact of New Brunswick life throughout much of the nineteenth century, it peaked during the years of the Irish famine.[35] The population of New Brunswick in 1845 was approximately two hundred thousand. In 1847 alone, seventeen thousand, mostly Irish, immigrants arrived in the province.[36] While the greatest proportion of these mainly Catholic immigrants settled in Saint John, the city of Fredericton can be used to illustrate their impact on the province generally. Almost 80 percent of the immigrants to Fredericton were Irish. An almost exclusively Loyalist city formerly, the Irish Catholic population swelled, until the city was picked to be the site of the first Roman Catholic cathedral in the province. By 1861, when the first census recording religious affiliation was taken, Catholics far outnumbered those residents of Fredericton who claimed allegiance to the Church of England.[37]

One of the consequences of the economic downturn, coupled with the waves of Irish Catholic immigration, was the rise of ethnic division and, eventually, violence. The powerful Orange Order, which counted over 150 lodges by 1850 in New Brunswick,[38] organized mobs and demonstrations aimed against the new Irish Catholic inhabitants. These demonstrations culminated in the 1840s with a number of bloody and deadly riots.[39] Armed clashes erupted in the previously almost entirely Loyalist centers of Woodstock, Fredericton, and Saint John, leaving dozens dead and countless more injured.[40]

It was into this economically stressed and racially charged environment that John Medley entered in 1845. As a man tarred with the Tractarian brush, he was immediately distrusted by the powerful Protestant body in the province. One could not have imagined a worse time for a bishop linked to a movement suspected of Romanist sympathies to arrive in New Brunswick. Newman's secession, in that same year, and the others that followed could only have exacerbated an already tense situation.

Medley's critics were not hesitant to voice their suspicions.[41] Throughout his episcopate Medley refused to descend into partisan controversy. Medley generally preferred toleration to doctrinal rigorism with regard to disputes within the church. Medley extended this argument for toleration toward Roman Catholics on the one side and Dissenters on the other. He called for his clergy to abandon "ceaseless vituperation of the Roman and Oriental Churches."[42] This certainly struck a different note from the virulent anti-Romanist tirades of the New Brunswick Evangelicals. How much more striking were even more explicit comments: "Both [i.e., the Roman and Eastern Churches] originally descended from the root of Jesse; both have their witness in the Scriptures; both have made us their debtors by 'imparting spiritual gifts', both profess to worship one God in Trinity, and Trinity in Unity; both acknowledge one Redeemer, one Spirit, and one Baptism; both unite in the three Ancient Creeds, except in one Article, and that capable of a milder interpretation; both own the weight of the moral duties of the Gospel, and look forward to the coming of the Lord to judge the quick and the dead; both have the witness of the Spirit 'working with them,' by the possession of great Saints and illustrious Luminaries."[43] In a time and place where the predominant Protestant characterization of the Roman Catholic Church was that it was the very living form of infidelity and the manifestation of a grand anti-imperial conspiracy,[44] Medley's words were both revolutionary and brave. Delivered just months after the bloody Saint John riots, Medley's *1850 Charge* went on to condemn Protestant intolerance: "We know indeed full well the injustice, and the narrowness of the Tridentine decrees; we know how that famous synod (for council it can hardly be called) was gathered together, awed, and silenced: nevertheless I maintain, that not to extend to the great body of the Christian world our sympathy, our wishes, and our prayers, to repeat for everlasting ages the same hard and bitter words, to mistake the thunder of the English guns for the rights of bishops, and to trample on the rights of Ancient and Apostolic Churches, by reason of our might, and our knowledge, and our wealth, is as unwarrantable as were the canons of the Council of Trent."[45] To speak such words at this time was remarkable enough. To be suspected of Tractarianism and to speak them in the context of a New Brunswick that showed many of the symptoms of sectarian civil war required more than ordinary courage. Medley paid the price for his courageous stand in the strident opposition of the Evangelical press.

With regard to the other side of the religious coin, Medley argued that however mistaken Dissenters might be with regard to points of doctrine or church order, "they cannot be mistaken in their Piety."[46] This toleration, combined with Medley's growing repudiation of the privileges of establishment, began to earn the regard of other religious bodies in the province.

The same tolerant spirit was demonstrated in Medley's own life. For example, he developed a close friendship with Dr. Brooke, a prominent Presbyterian minister in Fredericton. The regard between the two was mutual. At one time a rumor had begun to circulate in Fredericton that Medley had been bankrupted. Dr. Brooke and his wife promptly made their way to Medley's residence and placed their life's savings at the bishop's disposal. The rumor being false, the kind offer was not needed, but Medley deeply appreciated the gesture.[47] Medley regularly visited the Brooke home, caring for the senior gentleman in times of illness and then, after Brooke's death, continuing to care for his widow.

Over the course of his lifetime Medley's solid refusal to descend into the bitterness of partisan religious strife, either within his own church or with those outside, gradually yielded fruit. The opposition within the diocese, based upon his presumed Tractarianism, eventually ebbed, to be replaced with a genuine respect from even his former opponents in the Evangelical camp. In his refusal to argue for continued privilege to be extended to the Church of England in New Brunswick, Medley assisted the aspirations of other religious bodies in the province to gain equal status in civil society.

New Brunswick's principal divisions were between Catholic and Protestant on the one hand, and French and English on the other. The Church of England was never a strong presence in predominantly French communities, so Medley's interaction with a large segment of New Brunswick society was slight. While tensions between Catholics and Protestants in New Brunswick receded from their mid-nineteenth-century high, divisions between French and English inhabitants of the province continued through the rest of the century and persist to the present day.

Building a New Diocese

In the depressed economy of New Brunswick the task of building dozens of churches was far from easy. As a consequence, funding was arranged on an ad hoc basis from community to community. Medley led the efforts to solicit donations from England. For example, he returned to England in 1848 for the first time since arriving in New Brunswick. This trip was largely directed toward fundraising. He came back to Fredericton having accomplished some, if not all, of what he hoped: "Two thousand pounds were subscribed for the Cathedral, the S.P.C.K. also voted £1,000; £50 a year for five years were granted for a travelling missionary, and £300 a year for additional efforts by the S.P.G. The University of Oxford gave £100 for the Cathedral Library; and benevolent individuals gave the Anglo-Catholic Library, and the Library of the Fathers, making in all about six hundred volumes. The Bishop also procured a small organ for St. Anne's Chapel."[48] Individual priests made similar trips to England, returning with lesser amounts. For example, James Hudson[49] traveled to England and Ireland in 1858 and obtained donations toward building projects from "the Bishop of London (12 pounds), the Archbishop of Canterbury (2 pounds), the Duke of Marlborough (12 pounds), the Archbishop of Dublin (2 pounds), the Duke of Buccleugh (10 pounds), as well as contributions from eight other English Bishops and over 10 pounds from the passengers of the steamer *Canada.*"[50] Clearly neither Medley nor Hudson was shy about soliciting support, even from strangers.

In addition to donations from abroad, active campaigns were conducted to receive subscriptions from local inhabitants. On many of Medley's confirmation tours, he would receive subscriptions of £25 or £50 from various communities toward the erection of a church.[51] These buildings were generally constructed of wood, using local timber and craftsmen to keep costs low. In addition, to encourage what Medley considered to be the proper, that is Gothic, church design, wooden models were constructed and made available to congregations to copy.[52] While most rural churches were constructed through local subscriptions, Medley regularly sought outside help toward furnishing them. For example, Medley had entered into an arrangement with "a Mr. Nichens, of London," to donate a full set of silver communion plate annually to the diocese. The bishop would then distribute these sets to needy missions.[53]

Many churches were built partially or entirely by means of Medley's own liberality or that of some other clergyman. St. Anne's Church, Fredericton, the most elaborate church building in the diocese after the cathedral, was constructed substantially at Medley's own expense.[54] Other clergy supplied materials for the building or furnishings out of their own more modest incomes. Rural missionaries, such as Hudson, were often physically involved in the construction of churches, to the extent of helping "to haul the lumber."[55]

When Medley arrived in New Brunswick there were no railways, no decent roadways, and few interior waterways capable of navigation. Travel was by ship around the coast, smaller craft up and down the principal rivers, carriage in a few cases, horseback in others, and often simply by foot. The harshness of the climate amplified the difficulties of any method of travel. Fredericton, located inland along the Saint John River, required long journeys along small inland waterways, or horseback rides along rough trails in some situations. Simply to go from Fredericton to a parish halfway across the diocese was a significant undertaking.

Medley kept a handwritten record of his daily business throughout his episcopate. Entitled *The Annals of the See of New Brunswick*, it is an invaluable record of his daily work.[56] Medley began the *Annals* with his own consecration at Lambeth Chapel on May 4, 1845. He recorded that he left Liverpool on May 20 and arrived in Saint John, New Brunswick on the night of June 7 after a short visit with John Inglis, the bishop of Nova Scotia, in Halifax. The next morning, Sunday, Medley preached three times in the city of Saint John at different churches and received, on the following day, addresses prepared by various parishes of his new diocese.[57]

Of these addresses, perhaps one in particular is worth noting. It was written by the Corporation of Trinity Church, Saint John. One of the oldest parishes and certainly the wealthiest in the province, Trinity Church was to be a thorn in Medley's side for many years. Staunchly Loyalist,[58] Evangelical, and strongly independent, it was clear from the beginning that it was not of one view with its new bishop on a host of matters.

While it had been known for some months that a new bishop was to be appointed for the province, the vestry records of Trinity took no notice of that important development. The first mention of the new bishop was not until a meeting held just prior to his arrival. It was resolved that an address would be presented welcoming Medley.

Tellingly, the address began, "As the representatives of the members of the established Church of England in this Parish . . ."[59] It was no doubt the case that the clergy and laity of Trinity had some knowledge of their new bishop's inclinations.[60] Certainly in later years the questionable character of the church as established was central to Medley's thought.[61] If this beginning had not raised a red flag to the new bishop, a later reference certainly would have. While expressing due allegiance and respect for Medley, the address continues, "Permit us, my Lord, while bidding you welcome to our shore, to pray that you may come to us 'in the fullness of the blessing of the Gospel of Christ,' and that all your efforts to preserve our revered Church in the purity of her faith and in the enjoyment of those forms and usages with which the pious feelings of Churchmen in this province have, from the earliest days been associated, may be abundantly crowned with success."[62] This concern for the preservation of existing "forms and usages" was an early signal of the apprehension about possible Tractarian leanings in their new bishop. The rector of the parish, the Reverend J. W. D. Gray, had his own aspirations to be the first bishop in New Brunswick.[63] Not only had he lost out, but a man reputed to have Tractarian sympathies had won the position.

The day after the addresses were presented Medley set sail up the Saint John River for Fredericton.[64] He arrived in Fredericton on St Barnabas's Day, June 11. The letters patent were read, and he was installed in the "Cathedral," which was, in fact, the parish church of Christ Church. He was greeted by the lieutenant governor and immediately celebrated Holy Communion.[65] Medley noted, "There were one hundred and fifty communicants, among them some coloured people, who had walked six miles to be present."[66]

In 1836, nine years before Medley came to New Brunswick, there were eighty parishes,[67] twenty-eight clergymen, and forty-three churches or chapels.[68] Thus, two-thirds of the parishes lacked resident clergy. By 1845, when Medley arrived, the diocese had increased incrementally to eighty-seven parishes, thirty clergymen, and forty-seven churches.[69] Still, twelve missions lacked Sunday services.[70]

The diocese of Fredericton was heavily dependent upon the SPG for financial aid.[71] Ketchum suggests that on the eve of Medley's arrival in New Brunswick not a single clergyman could claim independence from this support.[72] It was the suggestion that this support could not continue indefinitely that led to the establishment of the Diocesan Church Society in 1836.[73] Of the founding of the Diocesan Church Society in 1836, Ernest Hawkins, later Secretary of the SPG, remarked that it was "the first systematic attempt made in a British colony for the more full and efficient support of its own Church."[74]

Over the next few decades, SPG support continually declined, leading to the need for New Brunswick, as well as other colonial dioceses, to assume a larger responsibility for their own maintenance. This transition was far from painless, however. Medley's correspondence with the SPG was often tinged with anger at the church in England for, in his opinion, having turned away from a responsibility that it had assumed. Thus Medley wrote to Ernest Hawkins in 1856:

> It may do very well for gentlemen to sit at home in England, many of them with large private means, [and] to go down to the Board and vote away our aid and exult over the new principle of self government, but it is death and starvation to us. We shall resemble the American Church in which the small villages are, scarcely without exception, abandoned to dissent, infidelity and indifference. The Church then betakes herself to the towns, but we have no towns, except Saint John and Fredericton, of any wealth or importance. But the principle seems to be 'first experimentation' and we shall see the result. Parents will not send their sons into professions where they are worse paid than the commonest clerks in second rate stores.[75]

The situation was to become worse in the 1860s. Despite promises given in the 1830s to missionaries about a guaranteed level of income, the SPG had proposed in 1865 to reduce their meager stipends by twenty-five percent. The missionaries and Medley regarded this as a breach of faith. The consequence would be ruinous to those dedicated and now older missionaries, whose incomes were already modest. Medley immediately set off to England to meet the committee. He was furious at the SPG's callousness: "Much of this is no doubt owing to the persevering efforts of a few zealous members of the Committee, bent on withdrawing all aid to the North American Colonies, at all hazards, and aided in this resolve by the profound ignorance which everywhere prevails amongst educated Englishmen of our place, our usefulness, our feelings, and our interests; and by the conviction entertained by many at home that it is necessary, as they more pithily than compassionately express it, to turn the screw on, and to screw us hard, or we shall do nothing for ourselves."[76] Medley both appreciated what the SPG had done for the diocese and pointed out how much more could be done by the Church of England to advance the interests of the church abroad.

Over the years Medley continued to struggle with the withdrawal of SPG financial support. Repeatedly he called for the establishment of a diocesan endowment fund, similar to those in place in many of the episcopal dioceses to the south. However, New Brunswick never developed a robust economy comparable to that of most American states and, as a consequence, the diocese of Fredericton was always correspondingly poorer than its American cousins. Medley's longed-for endowment fund never materialized.[77]

In addition to the physical obstacles initially facing Medley in New Brunswick, there were spiritual impediments to church growth. The church in New Brunswick was divided between High Church and Low Church parties prior to Medley's arrival.[78] Evangelical clergy were chiefly located in and around the prosperous port of Saint John. The moderately High Church clergy were located in Fredericton and in the northeast part of the province. Archdeacon George Coster was rector of Fredericton. His daughter in later years described her father's churchmanship: "As a churchman he was far in advance of his time. He was the first to introduce anything like strict adherence to the rules of the prayer book with reference to more frequent celebrations of the holy communion, the offertory, holy days, and services in the week, and many other things now so common in the Church in America."[79] Despite this picture of Coster, it is to be remembered that he had made no move to add a chancel to his church in Fredericton, or otherwise alter its arrangement until just prior to Medley's arrival in the diocese. A divinity student visiting Christ Church, Fredericton in 1843 found the services far from any High Church ideal. The congregation did not make the responses, this being done by an elderly clerk. Few people knelt for the prayers.[80] Here and elsewhere in the diocese, music lacked imagination and was chiefly drawn from the metrical psalms of Tate and Brady.[81] Medley described even the High Church parishes in scathing terms: "The high church of this province is a miserable production—being *high talk* and *low action* in many quarters with great bitterness to dissenters . . . Close to Fredericton is one Church deserted—one more only three miles off, where the Sacrament has not been administered for three years. The Sunday School has only fifty children—and hitherto hardly any poor attend the church."[82] While the assessment of a relatively young bishop intent on reform cannot be said to be dispassionate, it is clear that the church in New Brunswick was hardly robust. Its expansion was slow, its finances (outside of one or two prosperous parishes) perilous, and it lacked a strong central vision to unite it. The harsh climate, long distances between missions, and the depressed economic state of a largely rural area all intensified the difficulties the church faced.

Opposition to Medley

One of the tasks that Medley first set about to accomplish was the building of a cathedral. He chose Fredericton for a site and thus ignited a storm of controversy. Opposition to the cathedral project was wide and varied in its origin. The existing parish church congregation resented the encroachment of the cathedral on their own space. Others objected to the cost of such a project.[83] From Saint John, criticism was based upon other grounds, for it had long been the commercial center of the province. Although the seat of government was at Fredericton, and thus Medley's letters patent directed him to have his residence there, Saint John believed that it was a more suitable location for a cathedral than the less sophisticated lumber town of Fredericton. Medley replied that Fredericton was more centrally located, thus making travel easier for the bishop, and the price of land in Fredericton was a fraction of the cost in Saint John.[84]

The Saint John *Courier* thundered that the people of Fredericton, in desiring their city for the location, were acting "beyond any love they bear the Church or its advancement."[85] This was reflected in the vestry minutes of Trinity Church. Having received Medley's request for financial assistance toward the cathedral (which they were well able to give, as the richest church in the province) they responded coolly. Perhaps Medley was less than diplomatic in his letter to the parish saying, "There is at present not one single church in the Province worthy of the name of a Temple."[86] He went on in his letter to exhort them to "rise above all party jealousies." At this last phrase they certainly took umbrage, responding curtly that they held no such jealousies. They eventually formed a committee to study the bishop's request and returned the response that the committee had recommended that no direct financial assistance be offered. Instead, they would make his request known to the parishioners and the city at large in case anyone cared to make such donations.[87] In closing they informed the bishop that in their estimation "the amount of subscriptions in this city will be so small as to be of little avail."[88] Months passed before the cathedral was ever mentioned again at vestry meetings. In November a motion was made to have a new pulpit built for Trinity Church and have it positioned "in the centre of the space in front of the Chancel."[89] This was a hallmark of Low Church architecture, whereby the pulpit, not the altar, had visual prominence. It is hard to imagine how they could have more directly signaled their opposition to Medley.

There was yet another ground for opposition to Medley's plan. This was one that united even the people of Fredericton and Saint John. Medley had made his opposition to pews and pew rents widely known. He had already published an influential work on the topic. He also declared that the seats in his new cathedral were to be "free and unencumbered forever."[90] This position was a tremendous irritant to many of the existing parishes, including the most influential ones. The reason is obvious when their financial statements are examined. For example, in 1842 the annual income of Christ Church Fredericton was just over £700. Of this amount half, £346, came from pew rents. Land rents accounted for another £194. Monthly collections made up just £187.[91] The situation at Trinity Church in Saint John was even more extreme. In 1845, the year of Medley's arrival, total income of the parish was over £1400. Of this, pew rents supplied £668, while land rents generated another £575. Sales of pews and sales of burial plots produced £141. Quarterly collections accounted for just £40. To abolish pew rents and substitute a weekly offertory appeared to be a disastrous course viewed in light of these figures. It may have been that Medley was unaware of the context into which he had been placed. Or, as some critics have suggested, he was simply bullheaded when it came to what he perceived as matters of principle.

Finally, opposition was directed at Medley because of his suspected associations with the Tractarians. Even Ketchum, otherwise loathe to speak of controversy, was forced to acknowledge the existence of this fact. According to him, Evangelicals "supposed that real vital religion could not exist in connection with High Church views [such as Medley's]."[92] He went on to say that Medley made no attempt to "disguise . . . the principles which ruled [his] mind." As a consequence, "By the Evangelical party he was regarded with distrust, which was felt the more, as accounts came of the terrible secessions to the Church of Rome, on the part of the most prominent of those concerned with the Oxford Movement. All this was diligently set forth in the public press, and in much public teaching. It had its weight in many parishes, and with many minds. For a while they watched rather than yielded to the Bishop's teaching. He found it hard, in many instances, to bring about the most desirable and harmless changes in the mode of conducting divine service. Such changes were often earnestly desired by the clergy, but opposed by the congregations. Any proposed alteration was called the "entering wedge," "the step by step system."[93] Even public figures were not without their concerns about his Tractarian ties. Sir Edmund Walker Head, lieutenant governor of the province, remarked upon one of Medley's fundraising trips to England, where he had gathered support from many of his erstwhile colleagues, "*Timeo Danaos et dona ferentes!*"[94]

Even prior to Newman's secession, even in faraway New Brunswick, suspicions about creeping Romanism occupied the minds of many Churchmen. Medley had scarcely arrived in his new diocese when he was called to mediate a dispute over a matter of ritual. The rector of the parish of Hampton had written to Medley in August of

1845, asking him to pass judgment on the wearing of the surplice to preach, which the incumbent had evidently introduced. The wearing of the surplice was hotly controversial in England, with its use during preaching being understood as an expression of High Church ritualism. Medley's response to this letter is one of the earliest pieces of private correspondence we have from Medley's episcopate. The response, addressed to the rector but intended to be read by both parties, is of sufficient interest to print in detail, inasmuch as it illustrates the pastoral approach that the new bishop was to adopt throughout his tenure in Fredericton.

My dear Mr. Walker,

My advice has been asked on a matter respecting which differences of opinion have existed, viz, the wearing of the surplice in preaching. I take it for granted in appealing to me that both parties in the case are willing to abide by my decision: otherwise there would be little use in the appeal. Abstractedly there can be nothing wrong or irregular in using the surplice in the pulpit: it is a decent comely garment, and is universally used without offence in all other parts of the service, nor is there any law or canon of the church which forbids the surplice, or enjoins the gown. In many parts of England it is always used throughout the whole service, and has been so used ever since the reformation. Nor does it appear to me that it should be looked on with suspicion as indicating a leaning to doctrines at variance with those of the Church of England inasmuch as it is not usually worn by those who differ from us.

I may add that the rubric in the beginning of our Prayer Book which requires that "such ornaments of the Church and of the ministers thereof, *at all time of their ministrations*, shall be retained and be in use, as were in the Church of England by act of Parliament, in the second year of the reign of Edward the Sixth" is commonly supposed to favour the use of the surplice in preaching, because the surplice is one of those ornaments which were directed to be used in the second year of Edward the Sixth. Still it must be admitted that a doubt may exist whether the words "at all times of their ministration" apply only to all the rites and offices of prayer, or to preaching as well as prayer. In the fifty-eighth canon (which is to be found at the end of the large Church Prayer Book), it is ordered that "Every minister saying the public prayers, or ministering the sacraments or other rites of the Church shall wear a decent and comely surplice with sleeves, to be provided at the Charges of the Parish." The expressions "saying the public prayers" and "ministering the sacraments and other rites of the Church" do not necessarily include preaching, and perhaps were not intended to apply to it: but there is nothing in the canon which forbids the surplice.

The twenty-fifth canon regulates the order of Cathedral Churches, the members of which all wear the surplice in preaching, but it may be doubted whether Cathedral Churches are the model for Parish Churches,

> or whether they are to be regarded as an exception to the general rule. In that Cathedral with which I have been connected,[95] the custom has been that all members of the Cathedral body should wear the surplice in preaching, but that all others should wear the gown.
>
> Seeing then that there is no positive law of the Church forbidding or enjoining the surplice in the pulpit, my judgement is that it may be reasonably left to discretion to decide: and though I do not think that the clergyman is to be censured for acting, as he conceived, in obedience to the directions of the Church, I think he will do well in yielding in such a matter to the wishes and even prejudices of his parishioners. For it is written, "Give no offence, neither do the Gentiles, not to the Church of God." But where a plain direction of the Church is found there all should submit their judgement: for it is written again "If any man seems to be contentious, we have no such custom, neither the Churches of God." so that it is an Apostolic rule, that the order of the Church should be obeyed . . .
>
> Having now given my judgement upon both the points which have been raised, I earnestly implore all members of the Church in the Parish of Hampton, to abstain from everything calculated to give pain to their Pastor, or to provide disorder. We have all but one interest; as we have but one church let us all be of one heart and mind: that "whether I may come among you or be absent I may hear that ye stand fast in the Spirit, striving together for the faith of the Gospel." "Now may the God of peace be with you all, now henceforth and forever." John Fredericton[96]

Unfortunately we do not have a record of the outcome of this matter. What is remarkable is the judicious tone of the young bishop. While popular New Brunswick diocesan lore portrays Medley as stubborn and tactless,[97] this episode displays a considerable degree of gentleness and prudence. Medley could have imposed the wearing of the surplice, as Phillpotts had done at Exeter, yet he recognized that there were higher priorities in his new diocese. It was this reluctance to force his point of view on peripheral issues that allowed him to eventually win over most of the Low Churchmen in the diocese.

While Medley certainly did have the capacity to speak bluntly, his ability to adapt to new circumstances and realities ought not to be discounted. He certainly had no illusions that his particular understanding of the church, its liturgy and aesthetic principles, could be easily transmitted to the new diocese. Thus, he reported to the SPG in 1851:

> The difficulties connected with the establishment of a new mission are greater than anyone accustomed to the quiet orderly system of an English village can readily conceive. Imagine a number of independent freehold farmers, but of several means, left to themselves, as is often the case for some years, without any religious ordinances, or divided into sectional

> parties of . . . very doubtful Churchmanship, Baptists, Methodists and Presbyterians . . . They have, as it were, to make their religion as they make their farm, and both are left in very imperfect cultivation. To gather all or any portion of these people together, soothe their prejudices, invite their cooperation, secure their attendance, and induce them to build a church and worship in it steadily, is a great effort, which can only be understood by those who have seen and felt the difficulty.[98]

Although a new diocese, the church had existed in New Brunswick for decades and certain patterns of churchmanship had established firm roots. Therefore, Medley had not only to contend with competing denominations in this pluralistic society, but also to wrestle with a form of churchmanship that was deeply suspicious of his own.

The Tractarians were attacked in public in strident and personal tones. One publication that led the charge against "Puseyite" religion was the *Church Witness* of Saint John.[99] Commencing publication in 1850, it was edited by the Reverend J. W. D. Gray, rector of Trinity Church and the de facto leader of the Evangelicals.[100] From its very first issue, the *Church Witness* took aim at the Tractarians and all who sympathized with them. While never attacking Medley by name, it often used Henry Phillpotts as a surrogate target. Indeed, in the first three pages of the first edition of the paper, Phillpotts is attacked five separate times for various "Romish" excesses. As far as the *Church Witness* was concerned, there was no difference worth mentioning between High Churchmen such as Phillpotts and the worst of the Tractarians. Those who seceded to Rome were generally described as "perverts," and the paper reported with barely disguised glee each time a new secession was made public. Generally the *Church Witness* concerned itself with the affairs of the church in England, but it was clear that those events had implications for New Brunswickers.

Indirect rebuttal to Medley's various positions and proposals was possible by referring to the same ideas in their English manifestations. Thus, instead of Medley, Pusey was attacked as a "semi-papist,"[101] the Bible Society was defended against Tractarian attack;[102] and synodical government was frequently decried as undermining the ecclesiastical establishment.[103] A favorite target of the *Church Witness* was St. Barnabas's Church, Pimlico, which would figure in Medley's own intellectual development.[104] The opposition to synods, the "sacramental system," and episcopal authority formed the core of Gray's position. However, the paper occasionally reminded its readers that the threat was not just from afar: "I alluded to the great fact of Puseyism having marked for its victims the Colonies of Great Britain; also, the inevitable conviction that our own Province must be considered one of those indoctrinated more or less by this new propaganda Society."[105] Short of naming Medley directly, Gray was as explicit here as he dared to be with regard to his own diocesan bishop.

Much of this animus had a racial overtone. The city of Saint John had a Protestant majority that was in the process of being overwhelmed by Roman Catholic immigrants from Ireland.[106] Thus, any opportunity to link the Tractarians with Irish "Papist" outrages was seized upon. The paper went so far as to regularly publish crime statistics from Ireland, observing after one particularly violent year, "The criminal returns from Ireland are characteristic."[107] Gladstone's support for Irish emancipation and his links to the Tractarians served as further proof of the Irish-Papist-Tractarian conspiracy.[108]

The *Church Witness* was not the only voice representing this camp. Even more mainstream papers such as the *Courier* regularly printed letters lamenting "the architectural Puseyism" of Medley's churches and even asking outright, "Is the Right Reverend the Bishop of Fredericton a Puseyite?"[109] One correspondent to *The Loyalist*, another Saint John paper, identified "his Lordship's tastes, feelings and purposes as identical with those of a dangerous party in England."[110] Medley had his public defenders, but they were certainly muted by comparison.

Another early controversy that faced the new bishop of Fredericton concerned a charge of Tractarianism against one of his clergy. The Reverend James Hudson, missionary priest on the Miramichi River, had arrived in New Brunswick, sponsored by the SPG, before Medley's time. He was curate to the Reverend Samuel Bacon, who was an uncle of Medley's first wife. While Bacon was a mild man of moderate High Church principles, Hudson was temperamentally headstrong and of decidedly High Church, if not Tractarian, sympathies. He, like Medley, was an active Ecclesiologist, building several fine wooden Gothic Revival churches.[111]

Hudson was charged by his parishioners in Chatham with distributing Tractarian books, among other suspect activities. In a long series of letters which were made public and printed by a local paper (initially contrary to Medley's knowledge and permission), Medley and the vestry exchanged views on Hudson and his supposed irregularities. Medley wrote to the vestry at one point to say that he was "not aware that the Oxford Tracts . . . are either lent or circulated by Mr. Hudson or by any other clergyman in the province."[112] He went on to say that "if any clergyman be proved to circulate books which in my judgement are contrary to the doctrines of our own Prayer Book, I will admonish him of his error."[113] Two months later the same paper published another letter by Medley in which he explained that in importing books for the use of his clergy he had previously decided to avoid any "which entered into the controversy respecting the Oxford Tracts."[114]

The vestry had also accused Hudson of "Tractarian heresy." To this charge Medley replied: "Tractarian heresy may however mean anything, from the doctrine of Purgatory to the wearing of a surplice, from Papal supremacy to the simple reading of the Athanasian Creed. It is one of those convenient phrases which form a substitute for sound argument. Had you undertaken to show me that Mr. Hudson held Mr. Ward's 'non-natural' sense of the Articles or Mr. Newman's doctrine of developments [*sic*],[115] I should have agreed with you as to their erroneousness and their danger."[116] Throughout Medley's correspondence with the vestry, he never took the opportunity to defend the Tractarian positions that the vestry found so offensive.[117] Instead, he defended Hudson as not circulating Tractarian material. In the same letter quoted above Medley concluded with a passage that is thoroughly representative of his later position:

> I shall add no more but that no person has the right to brand me with the title of a party-man. Since my arrival in this diocese I have attached myself to no party; I have sought the interest of no party but the Church. I have not enquired who are high churchmen and who are low churchmen, I have taken everyone by the hand who had any sincere love for the Church to which he belonged without nicely calculating the shades of his belief. No man can with truth accuse me of unchristian and hard speeches towards Roman Catholics or protestant dissenters and I have received from both those bodies marks of respect and good will. I most deeply deplore that intolerant spirit in our Church which, while it is content to see every part of our Prayer Book violated, makes no allowances for those who act on their conscious conviction in doing it.[118]

There is no reason to think that Medley was being disingenuous here. In the next year his charge would contain the same renunciation of "party spirit" and he would continue to repeat it throughout his episcopate.

Despite this determined and vocal opposition Medley pressed on, undeterred in his building plans. The cathedral was completed and consecrated in 1853, just eight years after its beginning and despite considerable financial difficulty.[119] Through Medley's exertions and through large expenditures of his own resources, the cathedral was free from debt less than two years later.[120] Beyond Fredericton, the work of building up the diocese was carried out at an exhausting pace. Medley built and remodeled churches, recruited and ordained clergy, and traveled to the far corners of his diocese to baptize and confirm.

In his journal Medley gave detailed accounts of his travels. An example of a confirmation tour in 1846 gives some idea of the conditions he coped with:

> August 4—The Bp. set off on his tour to the North Eastern part of the Province. Having reached Boiestown he held services in the schoolhouse. Next day he confirmed 13 persons at Ludlow in an open barn—thence to Blackville and confirmed 2. Reached Nelson at night. Held service next day in the unfinished Church. Sunday 9th, confirmed 81 at St. Paul's Chatham. Preached in the evening at St. Mary's. Monday reached Bathurst. Tuesday confirmed there 32. Wednesday went to New Bandon, confirmed 16 and administered the Lord's supper to 50. Thursday reached Restigouche. Preached on Friday in the Courthouse, confirmed 6 and administered the Lord's Supper to 10, one of whom had not received it for 17 years. Preached at Bathurst on Sunday. Monday to Chatham. Tuesday to Baie des Vents . . .[121]

This tour, of only one part of his diocese, took Medley away from home for just over a month. He confirmed 467 altogether and traveled 939 miles.[122] For the year 1846 he traveled over twenty-eight hundred miles, in winter and summer, by boat, canoe, horse, and foot.

Severe winter conditions, which often lasted from November into April, made an already arduous work even more so. Medley's son Charles, who was rector of the parish of Sussex, recounted one occasion that illustrates the point:

> One very stormy and bitterly cold Monday in March last, the Bishop started with me for Dutch Valley. We had to break our road through about fourteen inches of snow for nine miles, and then climb up on our hands and knees to the church, which is on a steep hill—a feat not easily accomplished, for underneath the snow was a thick crust of ice, upon which we slid down almost as fast as we crept up. However, after many struggles and efforts, we succeeded in reaching the corner of the church, when a furious gust of wind sent the Bishop and his missionary flying down the hill again, with the Bishop's robe box following. When at last we managed to get inside the church, we found four men for a congregation. On the following day I met one of my most constant attendants at church, and asked him why he was not present, especially when the Bishop was there. "Well, sir," he said, "it was such an awful storm, it wasn't fit for a dog to be out."[123]

That this was not an isolated incident is confirmed by a study of the *Annals*, which recount many such storms during which Medley continued to carry out his pastoral duties.

Medley did not travel with a retinue, nor was he often received in stately homes. Many of his journeys were conducted alone, stopping at humble dwellings, preaching in barns, teaching in schoolhouses, and performing divine service in kitchens. Lyman Harding recounts a story that Medley told of those early years: "Approaching a farmhouse to inquire whether there were 'any Episcopalians' in the area, he was told by the lady of the house, 'I don't know, but the boys killed something out under the barn the other day.' "[124] In such a milieu, the finer points of English ecclesiastical disputes were largely beside the point. Although the relatively cosmopolitan press of Saint John were keenly interested in the nuances of Medley's churchmanship, in the rural areas of the province he became known and loved by virtue of his labor and personal attention to pastoral ministry. The long and taxing visitation tours of the province allowed virtually every active Anglican member of the New Brunswick church to have some personal acquaintance with his bishop. The *Annals* recount the record of Medley's daily work, most of which was "hands on" and little of which was conducted in committee rooms or salons.

Remarkable as this is, it is even more remarkable to realize that he kept up this same pace for forty-five years. As a comparison, in his summary for the year 1885, Medley recorded the following statistics: "confirmed this year by the Bishop 400. Bishop travelled 2747 miles."[125] In other words, at the age of eighty-one, he traveled as much as he had when he was forty years younger. The *Annals* make clear that these were not exceptional years. Virtually every year saw the same workload and many of them saw much more.

In 1881 Medley acquired a coadjutor, Hollingworth Tully Kingdon. In the first episcopal election in the diocese of Fredericton, H. T. Kingdon (who would go on to become diocesan only on Medley's death, after eleven years as assistant) was the single nominee put forward by Medley and then elected by the synod. Kingdon possessed impeccable Tractarian credentials, having been recommended to Medley by H. P. Liddon and R.W. Church.[126] A Cambridge M.A., he was a former student of Liddon's at Cuddesdon and vice-president of Salisbury Theological College.[127] He had been curate at St Andrew's, Wells St. London, under the vicar, Benjamin Webb, one of the founders of the Cambridge Camden Society.[128] While his scholarly credentials were outstanding,[129] his personal style and communication skills were less well developed than Medley's. As a consequence, following the long and successful episcopate of Medley, Kingdon was not as warmly received or remembered by New Brunswickers.[130]

Medley divided his own modest income in half to supply Kingdon. From then on until just before Medley's death in 1892, when the bishop became too infirm to travel, he and Kingdon shared the work equally. Medley traveled no less—the two bishops simply confirmed more frequently and traveled more extensively than one alone had done.

Medley always showed a particular interest in the poor, an interest that had already been hinted at in England. This was a large factor in his opposition to pew rents. With free seats, there would be "no violent thrusting out of the poor into inferior places, still less banishing of them altogether."[131] Pew rents eventually died out, chiefly due to Medley's refusal to consecrate any new church or addition unless all the seats in the building were free. As a consequence, one church remained unconsecrated for five years.[132] Medley established a Madras school in Fredericton, with each poor student required to bring in only a penny a week. Medley himself provided annual prizes of clothing and shoes.[133] There are stories of less public examples of charity. Ketchum relates one such: "There lived a widow, advanced in years and of limited means, some distance from the Cathedral. She was a good woman and a constant communicant. No want of a temporal kind was left unsupplied from the Bishop's hand. At regular intervals he sent a conveyance to enable her to be at the Cathedral to receive the holy communion. The day to be spent at Bishopscote, and then the poor widow was taken back to her home."[134] To this account could be added many more, including Medley's solicitude toward the black population of Fredericton, many descended from American slaves. One letter from a prominent Fredericton layman recounts that during the last weeks of his life, the last time "[Medley] was out of the house was in paying a visit to an old colored woman residing near Government house."[135] Medley habitually visited the sick and shut-ins personally, no less than if he were "the humblest curate in the land," according to one who knew him.[136]

The Later Years

Each year Medley built more new churches and remodeled others, in keeping with "Church principles." Opposition slowly diminished as he won the trust of the people of the diocese. The last significant battle concerned synodical government, of which more will be said in chapter 5. He remarried in 1863 to Margaret Hudson, a woman who was to be a redoubtable figure in her own right. The second Mrs. Medley was a very active participant in diocesan affairs. Indeed, in the infirmity of the bishop's last year, Kingdon complained to the SPG that "the Diocese was being 'run' by Mrs. Medley."[137] He had no children by his second marriage.

Honors came Medley's way in later years. In 1879, he was elected Metropolitan of Canada, a post he held until his death in 1892.[138] At Lambeth conferences he was accorded the respect due to a missionary patriarch. On his various visits home to England, he was celebrated and coveted as a preacher. In 1878, when he attended the second Lambeth conference, Medley was a guest of the primus of Scotland, the bishop of Lincoln, the bishop of Ely, New College Oxford, Wadham College, and Dr. Acland.[139] He preached at St. Mary's Oxford, Cuddesdon College, Exeter Cathedral, St. Peter's London Docks (for Charles Lowder),[140] All Saints' Margaret Street, St. Paul's Cathedral, and Ottery St. Mary. In addition, he visited his old parishes in Devon and Cornwall, preaching several times there.[141]

In 1877 Gladstone had evidently written to invite Medley to visit him while in England.[142] Medley was forced to write to Gladstone while at Lambeth to apologize for not getting in touch with him, due to his busy schedule at the conference.[143] He suggested that Gladstone would likely be too busy to fit in a meeting at short notice. The next day Gladstone responded to Medley and invited him for supper. An attached sheet indicates that Medley was to be joined by: the bishop of Bombay, the dean of Christ Church (Henry Liddell) and Mrs Liddell, Lady Cavendish (Medley stayed at the home of Lord Devon, Sir William Cavendish, the privy councillor, while in Devonshire), Mr. Balfour (probably the future prime minister, the young A. J. Balfour, with whom Gladstone was, at this time, friends),[144] Mr. Knowles (probably James Knowles, editor of the *Contemporary Review* and founder of the Metaphysical Society, a longtime friend of Gladstone's),[145] Spencer Lyttelton (Gladstone's private secretary and Mrs. Gladstone's nephew),[146] and John Ruskin.[147] It was a star-studded cast, but sadly, no record of the evening's conversation has been discovered.

On his visit to the third Lambeth Conference in 1888, at the age of eighty-four, he was again received with respect and honor. He preached at St. Augustine's College, from whence many of his ordinands over the years had come.[148] He was the guest of Bishop Wordsworth of Salisbury, where he celebrated on a Sunday. At Cambridge an honorary D.D. was conferred and another at Durham. He preached in the parishes of his sons Edward and John. In addition, he preached in his old parish of St. Thomas, Southleigh. Perhaps because of his age, he limited his preaching engagements to those places with which he had a personal connection.

By 1889, Medley's health was beginning to fail. His son Charles's death in that year was a blow from which he never fully recovered. For the first time since he began keeping his journal forty-four years previously, Medley ceased to write. Instead, Bishop Kingdon took over the journal for a time and recorded Charles's death on August 25.[149] Later, in the winter of that same year, Medley fell on the ice, injuring his right hand and arm. Characteristically, he then taught himself how to write with his left hand.[150] When he resumed his journal in March of 1890, it was clear that he was finally slowing down. Nevertheless, in September of that year he embarked on a confirmation tour, traveling 282 miles. In 1891, he traveled less, but still continued to celebrate, preach, and confirm. Finally, on February 23, 1892, he sent a pastoral note throughout the diocese acknowledging that he was no longer able to "undertake the labourious journeys which, up to a later period, God gave me strength to perform."[151] The spring and summer of that year saw increasing infirmity. However, as late as July 17, he traveled sixty miles to Saint John and preached. He finally entered into his final illness in August. On September 9, "he became unconscious and remained so until the calm and peaceful end" that same day.[152]

On Medley's death condolences and tributes poured in from around the Anglican communion. One of these was from Medley's old friend, Lord Chief Justice Coleridge, who wrote: "[Medley's] goodness, his accomplishments, his noble simplicity, I have seldom known approached in the experience of what is now a long life."[153] The testimonial from the bishop of Albany, William Croswell Doane, spoke to Medley's close association with the Episcopal Church in the United States: "I feel that to no man on the continent of America more than to him is due the great advance in all things that tend to the upholding of the Catholic faith and order in America. He was Nestor and Patriarch really among us all, and was more closely identified, I think, with the Bishops and with the interests of the American Church than any English Colonial Bishop has ever been in America."[154] Medley's stature in the American church had been strengthened by numerous sermons preached while visiting there and others contacts over the years. In forty-seven years, Medley had been transformed from a young bishop, suspected within his diocese of Tractarian excess, to a patriarchal figure, respected near and far, among all stripes of churchmen.

Many of the leading Evangelicals in New Brunswick contributed heartfelt letters to Mrs. Medley or sermons to their congregations, expressing their admiration for him. Significantly, one of these tributes was contained in a letter written to Ketchum by the rector of Trinity Church Saint John, the church that had so tenaciously opposed Medley in the early days. After remarking upon Medley's "saintliness of life . . . simple habits and unaffected piety," Canon Brigstocke went on to applaud Medley's dedication to the diocese of Fredericton: "The Bishop's attachment to his Diocese is the more worthy of notice, as the history of the Colonial Episcopate furnishes, Alas, so many instances of Episcopal resignations, and returns to the mother land! I do not believe that our dear Bishop ever entertained such an idea. It is well known that when he went to England for a visit, I think it was the last one, he stated that the happiest day he spent away was the one on which he put his foot on the steamer to return. *O si sic omnes*! The Church would then have a chance of taking far deeper root in the land, and growing and expanding as we desire."[155] This reaction from the rector of a parish once profoundly hostile to Medley is reflective of the change that occurred around the diocese among erstwhile opponents. Another Evangelical cleric wrote: "His countrymen of this province know now, if they knew it not at first, and learned it but tardily, that they have among them one who in any country and in any environment, could have stood in the foremost rank; not as a scholar, although his knowledge far outstrips many possessors of showy academical diplomas; not as an orator, though to listen to his preaching is the supreme luxury to a trained literary taste, and not one of his clergy even distantly approaches him; . . . but in that mysterious result which men call character, which transcends all that men can do in what they are."[156] Through one means or another, the people of his diocese were largely converted to a personal admiration of Medley, if not a complete acceptance of his churchmanship.

The Accomplishments of the Medley Episcopate

If we look at the diocese in 1892, the changes effected are remarkable for such a short period. The diocese had grown very significantly. In addition to the forty-seven churches that existed on Medley's arrival in New Brunswick, 107 more had been consecrated by him. The vacant missions were filled and new ones added. Medley made the improvement of the physical setting of worship a priority for his episcopate. All but one of the forty-seven years recorded in his journal as bishop of Fredericton saw the consecration of a new or remodeled church. This process began almost immediately, as we have seen. St. Anne's Chapel was completed in 1847 and the cathedral in 1853. In Medley's first five years alone, twenty-four churches were consecrated—half as many as had been built in the previous sixty years.[157]

The building up of missions, increase of clergy, and erection of churches was no small task. New Brunswick offered little by way of attraction to young clerics. The province was rough, largely rural, the climate was harsh, and it was chronically depressed economically.[158] On top of this, the SPG grants, on which the colonial church was reliant, were slowly withdrawn over the course of Medley's episcopate.[159] Despite Medley's best efforts, there was never a substantial system of endowments established. Taking into account the above factors, it is remarkable that after removing the largest source of church revenue (pew rents) in the pre-Medley church, the diocese grew at all, let alone as dramatically as it did. However, it never became truly prosperous.

The group of thirty clergy that Medley found on arrival in New Brunswick in 1845 had grown to seventy by 1871.[160] However, obtaining sufficient numbers of clergy was always a difficult task, as Medley reported to the SPG in 1846: "after filling up twelve vacancies I could find immediate and full employment for twenty additional clergymen without diminishing the labours of any one at present in Holy Orders. Unhappily I have at present neither the means nor the men; but it will easily be seen that when one clergyman attempts to discharge the duties of three, four, and even six parishes, it must be done imperfectly and unsatisfactorily; schools cannot be superintended, the sick and the whole cannot be properly visited and after hurrying from place to place on the Lord's day, the result is exhaustion of mind and body, without a due effect on the minds of the flock."[161] While part of his work was to attract more clergy to the diocese, Medley also wished to raise the overall level of clerical training. He welcomed the establishment of St. Augustine's Missionary College, Canterbury, at which young men were to be trained for missionary work. His old friend, Bishop W. H. Coleridge, who had spoken at the public gathering before he left for Canada, was at one time the warden and Medley addressed the assembly at its opening.[162] Of the approximately one hundred priests that Medley ordained in New Brunswick, sixteen were students of St. Augustine's.[163] A handful of others came from the United States. The vast majority of the rest of his clergy were trained at the University of New Brunswick in Fredericton (formerly King's College). In these cases, Medley generally had a direct hand in their education. He was a rigorous instructor, even correcting the grammar in students' personal letters to him before returning them.[164]

He personally examined each candidate for Holy Orders, and the *Annals* record the outcome of these examinations. For deacon's orders he required knowledge of "the Gospels in Greek, knowledge of Browne on the Articles, Pearson on the Creed, Proctor on the Prayer Book, Church history and some easy parts of the Bible in Hebrew."[165] He also expected high standards of those who had already been ordained. At every visitation, he exhorted his clergy to be diligent in their studies. In particular, he always stressed the value of biblical languages, other linguistic studies, and a thorough knowledge of the Bible. In this he set an example, taking up the study of German in his sixties[166] and in his seventies producing a new translation of Job.[167]

Church Music

While Medley's architectural interests have been well documented,[168] less well known is the nearly equal passion he had for church music. T. G. Cooper has said this of Medley's musical contributions to the church: "His compositions were representative of the best of nineteenth-century Canadian Protestant church music. Medley was the first prominent Anglican church composer in Eastern Canada."[169] In music, Medley cannot be said to have made as lasting an impact on the church as he did with his architectural influence. His achievements were not insignificant. He composed dozens of anthems and other pieces of liturgical music. He wrote many hymns and hymn tunes.[170] He was also a great student of music. The Medley Library contains a large collection of sheet music and works on musical theory. Oddly, Medley's compositions never received wide notice in Canada and his only published compositions appeared in England.[171]

Perhaps his greatest musical legacy to the church was not in his own writing, but in his promotion of liturgical music. The musical aspect of Anglican worship was rudimentary in New Brunswick prior to 1845. Medley immediately began to promote "choral services" and to cultivate musical tastes. He served as his own cathedral choir director for his entire episcopate, holding practices in his home.[172] In this novel undertaking can be seen Medley's willingness to act in a way that was outside of the accepted English episcopal model, if he believed the situation called for such innovation.[173]

The choral tradition that he favored was at first distrusted in some quarters, as were the hymns with which he intended to supplant Tate and Brady.[174] By the end of his episcopate choral services had been adopted throughout the diocese. Nothing illustrates the thorough impact of his tastes more than the service in 1890 at which the "surpliced choirs" of three Saint John churches, including Trinity Church, joined in a choral service.[175]

Church Government

What is interesting in light of Medley's theological conservatism is his openness to radical restructuring of the relationship between ecclesiastical and civil institutions. While the older High Church tradition had been solidly Tory, disestablishment attracted many Tractarians.[176] For most of them, this was motivated by a reaction against the perceived Erastianism of the Elizabethan settlement, borne out by the alleged subservient nature of the eighteenth-century church. Although, as Nockles makes clear, prior to the Tractarians there was already "a deeper High Church principle of the Church being a divine society, which ultimately did not depend upon its connection with the state."[177] With Medley there was a new element in political thought. As a colonial bishop, he was forced to consider the nature of the church in a pluralistic society, in a more immediate way than he would have had to in England. He recognized that the church in New Brunswick was in a context more like the Episcopal Church in America than the Church of England at home.

Before Medley departed for Canada, in his address to the public meeting at Exeter, he described the shadowy quasi-establishment prevailing in New Brunswick. It was clear that on this point his more radical Tractarian tendencies outweighed his more conventional High Church Toryism. From his first charge onward, Medley consistently warned the clergy against relying on establishment and exhorted them to the vision of an independent church. This took concrete form in the 1851 meeting of the bishops of Canada and their recommendation to request synodical government. At this point the Diocese of Fredericton simply was not prepared to accept this measure and Medley had to relent. Meanwhile other Canadian dioceses proceeded with their own synodical plans.[178]

The Colenso decision, or at least the interpretation that Medley placed on it, eventually forced his hand.[179] In 1865 the Judicial Committee of the Privy Council had ruled against Bishop Gray of Cape Town and in favor of Bishop Colenso of Natal. The deposition imposed upon Colenso by Gray's Synod was declared null and void, inasmuch as the Letters Patent granted to a colonial bishop granted him no "coercive jurisdiction" wherever there was a separate legislature.[180] For many Tractarians, as Chadwick observes, this decision of a civil court upon an ecclesiastical matter was an echo of the Gorham decision, with all of its Erastian overtones.[181]

When Medley finally called directly for the establishment of a synod in 1865, the majority of the diocese was ready to acquiesce.[182] Whatever it was in Medley's character that won Evangelicals over to neo-Gothic architecture and choral worship also prevailed in this instance. One of the leaders of the Evangelicals, who had resisted synods because of the fear of episcopal domination, the Reverend G. M. Armstrong of Saint John, eventually became a strong supporter of the

Synod and later served as Medley's commissary while the bishop attended the second Lambeth Conference.[183]

While New Brunswick was not the first Canadian diocese to incorporate a synod, it was not because of a lack of will on behalf of the bishop. In this case, Medley's prudence triumphed over his sense of principle and his decision not to try to force synod into premature existence probably eased its eventual acceptance. Medley lived to see the diocese join the Provincial Synod of Canada and died just before the Anglican Church of Canada was constituted, with a general synod for the entire country established in 1893.

Diocesan structures were also developed during Medley's time. Although he served as his own dean, he appointed successive sub-deans, commissaries, archdeacons, and canons, who exercised greater or lesser degrees of authority. At his first visitation he divided the diocese into seven deaneries and appointed the rural deans.[184] These were to be elected every three years in the future. A list of their quite extensive duties and responsibilities was given to them. Responsible for collecting annual returns for the parishes of their deaneries, they also were expected to inspect those same parishes and report on the state of the churches, glebes, and so on. They were also to gather the clergy at least quarterly "for the purpose of mutual edification."[185]

Another significant act, which certainly was controversial at the time, was Medley's decision to ask for, and after years of debate to receive, a coadjutor. Medley first raised the question with Synod in 1874.[186] In 1879, Synod acceded to Medley's request including the most controversial provision of it, that he nominate his assistant and successor himself.[187]

It is clear that the episcopate of John Medley was remarkable for its length and its activity. It is fair to say that he never slowed down until his health gave out, and that was well past the age of eighty. He was a gifted and charismatic figure who drew on the education and experiences that he had received in England to help forge a new church in Canada. Having discussed the outlines of Medley's life and ministry, it remains now to examine more closely his theology.

3

John Medley's Intellectual Context

Rationalism and Romanticism

One of the pitfalls of attaching such labels as "Enlightenment thinker" or "Romantic writer" to individuals is that they immediately cease to be individuals and become merely two-dimensional representatives. Such shorthand as these labels do provide is of course valuable in many ways. When one looks closely at figures so described, complexities and contradictions often (if not inevitably) appear. In applying general conclusions to specific individuals and circumstances, the historian can often seriously misrepresent them.

For example, one nineteenth-century churchman might be labeled a Tractarian. Another might be called an Ecclesiologist. Still another might be a seen as a social reformer and another as a Tory. What confounds this system of labeling is the existence of someone like John Medley, who could, with equal justice, bear all of the above labels, plus a few more.[1] At the same time, he did not completely fit into any of those categories. Medley has been called variously a Tractarian Patriarch,[2] a salesman of the Imperial ideal,[3] and an exponent of the Romantic movement, by virtue of his championing of Gothic Revival architecture.[4] Given the caveats above, this chapter will attempt to categorize Medley's thought, beginning with an examination of his understanding of the place of reason in Christian theology.

If it is commonplace to suggest that Romanticism was, in some measure, a response to the Enlightenment, it has become an equally accepted statement to say that the Gothic Revival in architecture is a child of Romanticism.[5] It was part of that wider return to past forms and the identification with nature expressed in poetry by Wordsworth, in painting by Delacroix, in music by Beethoven, and in philosophy by Rousseau. In all these different fields of endeavor there appeared within the span of two or three generations powerful manifestations of similar themes. Passion and a new emphasis on imagination as opposed to reason, a rejection of Classicism, an exaltation of the individual, a sense of the transcendent, an identification with the natural order—these and other, sometimes conflicting, themes were shared by men and women who made contributions in virtually every sphere of European culture. The Gothic Revival (or neo-Gothic) movement seemed to be part and parcel of this larger cultural phenomenon.

In wider society the Romantic movement sought to correct the perceived errors of the Enlightenment. These errors were often contained under the umbrella of what orthodox churchmen called "rationalism." In the most formal sense rationalism describes the first of the two great philosophical movements of the early modern period, of which the other was empiricism. Associated, for example, with René Descartes, rationalism suggested that reason alone—the mind reflecting on itself, apart from empirical evidence—could supply us with the ground of knowledge. This view is, of course, opposed in the succeeding position, empiricism, for which we might look to David Hume as a representative.

Both rationalism and empiricism combined (along with other elements) to form the groundwork for that great revolutionary movement, the Enlightenment, from which we are still experiencing the shockwaves. In broad terms, the Enlightenment represented a rejection of knowledge based upon received tradition or authority. Instead, all knowledge was to be the result of "scientific" inquiry. That is, the presumption made by the thinkers of the Enlightenment was that it was possible, and certainly desirable, to construct a worldview without "prejudice," relying only on those truths that could be demonstrated by reason.

When nineteenth-century conservative Anglican divines, such as E. B. Pusey or John Medley, spoke of "rationalism" they did not mean that formal school of philosophy, which we identify with Descartes (although he would almost certainly have been included in their understanding of the term). Instead they meant a much more general habit of mind, represented by the Enlightenment itself. To them rationalism was regarded as a way of thinking necessarily antagonistic to Christianity. It was that approach to thought that dispensed with all authority, including that of Scripture. It rejected miracles, revelation, and the supernatural in general. It exulted in the unaided power of the human intellect and considered that religion, as traditionally understood, could be dispensed with in a modern, rationalistic, and scientific age. This is precisely the cold, mechanical view of nature and religion that the Romantic movement opposed. It is tempting to connect forms of opposition to this rationalism that may not in fact be otherwise connected. Medley's rejection of one form of "rationalism," for example, should not necessarily be seen as identical in aim with the Romantic critique of reason in a wider sense.

Within the Church of England, which was affected by Romanticism in so many of its forms, the appearance of the Gothic Revival is connected with the Cambridge Movement in architecture and the Oxford Movement in theology.[6] Although the architectural movement has separate sources from the theological, because the two shared a similar antipathy to the Georgian or classical *ethos* and both appealed to older forms, they are often considered together. Indeed, many of the personalities associated with the Oxford Movement were also participants in the renewal of church architecture that began at Cambridge University.

That Tractarianism is connected to Romanticism is no doubt true in some measure. For example, Sheridan Gilley speaks of "the role of the High Church revival, as a sublimation of the dangers of Romanticism under a discipline of religious self-control."[7] While the Romanticism of Byron and Shelley was clearly repugnant to the orthodox Anglican mind, there was nevertheless an appealing *spirit* to the Romantic movement. Gilley explains how Keble appropriated this spirit to his own religious and didactic ends:

> The tender human Christ of Keble, speaking to the heart and affections, transformed the High Church tradition, which would henceforth deliberately seek to transmit the divine comfort and consolation through a more loving presentation of Church and liturgy. Faith was no longer mere rational conviction or tribal duty to set forms, but the bond of worship as sacrament linking Christ and the soul. This devotional revolution underlay the High Church repudiation of much in its rationalist and Erastian and Protestant inheritance; for the new Anglo-Catholic teachings after 1830 were to speak to the heart and imagination, transforming the life of doctrine by the life of devotion, changing what Anglicans believed by changing the manner in which they said their prayers.[8]

The revolution went beyond changes in devotion alone. Doctrine, architecture, liturgy, ecclesiology, and many other areas would be affected by this change in perspective. The essence of the Tractarians' Romanticism was the shift from reason to other criteria as the basis for religious certainty. These criteria included tradition (and authority generally), feeling, and more mystical modes of communication. It can at least be said that the Tractarians in general were skeptical of the claims of reason in regard to religion, if not actually anti-philosophical.

Peter Nockles considers the Tractarian criticism of the previous High Church tradition to be connected to their understanding of the place of reason, whereby "religion seemed to be placed in the understanding, rather than in the affections."[9] To correct what they perceived as an overreliance on mere reason, a greater moral depth was required in the student of theology. That this aversion to philosophy and speculative theology was embraced by the Tractarians (with ultimately destructive results) is demonstrated by Robert Crouse.[10] He argues that there was a conscious division among churchmen, between those who espoused the principles of the Enlightenment and those who opposed it. It was no less an authority than John Stuart Mill who claimed "that every thinking man was either a Benthamite, belonging to the school of progress, or a Coleridgean who upheld and expressed the wisdom contained in the sacred texts of the race."[11] If this rough characterization has any measure of truth, the Tractarians would generally be understood to fall into the latter of the two camps.[12]

For Pusey (and others), "there was therefore no ground of mediation between the traditional doctrine and the position of the rationalist critics, only a choice, as Pusey saw it, according to one's faith or one's lack of it."[13] As Nockles puts it, "The prerequisites for the reception of the truth of the Gospel were not intellectual attainment or rational enquiry, but the simplicity and teachable disposition of little children."[14] The problem with this position was that it was unable, by its very nature, to make any reasoned response to the emerging theological liberalism of the nineteenth century. Many sincere persons who claimed to believe the Christian faith held theological positions at odds with the older tradition. Apart from denying the genuineness of their faith, the Tractarians were not able to make any rational argument concerning their opposing interpretations of scripture or the tradition.[15]

It is significant that E. B. Pusey's notable early work was *An Historical Enquiry into the Probable Causes of the Rationalist Character Lately Predominant in the Theology of Germany*. That this "rationalist character" was destructive, Pusey assumed went without saying. Nevertheless, his motivations in publishing such a study were questioned by other High Churchmen, notably H. J. Rose, and a prolonged controversy ensued.[16] Pusey's intention had not been to vindicate German rationalism, as Rose charged, but only to demonstrate that not all German theologians were guilty of it. There were theologians in Germany whom Pusey judged to be orthodox. They were part of a neo-orthodox, antirationalist movement.[17] This had a long tradition in Germany and included writers such as Neander,[18] Tholuck,[19] and, most significantly, Schleiermacher.[20] Schleiermacher's epigram, "the effort to introduce philosophical systems into theology is generally at variance with a correct interpretation of Scripture,"[21] underlined the opposition of this neo-pietist movement to the ungoverned exercise of reason. Liddon tells us that this saying of Schleiermacher was often quoted approvingly, even late in life, by Pusey.[22]

Both Hankey and Crouse argue that the failure to view the church fathers philosophically and to understand the philosophical roots of patristic thought severely limited the value of Tractarian scholarship. As Hankey argues, "Dr. Pusey tried to revive the study of the Fathers without attending to the philosophical framework of their theological and moral decisions and called rather for 'devout perusal' and spiritual understanding.[23]" This refusal to engage the "intellectual substance of the old forms," while dogmatically appropriating their conclusions, led finally to opposing parties marked by "self-consciously arbitrary self-assertion."[24] This exploration of the philosophical character of the older forms was just what the Tractarians (and many other conservative Christians of the period, like the German pietists) "feared to do or thought they could escape."[25]

Opposed to this criticism of the Tractarians for their deficiency in this regard, stand other contemporary scholars, such as Bishop Geoffrey Rowell. Recognizing the same antipathy of the Tractarians toward a philosophical approach to Christianity, Rowell nevertheless finds in this phenomenon the Tractarians' glory and one of their signal contributions to the church.[26] However, even Rowell is also conscious that this entrenched dogmatism finally limited the ability of the heirs of the Tractarian position to communicate the faith to the society around them.[27]

Medley's Understanding of the Place of Reason

There were many strands that made up the Romantic thread, many of which seem incompatible and indeed were unable to coexist in a single individual. It is entirely conceivable, then, that a given individual could display certain affinities to what we take to be the Romantic position, while opposing other distinctly Romantic notions. For instance while Medley might have accepted the appeal to the aesthetics of a past age and the enhanced (even mystical) appreciation of nature that was prominent in Romanticism, at the same time he utterly repudiated the emotional subjectivity of the Romantics.

There was, in John Medley, an ambivalence to reason that led sometimes to confusing and apparently contradictory opinions. In his first published work he argued that the Christian Church continually adapts itself to "the every modification of the human mind, to every stage of civilization and intelligence."[28] However, it is evident from the context that these modifications to which the church adapted herself were in the area of *adiaphora*, and not the substance of the faith.

Medley recognized that the matter of the jurisdiction of human reason was central. Moreover, in a sermon preached at Exeter Cathedral in 1840 he declared that in the Church of England, "the great question of the bounds and limits of private judgement has never been settled."[29] This question arose, according to Medley, at the time of the Reformation. This "private judgement," which Medley characterized as one of those areas in which Dissenters had erred by excess, would be considered by him repeatedly over the years.

In Medley's view of church history, if the Reformation had brought mixed blessings to the church, the seventeenth century was worse. The civil war allowed men "whose minds were alienated from the Church and cast in the Genevan mould . . . [to seize the Church in order to] . . . subvert her institutions."[30] Even the Restoration did not bring the church to the state that Medley would desire. The nation "rushed into the opposite extreme of profligacy, and open shameless impiety." This age in turn was followed by "an age of cold and specious rationalism; men became more decent in their manners, but not more practically alive to the power of goodness."[31] What was missing in this age of "cold rationalism" was "the fervour, and devotion, and spiritual tone of our Church."[32]

Eventually, Medley went on to relate, the church was awakened from her slumbers. The agent of this awakening was not Keble, nor Newman, nor indeed any Tractarian, but John Wesley and the Evangelical Revival.[33] Medley retained this respect for Wesley throughout his life. For Medley, it would always be the case that zealous and sincere Evangelicalism was far preferable to dry formalism.[34] True and living religion, for him, could not exist without some degree of "fervour and devotion." At the same time, he heartily disapproved of the schismatic tendencies of Wesley's followers—"in their zeal to *bring in*, they forgot to *build up*."[35]

In this sermon Medley commended, in a footnote, "Norris on faith and reason."[36] In a letter to Pusey, written in the same year that the sermon above was preached, Medley again mentioned "Norris on reason and Faith."[37] Medley was referring to *An Account of Reason and Faith: in Relation to the Mysteries of Christianity* by John Norris (1657–1712).[38] He had recommended Norris to a woman he was counseling because "it meets the precise point of difficulty in those minds, viz, that we must not believe what is contrary to reason or above it, confounding the two."[39] The language used here by Medley was in reference to the key question in the late eighteenth-century debate between the Deists and the orthodox.

Norris, one of the Cambridge Platonists,[40] was an interesting choice for Medley and one that offers us some insights into his thinking at this time. Norris himself, on the cusp of the Enlightenment, referred to his time as "a cold, frozen age,"[41] words that, as we saw above, Medley later echoed. Norris directed his argument against a work called *Christianity not Mysterious*.[42] Written by John Toland, it was an influential setting forth of the deist position.[43] Norris's reply to it was one of many contemporary responses.[44]

In his book, Norris argued strongly for the orthodox faith, suggesting that a Socinian position would easily turn into deism and that a deist would turn into an atheist "whenever he pleases."[45] The problem with the deists, according to Norris, was that they confounded human and divine nature. That is, "either they *Humanize* God or *Deify* themselves and their own rational abilities."[46] Thus, the argument from the deists could be, by Norris, reduced to a syllogism:

> Whatever is above our Reason is not to be believ'd as true; But the reputed Mysteries of Christianity are above our Reason:Therefore the Reputed Mysteries of Christianity are not to be believ'd as true.[47]

Norris said that the syllogism was flawed because of the "contestable" and ultimately false major premise. Only the divine wisdom was infinite and able to be the measure of all things. It was not only impious, but manifestly absurd, Norris argued, to suggest that human reason was able to comprehend all truth.

He proposed to refute Toland (and the deists in general) both inductively and deductively.[48] The heart of his argument was his demonstration "that there may be some things True which are above the comprehension of Human Reason."[49] This statement was followed by a detailed and complex scholastic-style account of the divisions and categories of reason. (We might observe at this point that Medley either had a high opinion of his young woman's academic ability or was a particularly impractical pastor to recommend this difficult work as a religious aid to a lay person.) Norris proceeded by way of definition and distinction:

"By things above Reason then (as the expression is used in this Distinction) I conceive to be Meant, Not such as reason of it self cannot Discover, but such as when proposed it cannot Comprehend. And by things Contrary to reason I conceive such as it can and does actually comprehend, and that to be absolutely impossible. Or in other words, a thing is then above reason when we do not comprehend how it can be, and then Contrary to reason when we do positively comprehend that it cannot be."[50] In light of these definitions Norris affirmed that there are indeed things above reason which are nevertheless not contrary to it. That this is so can be simply demonstrated, he suggested. It is conceivable that a thing beyond reason may be true; if true, it cannot be contrary to reason.[51]

Norris's position was well suited to Medley's own theological inclinations. While opposing the radical rationalism of Locke or Toland, which would confine all truth within the bounds of human reason, Norris nevertheless wanted to avoid any suggestion that the Christian faith was irrational. Hence, although *above* reason, some of its mysteries were not *contrary* to reason. In advising his Socinian friend, Medley's aim was apparently to convince her both of the limitations of reason and the rational soundness of the church's teachings. Norris, after all, affirmed that nothing could be "theologically true which is Philosophically False."[52] Medley was not inclined to accept a simple pietism. Yet, at this stage of his life Medley was, like his Tractarian colleagues, deeply critical of rationalism.

This critique of reason's claims can be tied to Medley's overall position at this point in relation to the secular order. He went on, in this same sermon, to excoriate a state church that was compelled "to bury persons who never enter our churches [and encouraged] the custom of administering the Holy Sacrament to criminals just before their execution, when the evidences of repentance, if any, must necessarily be so few and imperfect."[53] There was at work here a rejection of the impurities and compromises that participation in the secular world entailed, in favor of a mystical and revealed religion, and a church that corresponded to it. Any independent institution or art was suspected as being hostile to the church. Medley thus attacked forms of popular literature, art, and history that were not consistent with Christian doctrine and morals.[54] He saw the church as in a desperate state, worse than any previous age.[55] "Difficulties press on us on every side. Questions which once slept have risen to perplex and agitate the world. The spirit of the age, restless and incessant in its movements, but unable to guide itself, is hurrying men forward they know not whither."[56]

Medley's language here is of interest. While acknowledging the spirit of the age, it was, for him, an undirected and (potentially) malevolent spirit. He later developed a more positive account of it, linking it more directly to God's benevolent providence. In the end, Medley expressed classical Tractarian principles and feelings. The church was an ark of spiritual purity in a hostile and sinful world. Secular institutions were to be distrusted. Rationalism would destroy the necessarily mysterious nature of religion. The only answer was to go back to the Fathers and the Scriptures, received as authorities.[57]

This apparent distrust of the merely human was intensified in Medley's early understanding of architecture. In his *Elementary Remarks on Church Architecture*, he saw the value of Gothic (or "church") architecture primarily in its ability to remind man "of his own littleness."[58] Earthly concerns were "petty" and the horizontal lines of classical architecture tended to merely reinforce that limited earthly perspective. On the other hand, Gothic architecture lifted us above the natural, and only then were we "fit for communion" with God.[59] Medley's concluding hope was that the Gothic style might be revived and churches erected that would again "lead men's minds naturally to the great purpose for which they come to worship, and tend to fill them with self-abasing thoughts of their own littleness, weakness, and guilt, and with high and becoming reverence for the majesty and mercy of their Creator."[60] This extreme contrast between human wretchedness and divine splendor was certainly also present in Pusey, with whom, as we have seen, Medley seemed to have shared a special bond.[61]

A Change of Perspective

In 1846, one year into his episcopate, Medley preached a pair of ordination sermons at Christ Church, Fredericton.[62] In the second of them we can see that a distinct shift had occurred in his understanding of reason and the secular order. It is almost as if he had cast off his earlier Romanticism, in order to embrace a more directly pragmatic approach to the church. He took up the question of theological education. Significantly, his account of education began by quoting a paragraph of "Lord Bacon" (from *Proficience and Advancement of Learning*). This was, at first glance, a peculiar authority for Medley to cite. Bacon was, in many ways, quite opposite to Norris in his philosophical position. There was, in Bacon, a complete rejection of any mystical theology and an espousal of a practical, rational philosophy. In Norris, Medley found a position that appeared to support Tractarian sacramentalism as well as the Romantic rejection of deist rationalism. In Bacon, the opposite was found. Bacon rejected, in the work cited by Medley, any philosophical approach that was not rationally understood and was not directed toward a practical end. He thus rejected scholastic speculative philosophy as well as "occult" investigations.

In the ordination sermon, Medley quoted Bacon to his congregation and to the ordinands before him.[63] Reason directed to a contemplative end was here derided as "a couch, where to rest a searching and restless spirit." Instead knowledge should be directed toward two proper ends: "[to be] a rich storehouse for the glory of the Creator, and the relief of man's estate." In regard to the knowledge of God, reason is not to speculate about it; that knowledge comes to us from revelation. On the human side knowledge is to be directed toward the practical end of improving the human condition.

Medley continued the sermon by elaborating on his account of knowledge. He paraphrased Bacon: "The getting of true knowledge [is] the union of contemplation and action in the glory of God and the good of mankind."[64] Medley's intention in the sermon was to argue for the value of practical knowledge. He referred to those who argued that the Apostles were unlearned men. Quoting Bacon ("[that] same great writer") again, he suggested that God only chose them to show more clearly His great power, in using the weaker vessels. Since they do not enjoy the Apostles' gifts of inspiration it is even more incumbent on later preachers to devote themselves to study. Not only did he commend study, but he made it clear that this study was to be of subjects both "secular and divine."[65] Even to study Scripture required "a large measure of secular knowledge," inasmuch as the "word of God is written in different styles, some part in poetry, some in prose, some part in history and biography, some part in mystical and symbolical language."[66]

Medley expanded on the same theme, emphasizing the importance of secular knowledge for the practical end of being a better evangelist and expositor of the word of God. This was followed by a summary of those fields to which the educated cleric must turn his attention: the content of Scripture, its proper interpretation, doctrine, Christian duty, church history, and so on. It is interesting that in speaking of the right interpretation of Scripture he did not here suggest the reading of the fathers, but rather an acquaintance "with the laws of Hebrew Poetry, in which the greater part of Scripture is written, [and] with the manners and customs of the Jews and of eastern nations."[67] This indicates that Medley had at least some familiarity with the new investigations of critical scholarship and approved of their potential value.[68]

Medley had, by this time, also revised his opinion of Newman, possibly as a consequence of the latter's secession. Juliana Ewing recalled in later years that Medley had taken this event as "a great grief."[69] Unfortunately we have no references from Medley himself about this. A sermon preached in 1847 sheds more light on Medley's new view of Newman, which appeared by then as a profound disillusionment.

In a sermon on the Reformation, Medley spent some time considering the place of the Anglican formularies. In criticizing those members of the church who did not faithfully follow the Prayer Book he added, "A great deal has been heard of late about the natural and non-natural sense of the Thirty-nine Articles, in consequence of an attempt to prove that it was possible for persons holding all Roman doctrine to sign the Articles in their own sense, that is, in fact, to strain them into a sense their compilers never intended. As soon as this doctrine was broached, it was, I think, generally felt by most sound-minded members of the Church of England, to be inadmissible. For the question immediately occurs, if such be the looseness of subscription, of what use is it to subscribe?—nay, of what use are the Articles themselves?"[70]

While Medley suggested later that the original author of this interpretation of the Articles was Paley, he was clearly mindful of both Ward's argument and Newman's *Tract 90.*[71] Here too we find an apparent paradox. While Medley seemed to call for a rigorous interpretation of the Articles (and later, the Prayer Book) elsewhere in the same sermon he espoused toleration.[72] Private judgment was a vexed matter for him over the years. He always decried "the unlimited right of private judgement."[73] Yet he also lauded the principle of religious freedom.

If Newman's writings in *Tract 90* and his subsequent secession caused Medley to reflect on the nature of authority, Newman's subsequent writings caused the bishop to take up the idea of reason itself. In his first charge to his diocesan clergy, Medley waded into the theory of development.[74] He first affirmed, once again, the place of reason: "We speak the words of "truth and soberness" and our positions must be built upon sound sense, and reasonable proofs, or mankind will reject them."[75] He then immediately turned to consider the place of authority, by questioning Newman's theory. He introduced the topic by referring to "the unhappy defections to the Roman Church which have taken place in our own times." Newman's theory was not, in Medley's estimation, a doctrine even approved by the Roman Church, but rather something devised by him and his sympathizers as "a bold and ingenious speculation to cover their retreat" (i.e., from the Church of England).This relatively harsh language indicates the distance Medley had come from the cordial relationship with Newman that he had enjoyed only a few years earlier.[76] But when Medley had been close to the main Tractarian leaders and was even recommending the *Tracts* to others,[77] *Tract 90* had already been published. We have no record of Medley being disturbed by its teaching in the early 1840s, or prior to his consecration as bishop.

It seemed to Medley that the doctrine of development was a contradiction of the traditional Roman understanding of antiquity and tradition. In the end, Newman had moved to a point that, if pursued to its conclusions, would "probably end in that rationalistic system, which, regarding Moses, Mahomet and Christ with equal respect, as in their own day illuminators of the human race, waits for a still higher mission, which will change the whole nature of Christianity itself, and utterly abolish its mysterious and sacramental character."[78] Medley thus linked Newman's development theory with an implicitly Hegelian account of history, which he took to imply that Christianity in its orthodox form is but a stage of a developmental path. This is, of course, a significant distortion of Newman's theory and can only be attributed to polemical excess on Medley's part. In this sermon rationalism was again the great enemy of the Christian religion, inasmuch as it threatens to "utterly abolish its mysterious and sacramental system." After this rare excursion into (almost) explicitly philosophical territory, it is no surprise that Medley's next sentence began: "But to return to our own practical duties."

While Medley asserted the importance of the historic faith, received and preserved untouched, he continued to argue that the clergy must be more than mere automatons presenting historic dogma. For, "the Church of England has nothing to fear from the spread of sound knowledge and a liberal education." In fact, "the wider and more comprehensive the range of thought, the less ground she has of apprehension for the result."[79] If society in general is more learned, then there is even more reason for the clergy to have a greater standard of education. Again Medley reminded his clergy, "We must be able to give a reason for all we say and all we do lest men imagine that we are deficient in common sense, and confound our religious earnestness with a blind enthusiasm."[80]

To further the goal of greater education of his clergy, Medley made it a priority to establish a clerical library to be held at the cathedral.[81] Later, libraries were established in each deanery. To be sure, these were well stocked with such Tractarian works as *The Library of the Fathers, The Library of Anglo-Catholic Theology,* and studies of church architecture. In addition there were biblical commentaries—patristic and reformed. However, he also acquired books on a wide range of secular subjects such as music, geology, geography, history, and literature.

In his next charge, Medley again commended to his clergy a broad, liberal education. He was even willing to extend this idea, and suggested that not only were diverse areas of study worthwhile, but that even diverse theological opinions had their place. Far from the harsh polemics being exchanged in England at this time, Medley argued for toleration: "Infinite diversities of mind and action there must be: even schools of Theology are admissible, if we understand them to mean not opposing systems, but habits of contemplating the same truth from opposite points of view: but where perfect Unity exists they will be blended and softened as the colours form one ray of light, as innumerable rays are blended in one landscape."[82]

This led to another admonition to the clergy to "abstain from bitter language and contentious provocations of one another."[83] Unlike his Tractarian colleagues in England, Medley was in no rush to argue disputed points of doctrine. One might observe that a bishop is naturally inclined to prefer diocesan unity over theological and ritual exactitude. However, Medley's old mentor Phillpotts was certainly never deterred from wading into controversy. Medley, by contrast, in encouraging the clergy to meet in rural deaneries warned them, "But I should caution you not often to introduce controverted subjects of doctrine into these little resting places of friendship. Surely life is short enough, and sad enough, without being embittered by never-ending strife. Spiritual improvement, not party contests, should be the object of all our assemblies."[84] Medley previously served in a deanery in Devon, where he had himself delivered a substantial paper on the apostolic succession, a "controverted" topic to many. The struggle for the very existence of the church in the harsh climate and isolated wilderness no doubt rendered many of the English ecclesiastical disputes less pressing, if not irrelevant, to Medley and his colleagues. In the context of a struggling colonial diocese, toleration was more valuable than doctrinal rigorism.

Regardless of his tolerant spirit, Medley was clear about the perceived defects in other positions. In his charge, he pointed to the danger of "private judgement" in the Nonconformist position. Once outside of the authority of the church, they are forced to "lean upon the puny arm of their own unaided reason."[85] We ought to be careful in reading this though. It is *unaided* reason that Medley saw as so susceptible to error. Reason had its proper place both as *preparatio* for the Gospel and handmaid to it.

In this same charge Medley demonstrated, in a different way, the attempt to hold together the spiritual content of sacramental religion with the concrete, natural forms in which it is transmitted. He condemned worldliness among his clergy. In managing their glebes (lands reserved by the Crown for church use), he charged that too many spent an inordinate amount of time "buying, selling and bartering."[86] Their ends should be heavenly, not earthly. Medley had serious reservations about the growing popularity of temperance societies. In them he saw "Manichæism revived."[87] That is, they tended toward a rejection of nature (or some part of it), as having the character of evil. For a man who saw in nature a representation and vehicle of the divine, such dualist tendencies were incompatible with the Incarnation itself.

While affirming the place of nature in Christianity, this same charge presented Medley's most direct attack to date on rationalism and it is worth examining in detail. Rationalism was introduced in the context of warning against "infidelity." The first form of this "evil" arose from simple ignorance. That is, when children were not taught, they did not come to believe the great doctrines of the faith. This, although prevalent and dangerous, was not the greatest threat to the church. Worse than that was explicit denial of the particular doctrines of the faith. Medley claimed that this "modern unbelief" was peculiar to Protestantism. This argument, although somewhat veiled, appeared as a defense of the Tractarians against their Low Church opponents. Medley did this by linking the Low Churchmen to rationalism, in that both positions would deny the "unseen" elements of the faith. In the case of the rationalist, these were declared to be inconsistent with reasonable religion; the Low Churchman declared them to be popish. In England the attack was on two fronts: "the denial of the Eternity of future rewards and punishments, and the denial of Sacramental grace."[88]

The sacramental aspects of this argument are examined below.[89] Here, it is enough to consider what this said about the place of reason and the natural. For him, once one had foresworn belief in the unseen, as some did when they denied such mysteries as sacramental grace, the position slid easily into rationalistic unbelief. It is important to recognize that his position, as expressed here, was not opposed to reason itself. Rather, he objected to the claim of the rationalists that their doctrine represented the "ascendancy of reason." His argument was that there can be no rigid division between the human and the divine. This Chalcedonian insistence on the union of divine and human was typical of Medley's understanding of the Gospel and of its expression in the church.[90] In objecting to "rationalism" Medley argued against that exclusive account of reason, which allowed no place for faith and no belief in the supernatural. He did not propose to remedy this by retreating intellectually to pietism or fideism. Instead, he advocated a position that attempted to hold faith and reason in balance, just as grace and nature, divine and human are maintained in respective relations to one another.

No sooner had Medley affirmed the reality of sacramental grace and the divine foundation of the faith, then he turned to assert the importance of the human. The gifts may be given by God, but they must be "improved" by man. This activity is primarily accomplished when clergy "improve and cultivate their minds."[91] Through intellectual refinement, the revealed truths of the faith are made practical in their application to particular circumstances.

Medley was fighting a war on two fronts. He wished to oppose those who argued for a thoroughly "spiritual" religion, with no natural form. At the same time he rejected the "worldly" manifestations of the faith, which altogether missed the supernatural. Thus, in another ordination sermon, he was most interested in opposing those who would limit divine participation in the natural. While he warned against those who "find in every event the superintending hand of providence," he was more concerned about the opposite danger: "Writers in our own age desire to reduce all supernatural accounts to the level of common occurrences; ascribe all things to secondary causes; put out of sight the agency of Divine Providence; and would make truth entirely *subjective*. In other words, such writers would have us believe nothing beyond our own self-consciousness, and the discoveries attainable by man himself."[92] In general, Medley saw unbelief as a greater (or at least, more prevalent) danger than superstition in his age. Since rationalism always ended in unbelief, in his view, its fruits were more dangerous than those actual errors that the Enlightenment sought to remedy. While he would not minimize the dangers of superstition,[93] his own championing of church architecture, sacred music, the apostolic succession, and baptismal regeneration, indicate from which direction he believed the greatest threat to Christianity came.

In the following decades Medley returned to this question repeatedly, marking out the place of reason and of faith with more precision. His position, by times, appeared liberal and then conservative, as he attempted to maintain an orthodox theology, while taking seriously the newer forms of scholarship and science. For example, in his 1856 charge, he opposed any revision to the Authorized Version of the Bible, arguing that such work would only serve the end of "German sceptics."[94] Nine years later, in another charge, he took the opposite position. Written during the height of the Colenso controversy, Medley was clear on his opposition to those doctrines circulated by John Colenso and condemned by Bishop Gray. Bishops did not have the right to alter the doctrinal content of Christianity, for they were but "trustees for the faith once delivered to the Saints." Even so, Medley had sympathy with some of the criticisms made of the Authorized Version. He took issue with the popular notion "that the English version of the Bible, in every syllable and letter of it, is as much the dictation of the Holy Ghost, as the Commandments written by the finger of God on tables of stone."[95] Not only were various translations flawed, it was a mistake to believe that the Bible itself could supply all information required by the Christian:

> On several important questions the Bible gives us no information whatever. It does not tell us, what is nevertheless an undoubted fact, that for three centuries after Christ's ascension, the canon of Scripture was not precisely and accurately formed; that wide differences existed as to the authorship of particular books; that the precise number of the sacred books was finally agreed upon by the voice of the Church, not made known to us by any inspired person; that many and important variations occur in the manuscripts of the New Testament, which no inspired author can help us to settle; that an important difference is found in the chronology of the Hebrew, Septuagint and Samaritan texts of the book of Genesis, which still remains unsolved;[96] that other chronological difficulties wait for a solution, and that in regard to the Scriptural account of the creation of our present world, we neither have sufficient information at what point of time the inspired narrative begins, nor has there yet been produced an interpretation in all respects satisfactory, which leaves no doubt that the author of the book of Genesis was inspired by God to teach mankind the system of the world, as indicated by the researches of modern science.[97]

Medley distinguished himself from the liberals, however. Whereas he admitted that there were difficulties in the interpretation of scripture, the resolution of which was "complicated and by no means easy," they did not "deprive the whole body of the sacred volume of all historical truth."[98]

Later in life Medley undertook to produce a new translation (with notes) of the book of Job, which he published in 1879.[99] That Medley should have chosen Job as a study is not surprising given the personal tragedies and trials that he had endured. He alluded to these in his introduction, referring to his work as "a book specially endeared to me by having been studied in past years in seasons of deep sorrow."[100] The purpose of this work was to clear up "obscurities of the authorized version." In it he relied on several contemporary English and German critics.[101] These were a select group however, showing a preference for those whose work was "not disfigured by the contemptuous rationalism which unhappily is found elsewhere."[102] His own work, although it took advantage of contemporary philological and historical tools and research, was conservative in tone and interpretation.

Medley refused to link unbelief to the rise of modern science, however. In fact, he was optimistic that science would ultimately affirm the scriptures.[103] For Medley, if there were apparent contradictions between the conclusions of science and those of scripture, it remained for science to be more fully developed. However, he also suggested that in many cases, where science and scripture clashed, the cause was not science at all, but a faulty or "traditional interpretation" of the Bible. He was here an unabashed believer in the progress of human knowledge and was confident of the service that that knowledge would perform for the faith.[104] Science, as we saw with reason above, was understood as a handmaid to scriptural study. Geology, geography, biology—these all served more accurately to interpret the biblical record. Reactionary responses to the rise of science and biblical criticism would ultimately fail. To attempt to suppress new thought through judicial measures was pointless, for "The strength of the Church lies not in courts of law, even if we could deprive every essayist of all temporal means of subsistence. Even then we could not quench the light of reason, nor by such means rekindle the torch of faith."[105] At this point Medley had clearly parted company with Tractarians such as Pusey as well as High Churchmen such as Phillpotts. After all, Pusey had actively assisted Bishop Phillpotts in his prosecution of G. C. Gorham on the question of baptismal regeneration.[106] Although Pusey had misgivings, along with other Tractarians, with regard to the jurisdiction of civil courts over doctrinal matters, he did not in principle oppose using coercive measures to oppose erroneous doctrine.

For Medley, the only proper response to the challenges of science and other "new learning" was increased education. Again he stressed the need for greater theological learning against the danger of well-intentioned orthodox preachers producing a "generation of ignorant and narrow minded fanatics, ready to condemn every advance in knowledge as an error, and to brand with heresy every liberal and ingenuous mind."[107] This was a remarkable statement, signaling Medley's commitment to a genuine spirit of toleration and an openness to at least the consideration of progressive theological thought.

This led Medley to an interesting and, no doubt to his clerical listeners, striking argument concerning history. He identified the "spirit of the age" with God's providence. While the "great fundamental verities" of the faith could not change, the understanding of those truths was "liable to fluctuation and progress, or decline."[108] His earlier condemnation of the theory of development should be recalled at this point. There was here an acknowledgment of some sort of historical development. But this development must be limited to *our understanding* of the revealed truth and not to that truth itself, which remained unchanged eternally. Since the movement of history was seen to be the working of God's providence it ought not to be resisted. Thus, the spirit of the age must be followed as far as its advances were "in a right direction." With this final caveat, it became clear that the doctrines of the church were ultimately the judge of the zeitgeist and not vice versa. The presupposition was that the mind of God was known by the church and the teachings of the church were therefore able to determine which changes were part of God's will and which were not. For Medley, it was to the primitive church alone that we should look to check the validity of any development in doctrine or practice. Only those positions consistent with "the faith once delivered to the saints" and expressed in scripture, the creeds, and the first general councils were to be received.

Two years later Medley took the other side of the dialectic. In a sermon on the Holy Spirit, he was anxious to emphasize the limitations of human reason, and thus of our ability to criticize revelation. "Whatever God reveals transcends our reason; and if viewed only in one aspect appears to be contradictory to it. The truth is, we have no measure of a Divine Being. He exists in a sphere above and beyond our own. Once admit a revelation, and what is revealed is a pure matter of faith with which reason has nothing to do, except to try to discover the meaning of the words in which the revelation is made. The thing itself is a matter for adoration, not investigation."[109] Read side by side, it could easily be assumed that this sermon and the 1865 charge were written by different authors. Medley alternated between the two sides of what he took to be a single position. He defended the value of nature and human reason. He also defended the absolute necessity of divine grace and our dependency upon revelation. He did not take one position to contradict the other, no matter how strongly he presented each one's claim. For Medley, it was when either side existed alone that difficulties occurred. Thus, to see the church as working *ex opere operato*, apart from the participation of human subjective freedom was a distortion, every bit as destructive as the denial of the objectivity of the faith. Here Medley drew an interesting distinction between how God operates on matter and how he operates on "mind." "When God works in nature, He works on Matter: it has no power to resist his will; it forms such combinations as he directs, and is subject to such laws as He imposes. But when He works in Grace, He works on Mind, to which he has vouchsafed a likeness in immortal being and attributes to Himself; to which He has given a power denied to matter—the power to reflect, to compare, to will, to hate, nay to work with or to resist, for its own good, or its own undoing Omnipotence itself. The destiny of matter is made for it. The destiny of mind, the mind makes for itself; though whenever it works for good, it must be aided and moulded by the plastic power of a higher, wiser, nobler mind."[110] This was probably the high point of Medley's humanism and certainly his clearest expression of human freedom. Unlike nature, mind was free and, in its freedom, possessed the capacity of "making . . . itself." This was to be contrasted to the view that God worked "arbitrarily, capriciously, tyrannically . . . on the world of mind."[111] He thus rejected the doctrine of "irresistible grace," which was "founded on a misconception of the whole nature of man."[112] But even here, though free, the unaided mind could not "work for good." Grace was still required.

The same themes were repeated in another form in his charge to the clergy in 1868. He began by praising the development of modern sciences. "History, geography, astronomy, geology, and other kindred sciences, have all been cultivated with an amazing success, and the results have been directed to the field of Biblical literature."[113] That the laity now were educated in their sciences entirely changed "the aspect of things." Clergy needed to respond with equal expertise in these and other related fields. Once again, he decried blind obscurantism or reactionary conservatism. He referred again to the spirit of the age, in slightly more veiled terms than earlier. While acknowledging the power of the spirit of the age, he now wanted to suggest that it may not necessarily be associated with providence. Nevertheless, progress was seen as a mighty river, whose course we could not alter. Thus "we are deeply responsible for the manner in which we meet this overpowering tide."[114] If the modern spirit was in fact the providential working of God's will, resistance to it constituted sin. While many Tractarians would condemn "doubt" in religious matters, Medley here defended it. "All men who doubt are not infidels," he declared. The proper response to the new sciences and new doubts was not to "dogmatize," but to investigate and inquire.

In the end Medley was still clear that the purpose of the cleric's inquiry was "to vindicate the truth, and bring it home to the understandings, as well as to the affections, of his hearers."[115] He was not naive enough to believe that all new developments were beneficial. Nor did he believe that the new critical spirit was necessarily good. Often it was accompanied by "a restless unquietness of mind, which is, no doubt, productive of much evil." As a result, "there is no subject of thought, political, social, civil, or religious, of which it may not be said that the foundations are shaken."[116] The proper response to this was not retreat from this ambiguous modern spirit, but rather advancement in learning. Medley, unlike some other Tractarians, rarely yearned for a past golden age.[117] His pragmatic personality caused him to abandon such Romantic inclinations in order to get to the business at hand—building churches, writing liturgical music, preaching the Gospel, and so on.

Even when it came to establishing synodical government, Medley aimed to balance his understanding of development with the conservative character that he believed to be essential to the church. Thus he counseled, "Synod will do well and wisely not to reject those changes which the general progress of mankind and the providential course of the world have rendered necessary."[118] In the end, though, these changes could only be concerning the "form" and not "the essence of truth." Here Medley's understanding of the development of doctrine was most clearly revealed. The actual revealed body of truth was understood to be unchangeable. Only the means by which that truth was communicated could be altered and developed. The confidence that Medley showed toward human progress was thus tempered.

Even if, later in life, Medley was less sanguine about the spirit of the age,[119] he nevertheless continued to maintain the necessity of clerical education to "keep pace with the general knowledge of the day."[120]As always, this served a practical end. If they failed to improve their minds the clergy would be despised by the better educated laity and they would have less likelihood of influencing them toward the Gospel. He therefore exhorted his clergy, "for the Church's sake, to be students to the latest hour of your lives."[121] In his last charge, at the age of eighty-two, he had not wavered from this sense of the importance of continually improved education. He argued that the higher standard of education and its broader availability to the masses demand better and more widely educated clergy. An earnest character combined with moral integrity was not a sufficient recipe for the effective modern cleric. He must be intellectually equipped to communicate in an age "where everything is called into question."[122]

Here, near the end of his life, Medley continued to be hopeful as to the church's prospects and offered practical measures to ensure its growth. Knowledge, even secular learning, was not to be feared, but sought and treasured. Clergy were not to content themselves with memorizing the formularies of the church. Instead. they must understand their doctrines and know how to communicate them to contemporary listeners.

John Medley was connected with a movement that is generally thought of as being distinguished by its conservative, if not reactionary, theology. In doctrinal terms Medley certainly was a conservative himself. Yet, he was also responsive to an intellectually, culturally, and scientifically revolutionary age. He sought to seriously consider this intellectual dynamism, while attempting to preach the historic Catholic faith. This led to a clear development in his thought, manifested as an increasing openness to the claims of reason, which he strained to synthesize with the demands of authority.

Medley's sacramental theology was the most visible expression of his doctrinal conservatism. His understanding of the relation between church and state more clearly reflected his openness to some of the progressive aspects of nineteenth-century thought, especially in its North American context. The next three chapters will examine Medley's thought concerning architecture, the sacraments, and the relation of church and state in detail.

4

Medley the Ecclesiologist

The Development of Ecclesiology

In 1839 two societies dedicated to the study and revival of Gothic architecture were founded. The Cambridge Camden Society and the Oxford Society for Promoting the Study of Gothic Architecture were the first of what would become many such organizations across England. While these ecclesiological societies signaled a new impetus for the study of ecclesiastical architecture, they actually only inherited ideas that had been present in English society for some decades previous to their establishment.

Of the many ecclesiological societies that sprang up, the Cambridge Camden Society, later called the Ecclesiological Society, was the best known. It established an influential journal, *The Ecclesiologist.*[1] The members declared, "The object of the society shall be the study of Gothic Architecture and of Ecclesiastical Antiquities."[2] The mere study of these forms soon evolved to the advocacy of them and a single-minded attempt to promote them in the construction of new churches and the remodeling of old ones.

James White argues that the Camden Society had its genesis in two intellectual currents: the Oxford Movement and Romanticism.[3] While it is important for our exploration of John Medley's thought to recognize and distinguish these two influences, some caution must be exercised concerning White's account. In actuality, the roots of the ecclesiological movement, and hence the Camden Society, go back prior to the Oxford Movement. Romanticism was certainly one element in this movement, as was a more general interest in medieval forms and the pre-Reformation history of the English Church.[4] Interest in reviving Gothic forms had been present in England from the last part of the eighteenth century onward.[5]

Given the Victorian churchman's general enthusiasm for societies, it is no surprise that there were a plethora of organizations dedicated to church architecture.[6] In addition to those at Oxford and Cambridge, societies devoted to the Gothic Revival were established at Lichfield, Salisbury, Bristol, and elsewhere.[7] One very active such organization was the Exeter Diocesan Architectural Society (EDAS). Founded in 1841, the EDAS quickly attracted both amateur and professional, clerical and lay enthusiasts.[8] It also attracted a large number of the leading nobility and gentry from Devon and Cornwall.[9] One of the prominent families involved in the society was the Coleridges of Ottery St. Mary. While it is not known when Medley's association with the family began, it was an important connection throughout his life.

The EDAS was able to enlist Bishop Phillpotts as its patron and gained tremendous influence in the diocese of Exeter by serving as a sort of review panel for new church designs that were submitted to the Diocesan Church Building Society.[10] The official architect of the EDAS was John Hayward, whose work was to be highly favored in the eyes of the Camden Society. Hayward had studied under his relative Sir Charles Barry who, along with A. W. Pugin, was responsible for the new Gothic parliament buildings.[11] Martin Cherry suggests that Hayward became an increasingly more sophisticated and exact student of Gothic architecture, largely through the influence of John Medley.[12] Like the Camden society the EDAS aimed both to educate the public about church architecture and also to directly promote building and renovation in the Gothic style. However, Cherry argues that the Exeter society was less rigorous in the insistence upon strict Gothic principles than was its Cambridge counterpart.[13] In fact, of the many church designs it approved, only one, St. Andrew's Exwick, was exactingly fashioned after the ecclesiological ideal.[14]

Medley's Early Interest in Ecclesiology

The founder of the EDAS was none other than John Medley.[15] It has been suggested that John Medley's architectural interests went back to his student days.[16] Whether this is in fact true, he was certainly a keen enthusiast of the Gothic style by the 1840s. He wrote two works connected with the new "science" of ecclesiology.[17] The first of these, *Elementary Remarks on Church Architecture* caught the eye of the Cambridge Camden Society.[18] They were even willing to put it in a class with J. M. Neale's works.[19] Medley would go on to contribute articles published in *TheEcclesiologist.*[20]

This short pamphlet on church architecture clearly indicated Medley's mind at this time with regard to the science. Medley's interest in it flowed from deeply held beliefs about the way in which natural forms were intended to be vehicles of divine grace and truth. For Medley, there was no question of nature existing independently of God. For example, the whole purpose of church architecture was to direct the mind toward God. He thus deplored "Grecian Architecture," which "presents to our minds no solemn associations, no inspiring thoughts; and is therefore eminently defective in the proper characteristics of a religious edifice." This was contrasted with "church architecture," by which he meant Gothic architecture, which "by its very loftiness, reminds man of his own littleness and of God's glory, and seems desirous to raise him above the petty business of earth, and fit him for communion with his maker."[21] Leaving aside the chauvinism of this opinion, with its somewhat superficial judgment of classical architecture, Medley's point was clear enough. Architecture exists not to glorify man but to place him in his proper relation to the divine.

These comments had an immediately practical significance as Medley's purpose was to criticize the Georgian style of ecclesiastical architecture that took as its inspiration classical forms. This had become the common style prior to Medley's time in England and was to be the prevailing shape of the churches he encountered in his new diocese when he arrived in Fredericton in 1845.[22] For him, and others in the Cambridge Camden Society and its circle, its defect was not only aesthetic, but theological. To be sure, they were offended aesthetically by the Georgian classical forms, but they also believed them to be morally defective. The prevailing style of church architecture was spiritually inadequate: "It has all the elements of sectarianism about it, and not all the stained-glass window-makers or restorative artists in the worlds can make it otherwise; and, from pure ignorance of church feeling, many people probably would be content it should remain so. But they will not be content when they are rightly informed. He who has once felt the solemn, unearthly associations of the church system will not desire to go back again to comfortable sleeping-boxes[23] and 'a worldly sanctuary.' He will not go to God's house to have his mind chained down to earth, but to have it refined and sublimated into heaven."[24]

In short, the correct form of architecture, i.e., "church architecture," existed to lift us from our attachment to the natural and place us in a direct relation to the divine. In these early observations Medley (who was thirty-seven at the time) seemed less interested in an equal union of the natural and divine than he was in an assumption of the natural by the divine. The natural order was seen as "worldly" and something to be overcome in order to participate in God's realm. Paradoxically, however, the very means by which this was to be done were earthly and concrete in the most literal sense. It would be through the work of human hands, through the Gothic cathedral, that our minds would be lifted up to contemplate the divine.

In Medley's view, the defect of the Puritans and those others who did not give proper attention to externals was a failure to allow nature to be capable of communicating the divine. Thus Medley wrote that the stones and clay of churches had "a spirit and a life in them when they are brought together, and stand upright; and even the '*disjecta membra*' shew the poetry that is within."[25] So, on the one hand, church architecture existed to "fill [men] with self-abasing thoughts of their own littleness, weakness and guilt, and with high and becoming reverence for the majesty and mercy of their Creator."[26] Human nature was seen as little and weak. Great churches existed to remind us of the contrast between us and God in His power and majesty. On the other hand, this very nature, which was so defective and small, was also capable of containing within itself the "poetry" that reveals the divine. As he said elsewhere, "All God's gifts are, in a mysterious manner, made dependent on our use and improvement of them. He provides the vessel, but we toil in rowing. And though we cannot bestow the gift, it may be improved by cultivation."[27]

In addition to this work, Medley published a second work on ecclesiology in 1843. First delivered as a paper to the EDAS, *The Advantage of Open Seats* took up a question dear to the hearts of Tractarians and Ecclesiologists alike.[28] The system of rented, leased, and sometimes purchased pews was abhorrent, on several grounds, to these reformers. John Mason Neale had written a work attacking pews and advocating "free seats."[29] The *Ecclesiologist* had also weighed in with its own opinion, "Pews are the ugly offspring of two ugly parents, Pride and Luxury, and both parents and offspring in a place dedicated to the worship of God, are insufferable."[30] Medley's contribution was highly valued by other ecclesiologists and his writings became authoritative on the subject of ecclesiology.[31]

Medley's own interest in the question of pews was not entirely motivated by aesthetic or antiquarian concerns. His social conscience, which would later manifest itself in his episcopate, was certainly a factor here. His curate recalled how Medley "surprised the 'Gentry' and startled the 'Poor' by having all classes dine together on 'Clothing Club Day.'"[32] In *The Advantages of Open Seats*, he states, "The principle of spiritual equality between rich and poor is the very principle of Christianity itself."[33]

Medley argued in the same work that if the Puritans erred in refusing to allow the natural to be seen as revealing the divine, others fell into the opposite error of ignoring the divine and loving the natural for itself. This too was criticized by Medley: "The real object to be attained by Architectural beauty, [which] is not to please the eye or sense, but to render outward objects subservient to devotion."[34] Church architecture could never be merely aesthetic in character, but must always be "practical." As Finley observes, Medley used "practical" in a very particular sense when speaking of architecture.[35] He meant that church architecture must serve the ends of religion. It did not have an end in itself. The contemplation of a beautiful window could not be the end; it was only a means to the true end, the contemplation of God. Gothic architecture, in particular, was best suited to this transformation of our habits.[36] This ability of art and architecture was not universal, however. It existed when the object of art or the building wore "nature's garb."[37]

There was a clear sacramental implication in Medley's architectural position. Nature was subordinate to the divine. Yet it was through the means of nature that the divine was made known to man. There was, in Medley, no hint of any mysticism that would understand us as able to immediately contemplate the divine. Nature, art, architecture, institutions, reason, and sacraments all act as intermediaries of the supernatural. This was perfectly consistent with the general view of the Tractarians. That view of nature was expressed by Keble in *Tract 89*, "Of the Mysticism Attributed to the Early Fathers of the Church": "the works of God in creation and providence, besides their immediate uses in this life, appear to old writers as so many intended tokens from the Almighty, to assure us of some spiritual fact or other, which it concerns us in some way to know . . . they were pledges of some spiritual thing, if they were not means to it to us. They were, in a very sufficient sense, *verba visibilia*."[38] These *verba visibilia* were understood as natural mediators of the divine. Nature was not to be passed through quickly, in order to contemplate heavenly and eternal things, but was instead to be studied carefully. As Keble put it in the same tract, "the sum of this visible world [is] an index or token of the invisible."[39] It was this very necessary character of the natural component that would manifest itself in Medley's focus on the details of the physical arrangements of religion and worship. Architecture, music, preaching—these were all particular interests of Medley and themes that he would return to over and again in his various charges to diocesan clergy.

The EDAS was a vehicle for Medley to continue to advance the cause of the Gothic Revival. He was the first president and his curate the first secretary.[40] In time the society published a record of its proceedings.[41] In addition to articles, reviews, and drawings, the proceedings also reprinted the annual reports of the society. These reports, in the early years, were written by Medley.

While it may be the case that the annual reports of the EDAS did not simply reflect Medley's personal views, but rather those of the society or, at least, its executive members, they were perfectly consistent with the opinions we know Medley to have held. To review them is to add to our understanding of Medley's position at this stage of his life. In the very first annual report of the EDAS, Medley laid down the general goals of not only their own society but also the necessity to work in concert with others like it around England:

> What was so admirably accomplished by the Freemasons in older times must be attempted, at least, by us, in concert with the kindred societies now established in many parts of England. Our general principles must be the same: our manner of executing the various details of the style of Architecture must be harmonious: and we must communicate to each other and mutually agree upon the general external forms and internal arrangements of all Ecclesiastical Edifices. So that, making all allowance on the one hand for those provincialisms in art which are analogous to the minor varieties of dialect, and on the other for the very real differences in the details of execution which display the original talent of the artist, we may still hope to attain throughout the kingdom a harmonious and consistent style of building, which is as far removed from an ignorant affectation of vulgar originality, as it is from a servile imitation of ancient models.[42]

Medley went on to make clear that as much of the work of the society would need to be directed to things that needed to be "undone" as to those things that needed to be done. The report described the activities of the society in the past year, including educational visits made to various churches in the neighborhood of Exeter and a list of those building projects about which the society had been called upon to render advice. It also made reference to the generous assistance of the Oxford and Cambridge architectural societies for their moral support and donations of books and plates.[43]

The report concluded with a section that sets out policy and principles for the future. One passage in particular is significant in light of Medley's future architectural endeavors. "In the present revival of a taste for Ecclesiastical design it seems especially necessary that the principles of harmony of proportion and composition should be studied as much, if not more, than the mere details of the several styles. Not that any building can be good which is incorrect in its details, but that where a building is of small size, or the means inadequate, good proportion is of the utmost consequence. A certain rudeness and even ruggedness, provided the subject be well treated, is not always out of keeping, when the means are small."[44] Although unknown to Medley at the time he wrote these words, he would soon be placed in a faraway land, where he would have the opportunity to build dozens of churches. In that situation the "means" would certainly be "inadequate." The style of church that he would construct could certainly be described as rude, or even rugged, by English standards. Yet Medley would strive to hold to this sense of the importance of "harmony of proportion and composition."

The EDAS annual report of the following year recorded continued progress in the practical application of the society's goals in the diocese of Exeter. There had evidently been progress in the removal of pews and galleries and in the attention paid to chancels.[45] The words of this report prefigured ones that Medley would use in addressing the clergy of his future diocese in just a few years. As bishop in New Brunswick he would frequently remind his people not to put the church second in the use of their temporal means. As the 1843 report said, "[The Committee's] earnest desire is, that every House of God, as it is the noblest, so it should be the best furnished mansion in the parish: that it should be adorned, according to the means of the worshippers, with the best and most precious of their substance; that it should be as inviting to the eye as refreshing to the soul; the common home alike of rich and poor, easy of access, free from superstition, niggardliness and exclusion; full of a grave and reverend majesty, which strikes the beholder with awe, and send him to his knees, and fills his soul with comfort, knowing that (to use the words of our ancient laws) it is 'Domus mansionalis omnipotentis Dei.' "[46] The concern evidenced here for the social condition of the poor was one that, as we have seen, Medley repeated in his work on *Open Seats*. It was also evident in his practical parochial dealings in Exeter.[47]

The last report that Medley wrote was read at the annual meeting of the EDAS on May 9, 1844. By the following year, he was consumed with the preparations for his consecration and departure for Canada. This report was quite brief, restricting itself for the most part to the review of the past year's activities and with little of the "editorial content" of previous reports. Nevertheless, Medley took some time to lament the amount of work left to accomplish in undoing the "sad desecrations" that had been perpetrated on countless churches by earlier generations.[48]

The annual reports always ended with a list of the society's subscribers to that time. By 1844, the society included about 250 members, just under half of whom were clergy.[49] Among the subscribers were many who were prominent in their own right or would be prominent in Medley's life. These included: Sir Thomas Acland, John Bacon (Medley's father-in-law), Bishop W. H. Coleridge, Mr Justice J. T. Coleridge (Keble's biographer), J. D Coleridge (the future lord chief-justice of England), H. K. Cornish, Bishop Henry Phillpotts, Archdeacon Froude, William Froude (R. H. Froude's brother), Hon. Mr. Justice Patteson (John Coleridge Patteson's father), Frank Wills (noted Gothic Revival architect and student of William Butterfield), and E. C. Woolcombe of Balliol College (a primary contributor to Medley's diocesan libraries).

A quarterly report of the EDAS for 1846 began by offering fulsome praise to John Medley, who had, by that time, departed for Canada.

> Clear and loud as was the call for some interposing hand to stay the rapid progress of decay in our Ecclesiastical edifices, on the one hand to rouse the spirit of the careless, to whom any thing was good enough for a Church, any patchwork decent, and meanness excusable, and on the other to direct and improve the taste of those whose desire was to restore what was decayed, and to offer unto God of that which cost them something; loud and clear as was this call, it was the ready mind of Bishop Medley which first responded to it, and his energy which exerted itself at once to follow the example which had been set by our two Universities, and to form a nucleus in our own diocese, which might gather around itself those, who from purity of taste, knowledge of antiquity, acquaintance with examples, zeal in the pursuit, or from greater leisure than might belong to all, would contribute information upon the principles and practice of Ecclesiastical Architecture.[50]

The report goes on to record that Medley had always been among the most active members of the society when it came to visiting other churches where restorations were planned, offering "judicious comment upon plans and designs which were submitted to the Committee."[51] Prophetically, this homage to Medley concluded, "As of old the Bishops were the chief architects of our most glorious Churches, (witness our Cathedral) may his influence be successful in raising from the low state in which it generally is, the Ecclesiastical Architecture of our colonies."[52] Interestingly, in light of later developments, the report also made approving mention of the design for Medley's new cathedral, noting "that every portion of it is in harmony with the whole, and that the whole is a most beautiful specimen of an English parish Church of the Decorated period."[53]

Putting Theory into Practice

Medley's involvement in the cause of ecclesiology was not merely academic. As we know, Medley was not only active in the study and design of churches of others, he was also active in building and remodeling those under his own care. While vicar of St. Thomas, Exeter, Medley had remodeled the chancel, including, eventually, the addition of a striking monument to his late wife, made by his father-in-law, the eminent sculptor and EDAS subscriber, John Bacon. This work was done at his own expense.[54] While the effigy was the work of Bacon, the entire work, consisting of a tomb chest and elaborate canopy, was likely the design of Medley.[55] Medley also built a new chancel at a church in nearby Oldridge, this time with the financial assistance of his mother.[56]

His most significant early architectural achievement was the erection of a Gothic Revival chapel in his own parish, again built at his own expense. Of St. Andrew's Exwick, the *Ecclesiologist* said "it was the best specimen of a modern church we have yet seen."[57] Medley's curate recalled how Benjamin Webb and John Mason Neale were early visitors to the new church, expressing their enthusiasm for the project.[58] While John Hayward was listed as the architect of St. Andrew's chapel, Medley was regarded the "general designer of this beautiful church."[59] While small, the Exwick chapel was lauded for its correctness and attention to detail.[60]

The Architect as Bishop

When he became bishop, Medley's architectural hobby became a matter of serious business. He had been given a diocese in dire need of church building. There were simply not enough churches to accommodate the existing congregations. Those that did exist, for the most part, did not meet with Medley's understanding of "correct" church architecture.

Of the churches in the diocese when Medley arrived, the architecture tended to be simple and predominantly Georgian in character.[61] Most lacked chancels, decent altars, or fonts. As Ketchum wrote in 1893, "At the time of the Bishop's arrival there was not one church in the Diocese which, at the present day, would be considered properly arranged."[62] Many of them were modeled upon the Congregational meeting houses that had been familiar to the Loyalists from the New England states.[63] Thus, the pulpit was usually placed at the center of the church, often blocking the view of the altar.[64] Pews were rented, leased, or sold. The box pews were sometimes so constructed as to provide a sanctuary *from* the service. Those in St. Paul's, Bushville, were four and one-half feet high, thus effectively isolating each family from the others.[65] Of course, these arrangements were not limited to the New Brunswick church, but were common in the nineteenth century.[66]

Medley's intention was never simply to build churches in his new diocese; he intended to build particular kinds of churches, in keeping with his ecclesiological principles.[67] In 1851, Medley could write to Ernest Hawkins at the SPG, "I am bound to relate that more attention is paid to the decency and order of worship everywhere: that fewer churches are erected in which there is no provision for kneeling and in which there is neither font nor vessels for Holy Communion."[68] He hoped that his cathedral would serve as an architectural inspiration as well as a spiritual focus for the diocese. Recognizing the impracticality of stone structures in many cash-strapped rural areas and accepting the resources that a lumber rich province could provide, Medley developed a distinctive architectural style that expressed Gothic Revival principles in wood frame structures.[69]

Medley's son Edward inherited his father's interest in architecture and matched it with professional ability. Having studied under William Butterfield,[70] "he was immersed in the world of High Victorian Gothic."[71] In all, Edward designed seven churches in the diocese. It has been suggested that his designs "were unparalleled in North America" for their expression of advanced ecclesiological ideals.[72] Charles Medley, another son, also participated in the great family project, building a handsome wooden Gothic Revival church at Sussex.[73]

When Medley left Exeter he made clear that one of his chief tasks in his new diocese was the establishment of a suitable cathedral. Upon arriving in Fredericton he immediately made this his highest priority. This later became the occasion of the first major controversy of his episcopate. The vestry of Christ Church, Fredericton had anticipated the arrival of the new bishop and had recently enlarged their church, believing that it would serve, at least temporarily, as the cathedral. However, the building was certainly not considered suitable by Medley. His biographer offers a brief description of its inadequacies, "It had its galleries and square pews. There was no chancel. The altar stood in a narrow space between the reading desk and the pulpit."[74] This was a partial catalog of the ills that the Ecclesiologists had sought to eradicate from English churches.

On Monday, June 23, 1845, Medley "summoned a meeting of all persons friendly to the erection of a Cathedral Church."[75] At this meeting, and in the days to follow, £4500 was promised for the project.[76] This was to be added to the £1500 that was presented to Medley before he left England.[77] The congregation of Christ Church had always known that eventually the cathedral would be elsewhere.[78] What they did not anticipate was that Medley would decide upon the "Green," near the banks of the Saint John River as being the most suitable site for it. This was the very location of their own church. Medley proposed to move Christ Church and build his cathedral on the same site. This plan was rejected outright by Christ Church's vestry.[79] The vestry eventually conceded that Medley might build on the green, adjacent to Christ Church, provided "the Cathedral be kept at least 12' from the present fence of the Church."[80]

Medley must have accepted this offer, for just eight days later the cornerstone of the new cathedral was laid.[81] Eventually, the original Christ Church would be demolished, to the bitter regret of many of its parishioners. The Venerable George Coster, Archdeacon of Fredericton and long-time rector of Christ Church, wrote to the SPG about what he had endured: "I obeyed the order which closed my church . . . I accepted for my parish church a building which will not hold more than a fourth part of the parishioners and of which the

Even if Christ Church had been large enough, its Georgian lines and rented pews would have been sufficient reason for Medley to construct his own Cathedral. (This picture is published with the permission of the New Brunswick Museum.)

congregation when I took it had almost vanished before the superior attractions of the new Cathedral."[82] In this case an argument could be made that Medley had acted injudiciously, or at least tactlessly. Coster, after all, had been one of the stalwart High Churchmen, who had maintained their position in the early days of the diocese. He had helped to found the Diocesan Church Society, which paved the way for the establishment of the diocese itself.[83] A discontented group of the former Christ Church parishioners would eventually relocate to St. Anne's in order to avoid the cathedral altogether.[84] It took many years for this painful episode to be forgotten.

Certainly the speed with which Medley moved to begin his cathedral suggests that the idea must have been in the forefront of his mind long before he left England. Otherwise, he could scarcely have had opportunity to have developed the design for a cathedral by this time. In fact, we know that he had visited and selected an English model, St. Mary's Snettisham, Norfolk, before leaving for Canada.[85] This was to be a cause of a difference of opinion between Medley and some Ecclesiologists, who believed that a parish church was an inadequate model for a cathedral.[86]

Medley's choice of architect was Frank Wills.[87] He arrived in New Brunswick carrying plans for the new cathedral. However, the original plan to model it after St. Mary's Snettisham had to be considerably revised. How much of this is due to the criticism of English Ecclesiologists is not known. However, there were practical reasons for making some of the changes. Since St. Mary's was substantially in ruins, Medley and Wills borrowed elements from other churches to supply missing features. These included Selby Abbey and Exeter Cathedral.[88] Proportions were revised with regard to the nave and the chancel.[89] The nave roof was raised up above the level of the chancel roof, a modification more befitting a cathedral, according to the Ecclesiologists. Overall, the changes improved the Ecclesiologists' estimation of the design. In the end, they judged the cathedral to be a model example of the "Pointed style."[90] Medley's own former colleagues in the EDAS, who had formerly lauded the original design, expressed themselves much happier with the revised version, inasmuch as it was more suitable to use the lines of a true cathedral than a parish church.[91]

While the cathedral was being built, Medley had constructed another, smaller, church in Fredericton. St. Anne's Church was built to be a chapel for the bishop while the cathedral was being constructed.[92] St. Anne's would later become the parish church once the cathedral was complete.[93] Its seats were to be free, as it was to exist "for the accommodation of the poorer inhabitants."[94] Also designed by Frank

Christ Church Cathedral, Fredericton.

Wills, St. Anne's bore the clear influence of the ecclesiological movement.[95] It was the first architectural project that Medley completed in his new diocese and bore many of the marks of the ecclesiological revolution. Although relatively small, it was of stone, in contrast to the predominantly wooden churches of the province. It was also distinctively Gothic in character, in contrast to the Georgian style that was nearly universal elsewhere in New Brunswick. It included such "advanced" features as an elevated sanctuary (and altar), stone font, stained glass, and a rood screen.[96] Phoebe Stanton describes it as "the finest small North American Church of its date in the English Gothic Revival style."[97]

The relation of external form to spiritual reality was the subject of the sermon, entitled "The Staff of Beauty and the Staff of Bands," that Medley preached at the consecration of St. Anne's chapel.[98] Medley intended to speak of the proper relation of externals to spiritual realities. As was often the case with Medley, he chose to place a telling epigram on the title page. Rather than quoting Bishop Ussher (as with the sermon on the Reformation), this time Medley turned to Richard Hooker. "The sensible things which religion hath hallowed, are resemblances according to things spiritually understood, whereunto they serve as a hand to lead and a way to direct."[99] This was a concise statement of the Ecclesiologists' creed: that external or natural forms could convey spiritual content. Thus, great care must be taken as to the construction and arrangement of those forms, so that they might best serve their spiritual ends.

Medley had already run into opposition, which had started practically from the day of his arrival. This was rooted in Evangelical concerns about his alleged Puseyite leanings.[100] Undeterred by this, Medley pressed on with his intention to transform the rude, meeting-house arrangement of the churches in his diocese according to the ideals held by the ecclesiological movement. A sense of his determination in this regard can be gained from his first change to his diocese, in which he recounted his inability in many New Brunswick communities even to identify which building belonged to the Church of England because chapels of Dissenters appeared identical in every regard to Anglican churches.[101]

Medley prepared the ground of the argument in his sermon by asserting that the separation of physical space for the worship of God was grounded in our very nature.[102] He proceeded to give patristic support for the principle of there being a particular place for Christian worship.[103] He then launched into his main argument, which was a defense of Christian symbolism and the relation of symbols to things signified. In the first place, Scripture itself provided in its own form the first proof of the value of symbols: "Symbolic characters are inscribed on the pages of Holy Scripture from one end to the other: from the emblematic sword in Paradise, to the tree of life, the fountain of living waters, the golden city, and 'the twelve foundations' in the book of Revelations [*sic*]. The cardinal truth of Christianity, the atonement of Christ, is itself symbolically revealed. 'Behold the Lamb of God who taketh away the sin of the world.' 'I beheld and lo a Lamb as it had been slain.' What marvelous infatuation is it that men should print symbolism in the pages of books, and see nothing but beauty, and when the same truths are engraven on walls, or windows, should see nothing but deformity."[104] This was a none-too-veiled reference to the Low Churchmen and Dissenters of various persuasions, who dominated his diocese. Medley was responding to the argument that the outward forms were part of the law of the old covenant and had no place in the new covenant of Christ. "As long as man is capable of being acted on by outward impressions either for good or evil, so long as what is external is valuable, provided it does not take the place of what is internal."[105] Once again Hooker was quoted to justify the retention of ceremonies and laws.[106] The point was that nature itself was a divine creation and to use it properly as a road to God was not idolatry, but the very nature of religion itself.[107] The divine was not wholly separate from nature. Instead, properly understood, nature led to God.

The Tractarian account of this movement was most clearly expressed in Keble's *Christian Year.* Keble combined the ideas of the Romantic movement with the doctrinal spirit of the traditional High Churchmen.[108] So, Medley observed, "To worship the creature more than the Creator is idolatry: but to use the creature to dignify the worship of the Creator, *while the worship is paid to him, and Him only*, is not idolatry but religion."[109] If nature was a mirror of (and way to) God, then no less should art and architecture be directed to divine ends.

In opposition to Puritans who eschewed any external representation of the divine or any natural aid in the ascent to God, preferring an immediate union, Medley (consistent with the High Church as well as the Tractarian tradition) asserted the importance of the natural. Yet the natural was not to be enjoyed in itself; it appeared that "earth should be left behind."[110] Medley later suggested that this apparent dichotomy could be overcome by understanding nature in its proper relation to the divine. As long as it was seen as leading to God, the true end, nature was not merely harmless, but actually positive and helpful.

Medley took the common objections to this position in order and responded to them in the course of his sermon. To the charge that "external objects have no necessary connexion with spiritual religion," he responded that this was a straw horse—no one claimed that externals, by themselves, "produce religion."[111] The real question was whether "the giving to holy things and places the honour that belongs to them is not more likely to promote a religious frame of mind than the withholding of such honour."[112] Another form of the same objection asked, "Cannot God be worshipped in a plain simple edifice with four plain walls?"[113] Medley's response to this was practical. Of course, he replied, God could be worshipped in plain houses, or in the wild woods, but why would we do so, unless we had to? He suggests that the withholding from God of "the very best that we have" arose from "our meanness," rather than any high principle. The final objection often raised against any ornaments of religion was that they violated the second commandment, against graven images. Once again, the point was that the images should not become objects of worship in their own right, but rather should direct one to the worship of God Himself.[114]

This was an argument that Medley returned to throughout his life. In his charge of 1850, he took up the question of "Formalism."[115] He echoed earlier words of speaking of man's "compound" nature: "Is not man himself compounded of material form and immaterial spirit? And in our approaches to the Great Father of our souls, can we wholly abstract ourselves from all surrounding emotions, which are local, material, and visible? The attempt will always prove a failure. The feelings of man must always be of a mixed nature, so long as he is made of body and spirit: and any effort to divest ourselves wholly of matter, and to be all spirit, will only end in an unconscious self-deception."[116] He here opposed those who would construct a building, the only criteria for which "is to accommodate as many persons as possible."[117] In this view of religion, which Medley saw as arising from cold rationalism, hearing the sermon ("the love of mere preaching")[118] was the entire purpose of attending a religious service. "All surrounding emotions" were neglected. To correct this, form and order were employed to "promote . . . the higher graces of the heart."[119]

This Romantic perspective was restrained in Medley. It was balanced by an extremely pragmatic spirit. For example, Medley argued that while it was true that the Gothic form of architecture was "expressive of reverent feeling and faith," it was also "convenient for the use of man."[120] To build of stone was more prudent than to build of wood.[121] As he argued in his earlier work on church architecture, Medley suggested that in many cases it was from no theological reason that people opposed decorated churches. Instead, they were simply unwilling to spend on the church what they spent on themselves. Their own homes were lavishly appointed, with colored tiles and costly provisions. As usual, Medley spoke quite directly: "We are unwilling that our own houses should be poor and comfortless, because we love ourselves too well to wish them other than they are: why then should we be willing that the House of our God should be meanly served, if we love it as God's House should be loved."[122] To build the church out of shabby materials, while their own houses were built from the best available, was a shrinking from their religious responsibility.

More than this, Medley argued in various places that to worship with the aid of external forms was only to follow the pattern recorded in Holy Scripture. For example, with regard to music, Scripture was used to demonstrate divine sanction for Medley's proposed "choral services," a hitherto unknown form of ceremonial in his diocese. He cited numerous scriptural references as evidence of the place of song in Christian worship. The early church continued this practice, "down to the degradation of Cromwell, the regicide [Medley's permanent epithet for Cromwell]. Here surely is not a *catena patrum*, but a *catena omnium* . . . a galaxy of examples, in favor of a ritual, if not exactly the same, yet framed on the same principles, with our choral service."[123] The principle remained the same, whether one considered architecture, music, or ceremony. That is, external, natural forms were able to serve as vehicles for divine truth and grace. Rather than paring down all external forms in an effort to approach the divine without mediation, Medley would suggest that we were most able to approach this divine truth through the external forms, provided they were consistent with orthodox theological principles and that they were not mistaken for that which they signified.

Medley was certainly no materialist or mere sensualist. His stern condemnations of "worldliness" ring through virtually every charge he delived to his clergy. For example, a few pages after the passage quoted above, Medley admonished his clergy not to "become wordly, careless, time-serving Priests, striving to be popular by base arts and latitudinarian notions . . . and only desirous for more and more of the things that pertain to this life!"[124]

Medley expressed a full appreciation for nature and the arts that imitated it. He affirmed that those arts were vital aids for Christian worship and devotion. At the same time he asserted that this world was transitory and attachment to it was sinful. This tension ("to be in the world, but not of it") is a commonplace of the Christian life. But because of the peculiar historical circumstances of the Victorian period—with rationalism and Romanticism both vying for place—the resolution of this tension is loaded with implication.

In his later years Medley worked to develop a resolution of this tension. For example, in an 1867 sermon he was able to suggest the peculiarly Christian relation of form to spirit.[125] It was a test of faith to recognize the Holy Ghost working in "natural things and persons." Medley did not, at this point, limit this work to the sacraments. The suggestion was that the Spirit was operative in a variety of external forms—thus legitimizing the use of such forms by the church. This had, in some way, supplanted the older form of miracles. The "sanctifying" of external forms was a kind of miracle in itself. Following upon this, Medley also asserted that those natural forms, which are the subject of these miracles, remain unchanged outwardly. This respect for the integrity of the natural world was at the core of his understanding of the real presence, as we will see below. Medley himself affirmed that a single principle supported both the doctrines of regeneration and real presence.[126]

The sacramental implications of Medley's position with regard to ceremony and ornamentation are obvious. If external forms were capable of being vehicles of spiritual reality, then rather than being opposed to the divine, the natural was to be seen as both proceeding from God and as leading back to Him. Medley argued that externals were part of the original character of the Christian revelation and were supposed by the ancient, medieval, and reformed tradition of the Catholic Church.

What Medley Accomplished

Beyond the building of dozens of new churches in New Brunswick, Medley inspired or directly caused the renovation of numerous others. Chancels were added, altars improved, fonts introduced in some places and repaired and repositioned in others.[127] Even his former opponents in the Evangelical parished of Saint John eventually were persuaded to accept the new architectural style. When Trinity Church, Saint John was rebuilt after the great fire of 1877,[128] it was distinctively Gothic instead of its previously Georgian form.[129] Another Saint John Evangelical stronghold had been remodeled even prior to the fire. In November 1872 Medley preached at the reopening of St. John's Church. He noted in his journal, "A new Chancel had been added, the choir placed in it, with proper seats, the organ brought down from the west gallery and a more decent arrangement adopted."[130] Throught the diocese, other parishes followed suit.

As Finley notes, there were actually two moments to the Gothic Revival in New Brunswick:

> the first, and more ecclesiologically correct, revival of Gothic forms that characterized the Anglican experience, and a second, largely vernacular, adaptation of Gothic forms that occurred among the other Christian denominations. After 1850, country or carpenter Gothic began to appear throughout New Brunswick. Roman Catholics embraced Gothic forms wholeheartedly, if somewhat eclectically . . . Protestant congregations rarely showed an inclination to use Gothic elements consistently; there was little conscious effort to employ thirteenth-century models as a reference nor to adhere to the dictates of the Ecclesiological Society. [However] as the century progressed kirks, meetinghouses and Catholic churches were increasingly gothicized according to vernacular building pattern. Round-headed windows assumed pointed tops, clear window panes were replaced by stained glass, classic belfries were renewed as gothic towers sporting turrets, pinnacles and stylized tracery.[131]

The influence of the Gothic Revival in New Brunswick cannot, of course, be solely attributed to John Medley. It was a cultural phenomenon of which he was only a small part. Yet in New Brunswick he was the most visible and vocal representative of the movement. It is not unreasonable to attribute to him some measure of responsibility for effects that stretched well beyond the Church of England in the province.

Beyond the boundaries of New Brunswick, Medley's influence is harder to define, but nevertheless undeniable. He was named one of the four patrons of the New York Ecclesiological Society and Frank Wills was made its official architect.[132] Wills designed churches throughout the United States. Combined with Medley's friendship with leading High Church Episcopalians, it is reasonable to say, with Finley, that, "New Brunswick [was] a conduit for the transmission of neo-Gothic ideas and forms from England to North America."[133]

Medley left the ecclesiastical landscape of New Brunswick indelibly stamped with his vision of "Church Architecture." Not only Anglican churches, but those of Dissenters and Roman Catholics adopted the Gothic pattern. Following the great fire in Saint John, Baptists and Methodists, as well as Evangelical Anglicans, rebuilt according to the Gothic style.[134] Not only religious edifices, but secular buildings too, could be identified as Gothic structures. In regard to the wider implications of church architecture, the increased care for structure and form mirrored an increased sense of the holiness of place that was high on the High Church ethos. Prominent fonts and altars, elevated chancels, and rich stained glass were almost universal in New Brunswick churches by the end of Medley's episcopate, where they had been almost completely absent when he arrived.

5

The Sacraments and Ritualism

MEDLEY'S PARTICULAR UNDERSTANDING OF THE SACRAMENTS WILL come as no surprise, once one has understood his approach to ecclesiastical architecture. However, in studying Medley's sacramental theology, a deeper degree of subtlety and perhaps ambiguity can be seen. This chapter will explore both his understanding of the sacraments and his relationship to Ritualism. While Medley was relatively easy to label as an ecclesiologist, his sacramental theology is somewhat harder to define. At times Tractarian, at times Protestant, his position is instructive as to the limitation of ecclesiastical labels.

BAPTISM

For John Medley there were two sacraments: baptism and the eucharist. Although he spoke of the other "five commonly called Sacraments,"[1] they did not rise to the level of the dominical sacraments. For example, he said that ordination was not a sacrament because it lacked: "the *vis sacramenti*, the proper matter [and] the injunction upon all men to make use of the sign."[2]

In Medley's 1850 charge, he took up several doctrinal questions. However, it was to baptism that he directed his most substantial comments. That this would be at the forefront of Medley's mind is not surprising since the Gorham case and its aftershocks were still reverberating. In fact, the decision of the Privy Council had been announced just a few months prior to the charge.

The matter arose over the refusal of Medley's old diocesan, Henry Phillpotts of Exeter, to institute the Reverend George Cornelius Gorham to a living, on the grounds that Gorham did not hold an orthodox account of baptismal regeneration. This led to a celebrated court case, where the court sided with Phillpotts. However, upon appeal, the Judicial Committee of the Privy Council declared Gorham's position to be legitimate and ordered Phillpotts to institute him. Phillpotts refused and Gorham was eventually instituted by the Evangelical Archbishop of Canterbury, J. B. Sumner. The entire issue became a rallying point for High Churchmen, Tractarians, Evangelicals, and Latitudinarians alike. Several Tractarians cited the Gorham decision as the last straw, precipitating their secession to Rome.[3] The question of baptismal regeneration was one thing; another offense to the Tractarians was the notion that a civil body should even have jurisdiction over matters of doctrine.[4]

In New Brunswick the Gorham case provided fuel for Medley's critics. J. W. D. Gray's Evangelical weekly, the *Church Witness*, concentrated on it for months. The paper always took delight in casting Medley's presumed mentor Henry Phillpotts in a negative light. In this case, Phillpotts was guilty of two crimes: "popish doctrine" and episcopal high-handedness. Thus, on October 30, 1850, the *Church Witness* warned against "the *opus operatum* system of Papists and Tractarians on the subject of Baptismal regeneration."[5] Phillpotts himself was just a mouthpiece for "the Exeter Tractarian party."[6] All along, there were repeated attacks on Phillpotts's abuse of power.[7]

Medley himself took up the question of baptismal regeneration at this time. Medley's second triennial charge, even more imposing (at fifty-three pages) than its predecessor, is remarkable for both the breadth of its subject matter and the depth of his exploration of particular themes. The first third of the charge dealt with matters of personal sanctity and of relations with other Christian bodies. Medley then turned to the matter of doctrine. That doctrine should be of vital importance was his initial concern. Typically, he began his defense of this point with scripture, and with the whole of Scripture understood, as in Hooker's conception, as "a doctrinal instrument of salvation."[8] He intended to refute those who preached only "the Gospel of Calvin," or otherwise restrict the full doctrinal content of the Bible.[9] This led Medley to renew his call for a more learned clergy, who would have a comprehensive understanding of the faith and would be able to teach it in its fullness.

Having laid the groundwork for his argument, Medley turned to consider "infidelity." More specifically, he wished to address that form of "modern unbelief [which] hides itself within our own camp."[10] This unbelief, "professes a general regard for Christianity, rears aloft the broad and spacious banner of Protestantism, but vehemently opposes every doctrine which is distinctly and clearly brought out."[11] The particular doctrines that this unbelief opposes are those "which rest wholly on what is unseen. These the semi-sceptic perpetually denounces: declares them . . . above all, impossible to be apprehended of reason."[12] Medley declared that it would be too large a work to trace out this infidelity in all its branches and settled for pointing it out in two forms: "the denial of the Eternity of future rewards and punishments and the denial of Sacramental Grace."[13]

For Medley this sacramental grace was "that portion of God's spiritual gifts which He has limited to two particular channels, Baptism, and the Supper of the Lord."[14] He wanted to make clear that he did not believe that God's grace was limited to the sacraments alone. Not only did it come regularly through such channels as prayer, but Medley also asserted that it could be received by those who were neither baptized nor had not received the Lord's Supper. Despite his earlier insistence on clearly defined doctrine, he charged that the great error of Rome, and of the Lutheran Church, was that "they have, in respect to one Sacrament, attempted to define the manner of this communication."[15] Medley would later refer to this position again.

He first took up the sacrament of baptism, cataloging the passages from Scripture used in the Prayer Book baptismal services, briefly summarizing their doctrinal purpose. He then turned to consider Peter's sermon on the Day of Pentecost,[16] offering a commentary on it. The thrust of this commentary was to demonstrate scriptural support for the doctrine of baptismal regeneration and to distinguish it from conversion.[17] Medley proceeded to offer a defense of the classical High Church understanding of regeneration. The central character of this position was the assertion of the universality and objectivity of the efficacious grace of the sacrament. He declared, "To limit this blessing to certain elect infants, the subjects of a prevenient grace, of which there is no special warrant in the Word of God, and to deny it to other infants, against whom no ground of separate exclusion can belong, and to call this unscriptural limitation the 'judgement of charity' is, to say the least of it, a sad misnomer. To me it appears the judgement of unbelief. The absolute and positive declaration of the regeneration of every infant in Baptism, by our formularies is, I think, a strong reason against a hypothetical Regeneration."[18]

Medley listed, in passing, those Anglican divines by whom the Prayer Book doctrine of regeneration was affirmed in its "literal sense." These include Ridley, Latimer, Pearson, Sanderson, Sheldon, Cosin, Heylin, Sparrow, and Thorndike. In particular he cited the response of the Anglican divines to the Puritans at the Savoy conference.[19] There was no full *catena* of authorities at this point, simply a mention of their names. He defended his reluctance to cite them. There were ample examples available from the early church, as well as the Reformers, in support of the doctrine, but these authorities were not recognized or understood by "plain honest men in our congregations."[20] Instead he believed that the argument must be based upon the plain, literal sense of the scriptures and the Book of Common Prayer.

Curiously, Medley offered little scriptural evidence for regeneration. It initially appears that Medley introduced the topic of baptism with regard to local errors. Ostensibly he intended to guide the clergy in responding to erroneous doctrines taught by other religious bodies in New Brunswick. In reality, he really had in mind the Gorham decision and those who held erroneous positions within the church. Thus, he did not try to defend baptismal regeneration upon theological grounds, beyond a cursory statement of orthodox teaching on the point. Instead, he was most concerned to demonstrate that baptismal regeneration was the doctrine of the Prayer Book and thus the Church of England. The entire argument was directed toward those who were members of the church, not those who were outside of it. Thus, in his pointed conclusion, he stated that even Dissenters acknowledged that regeneration was plainly taught by the Prayer Book. That was, after all, one of the grounds upon which they so desired Prayer Book revision.

At this point Medley wanted to simply make clear what the church actually taught about baptism. The church *did not* "hold that regeneration ensures the salvation of adults, or supersedes the necessity of repentance, faith, and a regenerate life."[21] These points were self-evident, to the extent that they were accepted by all as not the teaching of the Prayer Book. To this list Medley added that the church just as clearly *did* teach that all who are baptized were regenerate and "in an important sense . . . saved." This, of course, was just the point of contention in the Gorham case. While High Churchmen and Tractarians accepted such a statement of regeneration, Evangelicals rejected it, lest it should rule out the necessity of personal faith and Latitudinarians felt that such a position carried the odor of superstition.

Medley added as an appendix to his argument a brief *catena*. Aiming to depict a broad consensus of Anglican divines—both Low and High Church—he listed as supporters of the doctrine of regeneration Cranmer, Ridley, Jewel, Hooker, Taylor, Ussher, Pearson, Davenant, Andrews, and Bishop Ward. His final authority was none other than J. B. Sumner, the very archbishop of Canterbury who had opposed Phillpotts and finally himself instituted Gorham.[22] It was only at the end of the *catena* that Medley made direct mention of the Gorham case: "I earnestly protest against the doctrine avowed in a late decision, that our church speaks with the stammering lips of ambiguous and uncertain formularies."[23] It is interesting that Medley did not here take up the constitutional question—whether a civil court had any real authority over the church. As Chadwick puts it, some High

Churchmen were asking, "Was the pronouncement of the judicial committee no more relevant to the church than a pronouncement by the Great Mogul . . ."[24] Even Gladstone (who had himself been a convert to the doctrine of baptismal regeneration)[25] was shaken by the court's decision. "The Church of England is gone unless it releases itself by some authoritative act," he declared to Manning.[26] Medley developed quite firm views about this very question, but they were either not yet formed, or he chose not to express them publically at this time.[27]

Medley continued to hold and teach a high doctrine of regeneration throughout his life. More than twenty years into his episcopate he was still defending the doctrine to his diocesan clergy. He argued that the doctrine of "Sacramental Religion" derided by some, was none other than that which "Cranmer, Ridley and Jewell held to the last hour of their lives."[28] To use the word "regeneration" was only to affirm belief in the presence of the Holy Ghost. In the end it was all about "our transplanting from a state of nature into a state of grace, and our admission into all the privileges of the sons of God."[29] Note that Medley again used those authorities that the most Low Church of his listeners would accept.

The Eucharist

When we turn to Medley's direct references to the eucharist, the same principles are in evidence. One of the earliest extant statements of his views on the topic was in a sermon on the Reformation preached in 1847, just a month prior to his sermon on "The Staff of Beauty." Why Medley chose to preach on the Reformation on this occasion is unknown. However, in his dedication he made mention that it was preached in the [old] cathedral before the members of the House of Assembly and other prominent members of the New Brunswick government. Given that Newman had converted to Rome less than eighteen months previously, and other secessions had either taken place or were rumored to be imminent, and given that Medley was well known as being connected with the Tractarians, one might suggest that this sermon was delivered to its important audience with the aim of affirming his own allegiance to the reformed Church of England. Such political artfulness does not elsewhere seem to be part of his character. On the contrary, a sometimes startling candor belongs to his characteristic style. In addition, the opinions expressed in this sermon are nowhere contradicted and are in fact supported elsewhere in Medley's writings and speeches.

On the title page of the sermon, Medley placed an epigram of Bishop Hall, who was later in the sermon described as "that excellent and amiable divine":[30] "We desired the reformation of an old Religion—not the formation of a new." Although these are sentiments that lie at the heart of the Tractarian position, much of Medley's sermon could have been preached by the most fervent Evangelical member of the Church of England.[31] Directed at the Reformation in general, Medley treated the sacraments in passing, particularly the eucharist. After a forceful condemnation of the two chief errors of the Roman Catholic Church—the claimed supremacy of the bishop of Rome and the intercession of the Virgin Mary—he turned to "other corruptions." Chief among these was "the definition of the presence of Christ in the Lord's Supper to be the conversion of the whole substance of bread and wine into the whole substance of Christ's body and blood." To Medley, this violated the sacramental principle that required not only an invisible grace but a visible sign.[32] He thus did not oppose the real presence, but only the loss of the real substance of the natural sign.

Medley was equally determined to refute the Low Church account of the eucharistic presence. At this point Medley added in a footnote a lengthy quotation from Archbishop Ussher, "a man who had as great an aversion to the Papacy as most."[33] James Ussher, the seventeenth-century archbishop of Armagh was of decidedly Calvinist sympathies, yet in the passage cited by Medley even he affirms a sacramental presence.[34] The use of such an authority was common in Medley's work. While the Tractarians were not averse to using Protestant-leaning Anglicans in their own *Catenae* of authorities, there seems at times to be a purely rhetorical purpose for such inclusion. The intention was to confound Low Churchmen with the words of their own worthies and heroes. Medley's own views on the real presence underline that, at least in this case, Ussher was being quoted without any trace of irony. First, Ussher was not here being quoted out of context, as the Tractarians occasionally made their authorities appear.[35] Secondly, Ussher's position *was* Medley's position, with regard to the presence of Christ in the eucharist. Medley here categorically condemned the doctrine of transubstantiation and in doing so he applied the direct language of the Anglican formularies.[36] Interestingly, Medley used Ussher's words to supply the theological reason for his rejection of transubstantiation. His own arguments proceeded on the ground of authority.

In speaking of "significative" and "exhibitive" senses of the sacrament, Ussher actually intended the scholastic distinction between *sacramentum* and *rem sacramenti (res significata)*.[37] Ussher went on, in his sermon, to arrive at a quite unscholastic receptionism.[38] This position, however, was also received sympathetically by Medley. To stretch the literal meaning of the Article (XXVIII) so as to comprehend it in a "non-natural" sense[39] was "inadmissible" according to Medley.[40] He accepted the doctrine of the presence of Christ in the sacrament, as presented in the Articles and the Prayer Book, in its natural sense.

While Ussher appealed to scholastic theology, Medley's own words were based in a particular understanding of authority. First, the doctrine of transubstantiation (along with the other errors of the Roman Church that he had previously listed) was not supported by the supreme authority, scripture. Secondly (and here we have an echo of Tractarian rhetoric), these errors were not part of "the deposit of faith." Instead they were "corruptions of doctrine the English Church protested against and renounced at the Reformation."[41] They were unknown to the period that produced the three creeds and the first four general councils.

This sermon, delivered early in his episcopate,[42] reflects both sides of what will be seen as Medley's complex position. He was identified with the Tractarians and their emphasis on the *Catholic* nature of the Church of England. But, he was a confirmed Protestant and, unlike many of his Tractarian contemporaries, not shy about using the term.[43] It is this tension in Medley that makes the label "Tractarian" an uncomfortable fit.

Predictably enough, Medley used the occasion of his first charge, delivered in August of 1847, to spell out his program to his clergy. Medley drew a distinction that would have been familiar to those who had heard him before, "Neither a religion which is all form without spirit, nor a religion which is all spirit without form, can be intended for beings who are compounded of 'body, and soul, and spirit' and whose eternal happiness is incomplete without the reunion of the material with the immaterial substance. . . . In an age when decent respect is paid to forms, they think of nothing else: now that the emptiness of the form without the spirit is discovered, then can we do without them altogether."[44] The note of balance, seeking to find the mean between two extremes, was characteristic of Medley's approach throughout his episcopate. This may only have been a function of his consciousness of having to be a unifying force as diocesan bishop. Whatever the case, some of the more extreme positions of his earlier years were replaced by more irenic statements later on. In fact, at the outset of his charge, he declared that it would not be "conducive to our mutual good, that I should enter at length into that wide field of polemical theology . . . where it is easier to discover a partizan than to find a judge."[45] He added toward the end that he was "sick at heart of controversy on trifles."[46] While many nineteenth-century religious controversialists protested their aversion to controversy, in Medley's case his words appear to have been sincere. For while we might wish to have had his thoughts on many of the contentious ecclesiastical issues that boiled up in Victorian England, Medley seldom spoke directly of them.

One of the few private insights we have into Medley's sacramental thought serves to confirm that his public position was indeed his own and not simply one adopted for his audience. He wrote occasionally to his friend Cecil Wray, perpetual curate of St. Martin's in the Fields, Liverpool (and himself a correspondent of George Denison, John Keble, A. P. Forbes, J. M. Neale, and W. F. Hook).[47] In a social letter in which he enclosed a lecture for Wray's perusal and requested some choral music, Medley soon turned to the topics of the day.[48] Two controversies then at the center of ecclesiastical debates were the Denison affair[49] and the case of St. Barnabas's Pimlico.[50] Of the two, Medley told Wray that the St. Barnabas case was, in his opinion, the more momentous. It might appear curious that Medley would take greater interest in the "St. Barnabas case," than in the Denison matter.[51] It is entirely consistent both with Medley's character and theological position that this would be the case. Denison's aggressive pursuit of persecution would not at all have been amenable to Medley's personality.

As Chadwick relates, Denison tried to goad Bishop Bagot into charging him so that the doctrine of the real presence could be settled once and for all.[52] Not content to have his own position merely tolerated, Denison wished for the church either to formally affirm the real presence or to condemn the opposing view. Bagot was reluctant to do this and Denison continued to force the issue with a series of sermons until finally a Low Churchman was provoked into bringing a complaint against him.[53] Rather than seeking to avoid conflict, Denison "looked forward with joy to the fight."[54] Medley's judgment of this was forthright: "The Archdeacon is overfond of controversy and is pertinacious to a degree in my judgement."[55] Such an opinion was held by others connected to the Tractarians. For example, J. T. Coleridge, Keble's biographer and Medley's friend, thought that Denison's actions were "needless and unsatisfactory."[56]

Medley believed that in the case of St Barnabas's Pimlico "principles" were more at stake. Bishop Blomfield of London had issued a number of orders calling for the cessation of various Ritualist practices, including using colored altar cloths (frontals). The Ritualist priest Charles Lowder was one of the clergy resident there at this time. It may be that Medley and Lowder had met; they certainly had acquaintances in common. For example, Lowder and his family knew William Butterfield, the celebrated Gothic revival architect and Medley's collaborator on Christ Church Cathedral in Fredericton. The warden of St. Paul's Knightsbridge, of which St. Barnabas's Pimlico was a chapel of ease, was responsible for bringing many of the charges forward against Lowder. A full-blown controversy soon resulted.

Medley believed that "[the church warden] Mr. Westerton . . . under colour of attacking an altar cloth aims at the reverence due to the sanctuary." However, this was the lesser of the principles involved. What really concerned Medley was the attack on "the right of a congregation under due authority to judge for themselves in these matters." There must be, in his opinion, toleration within the church for such variation in matters of "taste and feelings."[57] He suggested that High Churchmen should not impose their tastes upon Puritans; nor should Puritans attempt to do likewise.

Having made this point Medley returned to the question of the real presence, raised in the Denison case. Wray must previously have expressed his views on the matter to Medley, for the bishop replied, "I entirely agree with your view of worship—I worship Christ not so much in the Sacrament as at the Sacrament." Nevertheless, Medley declared that he did "hold to real presence." It was precisely Denison's insistence on a particular (and narrow, in Medley's view) understanding of the presence that he objected to, as "this over-refinement distracts one's mind and withdraws it from the simplicity of faith."

Medley's position was not quite this vague, however. Upon quite specific theological grounds, Medley was at odds with Denison. As he went on to explain, his account of the presence in the sacrament differed with respect to the manner of the real presence, the adoration proper to the sacrament, and whether faith was required for reception of the body and blood of Christ. These were the three central points of Denison's position, around which the entire controversy revolved.

On the manner of Christ's presence, Medley believed that it was a "mystery" necessarily and not able to be spoken of. Denison's initial problem was his attempt to "define what [cannot] be defined." Not only did Medley say that we were unable to make such definitions; he disavowed any interest in being able to do so. It was sufficient to affirm that Christ was present, so Medley therefore counted himself as accepting the doctrine of the real presence. In the sheet attached to the letter he went so far as to say that Christ was present in the sacrament "really and objectively." Still, this was a "holy mystery" and resistant to precise definition as to "the mode and limits of this supernatural presence." This line of argument carried over to Medley's treatment of adoration. Medley at once affirmed a principle of eucharistic adoration but did not suggest any adoration due to the elements themselves.

Just as with his mature understanding of Christian architecture, Medley approached his sacramental doctrine with the intention of affirming both the divine and natural, both the objective and subjective aspects. While he declared the divine, objective presence of Christ in speaking of the "supernatural" character of the eucharist, he wanted also to assure the necessity of faith, on the side of the natural and subjective. There must be faith in order for Christ to be received. This faith was "the instrument of reception." To discount the importance of this was to reduce man to a "mere machine." Medley's position here was not unique. That he appears to have affirmed a mildly receptionist eucharistic doctrine is not surprising, even if he was a Tractarian.[58] Nevertheless, his repudiation of Denison on each of three major points is significant. In the end though, it was the narrowness and intolerance of Denison's position that Medley saw as most dangerous.

It is for this last reason that Medley saw the St. Barnabas case as of greater interest than the Denison matter. The ecclesiastical courts, in condemning Denison's position, had not, in Medley's estimation, threatened any important church principle. Rather, it was Denison who held the dangerous position. In the St. Barnabas case, the opposite was true. Although the points at issue may seem to us at a distance trivial, Medley saw vital principles at stake. In Blomfield's rejection of coloured altar cloths (as well as altar crosses and candles) Medley saw a double threat. On the one hand, Westerton (the warden who brought the charges) was actually attacking "the reverence due to the sanctuary." For Medley, this was no small thing. It touched on the proper relation between man and God. We might think back to his understanding of church architecture, the purpose of which was to remind man of his smallness in comparison to the majesty of God. Those forms of church design that Medley criticized were at fault because they encouraged "irreverence." He knew full well that outward symbols and ceremonies were not of any divine character. They helped mold our minds and "feelings" so that we would be able to approach the divine more easily and with the proper spirit of humility. The worship and rites of the church were but the "veil of the sign, the inward and significant grace which accompanies it."[59] The intimate and sacramental relation between the outward sign and the inward grace was at the heart of Medley's ecclesiology here and elsewhere.

On the other hand, by attempting to abolish the liturgical practices at St. Barnabas's, Mr. Westerton was interfering with the rights of another congregation. He was the warden of St. Paul's Knightsbridge, the parent church of the chapel of ease.[60] Medley never wavered from his affirmation of an acceptable degree of liberty with regard to ceremonial. He did not seek to suppress Evangelical forms in his own diocese or to impose High Church forms on Evangelical congregations (beyond encouraging the use of a regular offertory and daily prayers in the church). Indeed, later in his life he would attack the Public Worship Regulation Act because of its intolerant spirit. Perhaps particularly because of the circumstances of the colonial environment, Medley was acutely sensitive to the impossibility of strict religious conformity. This ultimately would find expression in his criticism of establishment.[61]

At the end of the letter to Wray, Medley appended a curiously formal paragraph, which seems to be an attempt to devise a clear statement, perhaps for later public use, although we have no record of him using it in this way.

> At the celebration of the Holy Eucharist I worship and adore Christ God and Man, then and there really and objectively (objectively, not subjectively only, i.e. He is an object of faith and worship at the Eucharist before he is received by the communicants) present in this holy mystery and offering to me his very body and blood for my spiritual food. Being ignorant of the mode and limits of this supernatural Presence I hesitate to define the very place of this presence, to which our adoring faith ought to be directed, as if our worship were due esp. to the precious gift of his body and blood and not also or it may be rather, to Him who is the giver of this holy food and who is undoubtedly present as our great high priest at this sacrifice.[62]

This position ultimately fit within the norms of High Church accounts of the eucharistic presence and certainly within the literal meaning of the Articles. It was certainly not a radical view and although apparently an account of Medley's sincere beliefs, it was a statement that might well have been able to be used to unify diverse positions within his own diocese, as well as beyond. It could easily be imagined that he was consciously trying to produce a conciliatory position that could be accepted by most people of High or Low persuasion in New Brunswick.

Ten years later, Medley felt confident enough to express publicly what he had written privately to Wray. In his two sermons on the Holy Spirit, he spelled out his position on the mode of Christ's presence in the sacrament.

> Again, by the words "real presence" we do not mean that the elements of bread and wine cease to be what in their own nature God has made them,

> but that the Holy Ghost descending upon them, and receiving them as our oblation to God, sanctifies them to a holy and spiritual use wholly different from their natural use, and through them communicates the Body and Blood of Christ spiritually to the soul of the faithful receiver; so that in a manner wholly incomprehensible to our natural faculties, Christ and His Spirit are truly present, and we do by faith "verily and indeed" spiritually feed on Christ our Lord. This is so often and so plainly stated in our Catechism and Communion office, that it is needless to quote passages familiar to all who use these offices, and the doctrine being there expressed, the words "Real presence" need not disquiet any serious mind, as though any change of the substance of the elements, or any adoration of them, or any carnal presence of Christ's body were implied or intended.[63]

Point by point, his position was that of a decade earlier.

His understanding of the eucharistic presence was analogous to his view of baptismal regeneration. Medley was at pains to point out the difference between regeneration and conversion. Conversion meant a turning from sin. Infants needed no conversion because they had committed no actual sins. Once they attained maturity they were subject to that lifelong need for repentance and "conversion." In this argument, Medley intended to offer a corrective subjectivity to the objectivity of regeneration. There was still required the subjective assent of the will in the rational adult. Medley would spend some time arguing for the "resistibility" of divine grace. Were divine grace irresistible there would be no need for the participation of the human will and the entire Christian Gospel would be made pointless.[64]

While Medley was as strong about matters of principle as one could be, he never failed to express remorse at public division in the church. Certainly the Evangelical opposition to him, especially during the early years of his episcopate, furnished sufficient provocations that he could have continually resorted to the courts and other forms of disciplinary proceedings. But he refused to do so. His desire to avoid confrontation may be illustrated by his repeated calls to avoid "party spirit." Years of experience as a bishop, during which he faced significant opposition over small points of ritual and practice, did nothing to harden his heart, or incline him to a more aggressive stance with regard to the imposition of uniformity. In fact, his experience as a bishop only enforced his sense of the necessity of toleration. In order for a diocese to function as an effective tool for spreading the Gospel, there must be a pragmatic approach to matters of lesser importance. As a bishop Medley naturally sought to promote unity within his diocese. In the end, it was Medley's sense of the church's missionary calling that outweighed any inclination toward the "wedge politics" of someone like George Denison.

Ritualism and the Value of Toleration

We treat Ritualism along with the sacraments, because they both flow from a single principle: the claim that external forms can be means of spiritual blessings. This was at the heart of Medley's understanding of "church architecture." It was also the principle upon which he built his sacramental theology. The externals were not merely accidents, but important in their own substance. Thus it reflected a difference in one's understanding of the divine, if one used Gothic arches or classical columns.

So, it is not surprising that Medley, even though no Ritualist himself, should defend the Ritualists. While we do not have detailed accounts of the ceremonial used by Medley in his cathedral, the relative lack of controversy surrounding the same suggests that nothing very novel was being done. Early in his episcopate Medley expressed surprise at the criticism from Evangelical circles for, as he said, "I have not ordered the surplice nor pulled down all the pulpits, nor turned to the East, nor crossed myself."[65] Medley was the object of intense criticism from Low Churchmen during his episcopate. He was attacked in various Evangelical periodicals, which seldom failed to notice even the slightest hint of "Puseyite" or "Romish" behavior. But there were no charges of elaborate Ritualist liturgical practices, even from that extreme quarter. Medley introduced choral services, the daily office, weekly communion, and altar candles to the cathedral and he advocated wearing the surplice. Beyond that, there is little indication of any advanced Ritualist practices. As far as the vaunted "six points"[66] of Ritualism are concerned, there is evidence only that he employed altar candles. Yet, particularly in his later years, Medley became one of the few public episcopal defenders of the Ritualists.[67]

Medley's early instances of defense of ritual have been noted above. The idea of a religion that is both "form and spirit," that brings about a "reunion of the material with the immaterial substance,"[68] was at the heart of his ecclesiology. This argument was directed at those who would deny any place to externals in worship. But what about those who would allow a due measure of outward form, as long as it did not exceed Anglican formularies? In other words, where did Medley part company with those conservative High Churchmen who expressed concerns that the Ritualists had gone too far?

Peter Nockles argues that the High Churchmen were not as much a source for the Ritualists as were the "Camdenites."[69] While Medley certainly had High Church connections, his ties to the ecclesiological movement were even more direct, as Finley has demonstrated.[70] Despite Medley's firm convictions concerning what constituted proper form and ceremony, he was tolerant in the enforcement of the same in his own diocese. In his first charge he asserted that "to be unable to distinguish between the things which are vital, and those which are accidental, and alterable, is mere blindness or obstinacy."[71] Clearly considering ritual as among *adiaphora*, Medley returned to this argument more directly later in his life, at a crucial time for the Ritualists.

It was in his charge of 1868 that Medley first addressed the topic of Ritualism directly. The Ritual Commission had been created in England the previous year in order to investigate liturgical variations and the question of ritual was prominent in public discussion.[72] Medley began his argument concerning the Ritualists in an interesting way. He first set out to speak about advances in learning. This was introduced after a reference to "the perilous crisis through which our Church is now passing."[73] He again suggested that the general advancement of learning, especially the increased spirit of "inquiry on all subjects," was part of divine providence. He then gave a catalog of those sciences—history, geography, astronomy, and geology—that had been developed and applied to the study of scripture.[74] Other conservative clergy at this point might have followed this with a denunciation of this new critical spirit. Instead, Medley offered a spirited affirmation of the pursuit of knowledge and a condemnation of obscurantism. "We may lament over, or we may rejoice in, this altered relation; but we cannot 'force the course of a river.' What I wish to impress upon you all is, that we are deeply responsible for the manner in which we meet this overpowering tide. To meet it with unmanly lamentations is worse than useless; it is actually sinful, if the new order of things be part of God's providential government. It is equally useless to meet it with simple denunciation of infidelity. All men who doubt are not infidels. Ignorance and self doubt often dogmatize, when the wiser and more reverent mind is endeavouring to discover where the truth lies."[75] This was not a startling position for Medley, though it may have been for many other conservative Victorian prelates. He had always encouraged his clergy to study secular subjects and to have as well-rounded an education as possible.

It is the obscurantist or intolerant position that Medley meant to criticize with regard to the Ritualist question. The Church of England was "a compromise," designed always to be "as comprehensive as possible."[76] This was contrasted with "Rome and Geneva," both of which positions insisted upon rigid uniformity. According to Medley, for the Church of England to imitate these models would imperil its very existence. "The whole history of our church is a history of the failure of the enforcement by law of absolute uniformity."[77] Medley proceeded at this point to furnish illustrations of the destructive consequences of attempts to impose absolute uniformity on the English Church since the Reformation. Among the instances named were the efforts of Archbishop Laud, which resulted, in Medley's view, in both the church and state being brought low. Also, the church failed in not accommodating Wesley's revival; "Again the sword of uniformity was unsheathed, and again a vast breach was made in our ranks."[78]

This brought Medley around to the conclusion that this fairly elaborate argument had been designed to reach. Comparing the Church of England to Romanism and Puritanism, he argued: "If our Church professes to be built on a more popular basis, it is plain that we cannot evade the necessary conclusion, that whether a man be called Low Churchman, High Churchman, or Ritualist, there is comprehensiveness enough in our Church to embrace him, and there ought to be charity enough to make use of his zeal and piety, though as to the means he makes use of to promote the glory of God and the salvation of souls, our conclusions may widely differ."[79]

It is noteworthy that here, and elsewhere, Medley did not enter into a defense of particular Ritualist practices. Few of the advanced forms of ritual would have been congenial personally to the conservative Medley, nor were they in use in his diocese.[80] His position is as it was with regard to the controversy at St. Barnabas's Pimlico. The repression of particular and local variants in regards to the "accidents" of the faith was what he opposed. The notion of comprehensiveness in dealing with liturgical variation continued to be a theme of Medley's in the years to come. Finally, it is surely significant that this charge was published in England and meant to be read there.

He again took up the defense of the Ritualists in his next charge in 1871. This was the year of the Purchas Judgment, in which many of the Ritualists' "six points" were condemned by the Judicial Committee of the Privy Council. No doubt Medley had this in mind when he again spoke explicitly of Ritualism. After speaking of the Ritualists as "remarkable examples of self-sacrifice and continual devotion to their holy work, and from whom many who rail at them might learn much," he suggested that the errors of the Ritualists were less offensive than those errors committed at the opposite end of the liturgical spectrum: "But I think we have far more to fear from the dead level of cold worldliness, which eschews all reverence, and sees no reality in the Church and its Sacraments, and reduces the whole act of worship to a meagre performance by a minister, than we have from any excesses of ritualism. Mere outward show, for show's sake, is certainly to be avoided in divine worship; but our Lord reserves for his severest displeasure the lifeless Church, which He will 'spue out of his mouth,' the cold lukewarmness of respectable and fashionable worldliness."[81] He noted that the Church of England had generally been inclined toward "excessive carelessness rather than excessive ritualism." Medley's defense of the Ritualists was twofold: first, a general defense of the existence of ritual in worship; second, a call for toleration and a condemnation of the intolerant spirit that produced the Act of Uniformity and in a few years would produce the Public Worship Regulation Act.

In his defense of ritual there was an element of Romanticism. But there was also an echo of Wesleyanism and its call for the engagement of the feelings in worship. Medley recognized the contribution of the Wesleyan revival even as he regretted its eventual outcome. Even there though, he placed the blame for the schism on the bishops who failed to make a place for Wesley's position. Medley was always at pains to remind his listeners that Wesley remained a loyal churchman to the end of his life. It was through fear of "enthusiasm" that the hierarchy of the church forced Wesley's followers to leave.

Whether through ignorance or design, Medley claimed that the Ritualists' aim had been simply to bring worship up to the level of "the plain, positive, undeniable direction of the Prayer Book."[82] In fact, many of the Ritualists had gone significantly beyond the "directions" of the Prayer Book and some did not hide their utter disdain for the reformed liturgy.[83] There is no indication that Medley had any sympathy for the more "advanced" observances of the Ritualists.

Medley had introduced his own modest liturgical innovations as bishop. He alluded to them in this same charge, referring to an occasional form of service that he had produced for use on Good Friday.[84] Medley defended this practice by claiming that bishops of the church had always enjoyed the privilege of providing such services "on special occasion."[85] It had also been his practice, which he regarded as unexceptional, to draw up particular forms of prayers for "occasions of general humiliation or general thanksgiving."[86] Medley admitted that this practice had come under criticism, as people appealed to a Provincial Statute, which provided for "the grave penalty of deprivation on all who use any other service than that found in the Prayer Book."[87]

By 1874 the Public Worship Regulation Act (PWRA) had become reality and Medley was to direct his occasional attention to it throughout the rest of the decade.[88] In his charge for 1874 he again took up the question of ritual. After thanking the clergy for their condemnation of Bishop Colenso, Medley again repeated the argument that absolute uniformity with regard to ritual was both impossible and undesirable.[89] But he went somewhat further with regard to the Prayer Book on this occasion. He had previously argued that the whole effort of the Ritualists was to bring practice in line with the plain literal directions of the Prayer Book. Now he suggested that the Prayer Book directions were not sufficient. The rubrics did not provide for "every duty and custom." He did not say whether he believed that this was by design or fault, however. All manner of practices, used by churchmen of all parties were not covered by the rubrics, e.g., "preaching in a pulpit, for communion rails, for seats, for the patterns and forms of furniture, for hymns, for metrical psalms, and . . . many other things."[90]

He reminded his listeners that he had not been hypocritical in the application of this principle, but had allowed latitude to both High Church and Low Church practices. It was on this point of toleration that he returned to the argument he had made on past occasions. In an oblique reference to the Church Association, Medley asked rhetorically if "any reasonable man suppose[s] that we should be driven to agreement by the formation of an association to prosecute brethren who differ, to drag them before the judgement seats, and to inflict on them ruinous expenses, or the extreme penalties of the law?"[91] He went on to predict that these sorts of tactics would "end in . . . a disastrous failure." Medley was certainly accurate in his prophecy as subsequent events were to show.[92]

Medley was conducting his campaign against the PWRA behind the scenes as well and we have a series of letters that he wrote to Gladstone as part of this effort.[93] At that time, as a result of the elections of that year, Gladstone was in opposition and opposed the act for political, but also heartfelt theological reasons.[94] Alluding to their collaboration on previous occasions, Medley expressed his hope that Gladstone's "powerful and eloquent voice may be raised against a bill so destructive of all principles of true liberty, and so harassing to a great number of the loyal sons and servants of the Church of England."[95] In his next letter Medley referred to Gladstone's "kind reply" to the previous request. Unfortunately all of Gladstone's letters to Medley, during this and other periods of correspondence, are lost. Medley argued in this second letter that Ritualist excesses were intended to "magnify, perhaps unduly, one of the sacraments." This surely was "a much lighter endeavor than to abolish, or render nugatory, one of the creeds."[96] This was in reference to attempts at that time to have the Creed of St. Athanasius removed from the Prayer

Book or at least edited so as to remove the passages threatening eternal punishment for disbelief.[97]

Medley wrote twice more to Gladstone, three years later. These letters were on the subject of Ritualism. In the first, Medley enclosed a sermon he had recently preached before the Provincial Synod of Canada. Medley related that the sermon had excited some criticism "in consequence of my having taken a different line from most of my brethren." He wanted Gladstone's opinion on what he had said about the Ritualists in it.[98] Medley's next letter indicated that Gladstone agreed with his position.[99]

The sermon Medley referred to was delivered on September 12, 1877 in Montreal. He had, by this time, been bishop for over thirty years, as he recalled the state of affairs in the church before the Tractarian and ecclesiological revival:

> In those halcyon days, there were occasional meetings on behalf of the society (as it was called), scantily attended. A safe, moderate and wealthy parson was usually invited to preach, and discoursed on the security of the Church of England, and the evils of dissent. At a small assemblage afterwards, held, after a few well turned compliments to each other, and a brief glance at foreign lands, which no one had any intention of visiting, and of which few knew anything, the meeting separated in the full spirit of Mons. De Talleyrand's direction "above all, sir, no zeal." It was taken for granted that Christianity and the Establishment were synonymous terms. One can scarcely think it possible that in one man's lifetime the aspect of things in the Church should have so completely changed. Hundreds of parishes in those days had only one service on Sunday; and thousands found the church door closed against them all the week. It seemed that man was made to worship his creator one day in seven, more than this would be fatal to the Protestant religion.[100]

This accords with the accounts of the state of his diocese that Medley gave upon his arrival in Fredericton in 1845. In particular the closing of churches through the week was perceived by Medley as an evil that he had fought throughout his episcopate. His reference to "no zeal" recalls the "dead worldliness" that he associated with Low Churchmanship.

Medley went on in the sermon to describe the dead state of a church that had not yet revived a decent understanding of ritual. He mentioned particularly several areas that had been at the center of his own reforming efforts. The campaigns against "pews" and Tate and Brady's metrical psalms were particularly recalled. In place of the latter he had promoted hymnody and congregational singing. These were days when "the Christian Year had not then been born." This was evidently a reference to Keble's tremendously popular book of devotional poetry, *The Christian Year*, and the effect that it was to have on popular devotion. Medley especially makes note of the infrequency of holy communion and the general ignorance of liturgy that had prevailed in those days. He had himself established weekly choral celebrations of holy communion in the cathedral. He referred to the Savoy Conference, which was important for him, as for the older High Church tradition, inasmuch as it gave the authority for the church's retention of Catholic practice against the Presbyterians. Meeting in 1661 and resulting in a rejection of Presbyterian ministry, its history had recently been documented by Edward Cardwell, whose work Medley referred to on several occasions.

Having thus far defended the Tractarians, Medley then offered one of the few direct public tributes to the great movement of which he was a part. However, he accepted no credit for this, speaking as if an outsider to it. Characterizing the church as having a "paralysis of spiritual life and motion," he said that "a few earnest and good men" set out to investigate the history and constitution of the English church. "These inquiries were, it must be remembered, made by men unversed in architectural knowledge, who certainly were not Ritualists. But the notion of any powers that were wholly spiritual, and independent of the state, appeared so novel and so foreign to men's minds, that men lashed themselves into fury at the thought. It would not be saying too much to describe them, like their predecessors, throwing dust into the air, and crying out, 'Away with such a fellow from the earth, for it is not fit that he should live.' "[101]

He thus places the Ritualist question into the wider context of the relation of the church to the state and the very catholicity and apostolicity of the Church of England. He wanted to make clear, as he did with his remarks on the Ritualist controversy surrounding St. Barnabas's Pimlico,[102] that much greater principles were at stake than mere outward observances. The result of this renewal was plain to see. Practices that once seemed scandalous had become widely accepted. Churches had been "restored to somewhat of their pristine glory, and every one rejoices." Fonts had been restored and "altars, duly vested, are substituted for mean kitchen tables." He said that the church had undergone a "second reformation." He focused here on the outward forms of this renewal: "No longer offering to God the meanest and the worst, 'the blind and the lame,' she humbly and reverently presents to His glory the best, the costliest of all His gifts to her."[103] Medley perhaps overstated the degree to which ritual observances had become universally acceptable, as prosecutions under the PWRA continued into the next decade.[104]

Medley declared that the chief threats to the church in the present age came from "within ourselves." Characteristically he listed "want of holiness" as the first of these dangers.[105] This was followed by "want of sound knowledge" and "want of love." Under this last heading he returned to the matter of the Ritualists. He charged that it was this lack of love that lay behind the "fierce fires of bitterness" and the "inconsiderate zeal of eager partisans" that plagued the church.[106] One of the consequences of this attitude was the tendency "to place things indifferent in the rank of principles." It was this confusion of *adiaphora* with true principles that he saw as behind the Ritualist controversy. While both sides might be seen as having fallen into this error, Medley clearly viewed the persecutors of the Ritualists as the chief offenders. "I am well aware that in addressing you *in cathedra*, I do not speak *ex cathedra*: yet shall I not withhold my opinion that in an evil hour for the Church of England, it was determined to stamp out one of the serious and earnest parties in our church."[107]

The English Church had long been in thrall to "that most fatal notion, that worship consists in seeing and hearing a preacher." The Ritualists attempted to correct this, inquiring by "what ritual, what postures of holy devotion, what significant and solemn symbols of [the] faith, we may most humbly, and most agreeably to the mind of Christ, adore our Incarnate God."[108] In speaking this way, Medley wanted to remind people that Christianity was neither a purely material, nor a purely "spiritual" religion. Spirit and form were understood to correspond respectively to inward and outward, divine and human. That Christians worshiped an "Incarnate God" mandated that natural forms be used in that worship. In trying to remind the church of this, it was not surprising that the Ritualists provoked controversy. "It is the character of all reforms to elicit differences of thought and action, and ritual is simply no exception to the general rule. This matter should, in my view, be dealt tenderly with on both sides."[109]

Medley's defense of the Ritualists had, on every occasion, been quite restrained to this point. He simply made modest claims on the side of toleration and a due place for external forms. In this sermon however, he permitted himself to express some depth of personal feeling. His criticism of the English episcopate was less veiled than earlier references. He was particularly disturbed that the Ritualists, alone among the manifold parties of the church, had been singled out for censure. He named Evangelicals, High Churchmen and "men of broader sympathies as representing the various parties of the Church, all of whom work together in Synods, in Congresses, in Consecrations and Holy Communions." Medley asked why the Ritualist alone should be isolated: "Why should he have a special scourge[110] [i.e., the PWRA] invented for his peculiar benefit, called by one of the many ironies of life, fatherly correction?"[111] He was willing to concede that the Ritualists themselves used "rude and uncharitable expressions . . . in haste and anger," but he insisted that they had been provoked to do so. As he said,

> I make great allowance for the feelings of men, who, thoroughly in earnest themselves, devoted to hard and often ill-paid work, seek to attract and to christianize rude and half-heathen populations, and having succeeded in this arduous task, and made up congregations of most unpromising materials, who are devoutly attached to their pastors, and delight in a service in which they can all join, find themselves prosecuted by people who send hired spies to watch, not to worship, in their churches, and are brought under the lash of a law which scarcely any of the Bishops themselves perfectly obey, and notoriously, those Bishops who put the law in operation obey it the least.[112]

He went on to underline again the exceptional personal qualities of many of the Ritualist priests (and laymen) and to contrast this with the unworthy behavior of their opponents. Finally, Medley suggested that "if a wholly different course had been pursued" in dealing with the Ritualists, one of prayer, patience, and charity, the outcome would have been a less bitterly divided church. Had this been done, he was sanguine that "a way would have been found for the tolerance of some things deemed by them essential, and the abandonment of others as idiosyncrasies, or eccentricities of hasty, impatient minds."[113]

While Medley did not perhaps consider himself a Ritualist, there can be no doubt that he identified with them to a degree. In speaking of the devotion of the Ritualist priests in the slums of England's cities who "devoted to hard and often ill-paid work, [sought] to attract and to christianize rude and half-heathen populations," he surely saw a parallel to his own missionary priests as fellow laborers in harsh circumstances. He had spoken before of missionary priests, willing to go where others would not, laboring in poorly paid obscurity. Beyond this, however, the sermon marked a departure for him. He had always suggested the need to avoid party divisions. In this sermon he actively employed party labels, with a clear intimation of who was the aggrieved party. While acknowledging the "rude and uncharitable expressions used in haste and anger" by some Ritualists, he nevertheless placed the greater burden of responsibility for the present discord on the shoulders of "those who call themselves Evangelical." Perhaps it was because this sermon was before the Provincial Synod in Montreal and not in his own diocese that he felt free to use language that would surely have reawakened controversy at home. None of his charges or sermons preached within the diocese contained attacks on any ecclesiastical party by name, despite the frequent and harsh criticisms directed toward him from Evangelical sources.

But if Medley only intimated in this passage that those who have authority in the church must bear responsibility for this strife, he became more than willing later to be explicit in his criticism of the English ecclesiastical and civil hierarchy. He listed all of those who, by their actions against the Ritualists, had damaged not only their opponents, but the church as a whole. The bishops, the Evangelical body, the Broad Churchmen, and the state all shared equally the blame, in his view.[114] The entire English establishment, in short, had behaved foolishly and uncharitably to bring about the present state of the church, "all torn and bleeding with continual dissension."[115]

While it has been argued that Medley had as his aim to disseminate the English ecclesiastical and imperial model in the new land and that all his actions served this end,[116] passages such as the above would suggest a problem with this interpretation. Medley had no illusions, by this point, of any inherent English moral superiority that would save its institutions from the worst forms of corruption. In fact the Ritualist controversy was only one element in a growing desire by Medley for ecclesiastical independence, which development we will trace below.[117] According to him, circumstances were simply different in the colonial church.

If the PWRA was folly in England, such an act would have been even more destructive in Canada, where such coercive power was unthinkable. Medley believed that "to attempt to force every man into the same narrow groove, would be little less than an act of insanity," in an unestablished milieu.[118] A theme that appeared in Medley's later years was the recognition of the voluntary nature of church membership. This was a consequence of living in an unestablished colonial situation, but also, as he recognized, part of the spirit of the age. Compulsion, if it ever was of value in religious matters (and Medley doubted that it was), would certainly not be useful in the modern world. If the church ought not to compel people to perform religious duties, much less should the state exercise such authority.

The year following Medley's appearance at Provincial Synod saw the second Lambeth Conference, at which the Church of England bishops worldwide gathered. He continued his defense of the Ritualists in the most prominent forum yet offered. The conference papers record that Medley was an active participant, intervening on several different occasions. On one occasion he spoke with reference to some of the evidently High Church ceremonial he had witnessed during his visit to England, using carefully calculated terms. He wanted at this point only to underline the positive character of the diversity of liturgical forms he had seen. These only expressed different styles of devotion, while not affecting the "verities of the faith."[119] Yet it was precisely these "varieties of devotion" that the PWRA was designed to suppress. Of course, this work was carried out with the active participation of the Archbishop (Tait) that Medley here addressed. For Medley, external expressions of devotion, although important, had always remained in the realm of things indifferent, and not of the substance of the faith.

Medley was to address the subject even more directly a few days later. Medley's biographer relates how the discussion had turned to the PWRA and Archbishop Tait, with the paternalism that was then unquestioned, "invited discussion on the part of the American and colonial bishops." Specifically, he requested the opinion of "the venerable Bishop of Fredericton."[120] Whether Tait anticipated the character of Medley's response is unknown. But, his response was typically lengthy and blunt. He reminded those present that the authority of bishops was limited. Priests were obliged to obey them in "all things just, lawful and honest" and no more, for "no man promises absolute obedience."[121] This clear rebuke was unlikely to have been missed by many of the English bishops, but there was more. "My opinion is that the Church of England will never enjoy any real peace until the Public Worship Act is *repealed*."[122] To this statement we are told, the room erupted with cries of "Chair! Chair!" and "Order."[123] Medley refused to yield and when the tumult died down pressed on with his argument. The PWRA "has brought forth injustice" and to continue it would only widen the divisions in the church.[124] Ketchum reported that the American bishops and the majority of the other colonial bishops "strongly supported the position taken by Bishop Medley." But they were in the minority overall.[125]

Medley proved to be prophetic, however. The PWRA, combined with the excessive zeal of the Ritualists' persecutors, soon turned the tide of public opinion. The imprisonment of several clergy under provisions of the act added to the feeling of revulsion. Archbishop Tait himself came to consider the act, which he had helped devise, a failure.[126] Toleration of ritual variation was, by 1890, considered the wiser course.

As Medley's long episcopate drew to a close, and the battle for toleration appeared to be largely won, he no longer devoted substantial time to the question. In 1880 he was able to make a veiled reference to the Ritualist battles of his own diocese, rejoicing "that the spirit of malevolent suspicion and perpetual insinuation of ignorance and faithlessness has been put down."[127] In the last charge that he delivered to his clergy, six years before his death, his position had not changed, unless to have become yet more expansive and tolerant. He conceded that although perfect agreement in the church was desirable, it was also "not to be expected." In the end, the church must "hold fast to primitive doctrine, primitive order, and practical piety . . . [even] while there is a considerable diversity as to the means by which reverence is promoted."[128] While discussion of theological issues would always be a feature of the church, Medley desired only that there be "that charitable construction of the actions and motives of others which each man unquestionably desires to be practised towards himself."[129] These words actually echoed his first charge of 1847, forty years earlier.

It was with joy that Medley was able to live to see much gained in the spiritual life of the church. He held that the dead worldliness that he found in the church of the first half of the nineteenth century had been reversed, although not altogether overcome, by the last decade of the same. In particular, "the value of our Services and our Sacraments is more fully realized by our members."[130] Given that this restoration of understanding was his life's work, he must have been truly gratified.

The aesthetic principles that Medley had first expressed through his interest in church architecture have been shown to have sprung from the same root as his sacramental theology. External forms had value just insofar as they were able to be vehicles for the divine. Yet they remained transitory and natural forms. That is, just as Medley could not accept transubstantiation of the eucharistic elements, he knew that even the most magnificent cathedral would fail to be an adequate host for the divine. He was able to raise nature up to mediate divine grace, but was fully cognizant of nature's limitations. With this understanding of the natural, in both its strength and weakness, Medley developed a critique of church government and proposed a remedy consistent with the theology described above.

6
Authority and Church Government

AT THE AGE OF THIRTY-ONE JOHN MEDLEY WROTE HIS MOST WIDELY known work, a short treatise on episcopal government.[1] Ten years later, he was consecrated bishop at Lambeth Palace. He was to serve as bishop of the missionary diocese of Fredericton for forty-seven years until his death in 1892. Thus it is certainly fair to say that church government occupied him for the greatest part of his life. In fact, along with his concern for the external form of the Christian religion (architecture, music, and the sacraments), it was to be his greatest interest. Medley's understanding of church government can first be understood in light of his view of episcopacy. But one can look at it from the standpoint of his more general understanding of the relationship of the church to the state. This chapter will address the former and then the latter.

EPISCOPACY

In 1835 Medley's slim volume on episcopacy was published and dedicated to "his fellow members of the clerical society in the county of Cornwall" by whose "unanimous approval" he had undertaken to produce "this little work." In the preface he explains that the work had its origins in "a few hints . . . thrown together by the writer of these pages, without the remotest idea of their ever appearing in public." According to a note in Ketchum's biography, the work was prepared at the invitation of Rural Dean S. T. Trist.[2] For Medley, the doctrine of the apostolic succession was no radical challenge to the prevailing opinion of the day regarding church government. Instead he placed it under the category of "allowed and moderate church principles."[3] This was characteristic of his position throughout his life, on a variety of topics. Except with regard to his later view of establishment, Medley was generally reluctant to make any statements that were consciously radical. Whether the position was a popular one or not, he generally presented it as being within accepted norms of practice or doctrine.

Tied to his insistence that his position was normative, Medley generally also suggested that those opposing that position did so in ignorance. That vast numbers of people were unaware of the meaning of the apostolic succession or baptismal regeneration, to name two doctrines, was a result of a lack of education. Medley did not accept that most churchmen who opposed these, and other positions, did so out of a reasoned consideration of the questions involved.[4] The cure for this disease was not the imposition of authority, but better teaching. The onus for this rested upon the clergy for "few of those who have knowledge communicate it to such as stand most in need of information."[5]

Medley began his argument by making a distinction that was, as we have seen, consistent throughout his life. That is, he separated "essence" from "form." The varieties of church government belong to the "form" of the church, not its essence; its *bene esse,* not its *esse.* This concern was integrated with his natural concern for the practical. "Beyond all doubt the question amongst whom, will be subordinate to the question *how* we have lived; the inquiry whether we are members of any particular church, is only a part of the inquiry whether we are living members of Christ's mystical body. Certainly we may be orthodox in sentiment and deficient in practice; we may have the form without the power of godliness; we may lay too much stress on non-essentials, and too little on vital points; we may be professedly churchmen, and yet practically infidels."[6] Medley thus recognized the force of dissenting arguments. The answer was not to be found in the abolition of form, but in its purification. While forms were of lesser importance than the great doctrines of the faith, they were nevertheless valuable and care needed to be taken for them. In fact, in his understanding of architecture, music, and the sacraments, the external was not merely accidental, but conveyed a spiritual truth and reality. It was not a thing "indifferent" in the contemporary usage of the term. Rather, it was reasonable to investigate the question as to whether one form was more suitable to religious expression than another.

Medley's view of church government was related to these principles. The first step was to discover what forms it took in the days of the apostles.[7] Medley was aware that such an inquiry would be charged with disturbing the peace. He was, after all, writing in the 1830s, when many Tractarians perceived that apostolic succession was an unpopular principle.[8] Nevertheless, he believed that avoiding the topic only encouraged "a false, delusive, dangerous security."[9] The issue was a volatile one inasmuch as it touched upon the relation of the state to the church and the independence of the church from the state.

Here, as always, Medley connected intellectual errors with practical consequences. Not only would the peace of the church be far more seriously disturbed by the toleration of error, families would be divided, simply because the truth was not taught clearly to the children.[10] This practical emphasis was a feature of most of Medley's polemical works over the years. Thus, he suggested that the question of church government "may not be in itself necessary to salvation, yet we see it has insensibly mixed itself up with the very essentials of Christianity, because our disputes and contentions on the subject are a reproach to the gospel which we profess, and a stumbling block in the way of unbelievers."[11] Medley expressed here the evangelical concern for the presentation of the gospel that remained with him throughout his life.

Medley went on to respond to those who suggested that if the apostolic succession was an essential doctrine it would have been more explicitly revealed in scripture.[12] Medley's answer to this, was to not allege some gnostic teaching of "reservation" of knowledge, but really quite the opposite. Referring to Butler's *Analogy*, Medley suggested that it was part of the divine plan that we are compelled to form some conclusions for ourselves. He argued first that God operated in such a way as to allow the possibility of human intellectual freedom. Secondly, he asked, "Is the truth ever so revealed, that unbelieving ingenuity will not find a plausible reason for rejecting it?"[13]

This was not an argument for an open-ended rationalism, which would allow all religious questions to be determined by natural reason apart from faith. For one thing, religious questions did not allow for the same sort of certainty as some fields of scientific inquiry. "He that believed this is ignorant of the first principles of all religion, the evidence for which, consists in an accumulation of probabilities, and not in mathematical demonstration."[14] His source for this argument was Butler.[15] If even the divinity of Christ was not placed beyond dispute, it was unreasonable to expect that "less vital" questions (such as episcopacy) should be completely clear.

Even though he was dealing with an explicitly theological question, Medley emphasized that the practical was foremost. What needed to be decided was "from which line of conduct may the greatest amount of practical good be expected."[16] He suggested that this may be determined by examining which approach to church government had, in the past, produced the greatest practical good. There was here, as elsewhere, a utilitarian overtone to Medley's argument. Hair-splitting differences of religious opinion could not but obscure "the simplicity of the Gospel."

While Medley was not indifferent to questions of theology and doctrine, they were secondary, almost added as an afterthought in this case. We can think back to Medley's defense of "church architecture." He did not argue on aesthetic grounds for the Gothic form, so much as he emphasized the practical value of the style. It promoted certain habits of reverence and produced practical spiritual effects in the worshiped. Gregg Finley brings Medley's pragmatism to the fore in his analysis of Medley's essay on *The Advantages of Open Seats*.[17]

Medley's theological argument was ultimately based upon scripture. Although patristic authorities were referred to, it was not in the manner of a typical Tractarian *catena*. He was only interested in the earliest of the church fathers, who could provide witness to "those good and pious men, who had seen the Apostles, and who knew what were their wishes with regard to church-government and discipline."[18] This was consistent with his later position, inasmuch as there was virtually no subject upon which Medley wrote polemically, that scripture did not provide the central core of his argument. In this case, Medley divided his argument into three points:

1. That we have reason to expect that there would be some determinate principles of church-government laid down in Scripture;
2. That an Episcopal form of government has the greatest countenance from Scripture;
3. That till within the last three hundred years, there was no Christian Church in the whole world, which was not governed by Episcopal authority.[19]

In arguing the first point, Medley followed Hooker.[20] He sought to "steer between the two extremes"[21] of suggesting on the one hand that in scripture "everything is as clear as we could wish it to be" and on the other hand "that no principles of church-government whatever are to be found in the word of God." But even, he argued, if the latter position were true, there would still be grounds for supporting episcopal government. Pointedly, he remarked that in addition to being accepted by the universal church for the first fifteen centuries, "it was approved of by the very men who established Presbyterianism."[22] He even quoted Calvin (generally vilified by Medley, later in life) at this point in support of episcopal hierarchy, properly understood.[23] In this same passage he referred to Bucer, Melanchthon, Luther, and "even Beza" as admirers of the English polity.

Medley argued that we need not rely simply on such evidence.

Scripture clearly indicated the need for order in the church. Using an argument that supported his understanding of architecture, he wrote, "God is a God of order, and not of confusion." He proposed that the very order of the "natural and moral world" suggested that the church could not have been designed by God to possess anything less than a similar order.[24] Here, the "natural and moral" world was taken as analogous to the spiritual world of the church. By implication the church was both the spiritual Body of Christ and an earthly institution with external forms. There was no radical disjunction between nature and spirit, but a sacramental reflection of the one in the other. Medley went on to argue: "Had any form of Church government been laid down, with all the numerous and burdensome rules of the Jewish ceremonial, we should have lost one link of the evidence for Christianity, one proof that all its harmonious parts were strung together by the same divine hand, by him who chose to rest its progress and ultimate triumph on the moral convictions of the human mind, rather than on any minute rules of a particular legislation."[25]

The point was that the participation of the human intellect was precisely part of what makes Christianity unique. Medley made clear that he was arguing "for the necessity of some principles and not for the laying down of minute and particular rules."[26] Because of the church's evangelical mission, such a rigid regimen of rules and forms would have been contradictory to the church's nature. The church therefore proceeded from certain principles, and then adapted itself "to every modification of the human mind, to every stage of civilization and intelligence."[27] This acceptance of the adaptability of the church to particular temporal circumstances would be particularly manifest when Medley later in life considered the proper polity of the colonial church in contrast to the established church in England. While very much a conservative, he was able to allow change in those areas that were considered by him as *adiaphora*.

This did not mean for Medley that all areas of inessentials were easily varied. Even if scripture did not expressly command certain things, there were still other grounds upon which they may be considered to have "the weight of actual commands."[28] Episcopacy itself, although not "so laid down in the word of God, that no other form of discipline could have been instituted," nevertheless had the testimony of the earliest practice of the church in support of what scripture at least suggested.[29]

At this point, Medley was not interested in distinguishing between civil and ecclesiastical powers in terms of those able "to make laws for the church." Just two years after Keble's "Assize sermon," and with the constitutional events of 1828–32 fresh in the memory, there was as yet in Medley no sign of criticism of establishment. He was content simply to argue that forms may be established, apart from clear scriptural direction, which are nonetheless binding on the Christian.

The argument then proceeded quite conventionally. Having established the general grounds for church order, Medley developed his second point, which was to show that "Episcopacy has the greatest countenance from Scripture." Examining the texts of the New Testament, he argued that Christ did not contemplate an equality among ministers.[30] His argument was not concerned so much with the particular powers of the apostolic ministry as with the basis of their authority. He thus exhibited those passages that showed the Apostles exercising their particular authority. This point must not be pushed too far in this case, since Medley's purpose in this tract was to speak of episcopacy in terms of government. Ironically, in light of Medley's later advocacy of synodical government and episcopal election, he also pointed to the fact that "there is no where any Scriptural evidence that the people selected and controlled their own pastors."[31]

The next stage of the argument was to make the connection between the apostles and their successors. He employed at this stage authorities as diverse as Mosheim, Hegesippus, Eusebius, and Cranmer.[32] He was trying here to demonstrate that the Apostles passed on their authority to specific individuals and not to the church in general. Primarily drawing upon the Epistles to Timothy and Titus, Medley furnished scriptural support for their having the power to ordain, superintend doctrine and conduct and regulate all matters not already arranged by Paul himself.[33] This set the stage for the final of Medley's three points: the subsequent practice of the church.

It was at this point of the treatise that Medley necessarily resorted to non-scriptural evidence. This was prefaced with a cautionary note, "We do not pretend that the Fathers were infallible: the age of blind and superstitious veneration for their writings has long since passed away."[34] This attitude suggested a more critical stance than that of Keble, for example. He had recommended that the proper approach to the fathers was one of "devout perusal."[35] Medley also advised, "let them [i.e., the church fathers] receive their due."[36] The non-juror Charles Leslie was cited at this point to support the argument that it was impossible that the early church fathers could have invented the doctrine of episcopacy out of whole cloth.[37] As Medley himself wrote, given the contentiousness of the early Christians with regard to sundry practices and doctrines, it was unlikely that one so momentous as episcopal government could have been quietly introduced. "We have before us records of the ancient differences among the early Christians. We may read till we are weary, of the Marcionites, the Basilidians, the Valentinians, the Patripassians, the Ebionites, the Ophites, the Montanists. Now can any one in his senses swallow so monstrous and absurd a proposition, as that a change so important, so comprehensive, should have been quietly got over in all the churches of the world?"[38] This primarily negative argument that the lack of evidence to the contrary proves the point was followed by a reassertion of the authority of the fathers, which Medley had thus far avoided.

Aiming presumably at Dissenters, he asked rhetorically whether the authority of the fathers was accepted in other instances by those who opposed episcopacy. He answered his question by the example of the canon of scripture, which, he argued, rests entirely upon patristic authority.[39] A *catena* of sorts followed at this point. While Origen in the third century supplied the most ancient catalog of canonical books, there were ample testimonies to episcopacy from still earlier authorities. Hegesippus, Ignatius, Polycarp, Irenaeus, and Tertullian all were furnished as witnesses.[40]

Typically, Medley wished to draw practical conclusions from the argument he had made. In this case, the practical conclusion concerned Dissenters. "The Church of England [has] a claim upon the Christian community in our country, superior to that of every sect among us, a claim independent of all connexion, with the State, and of every other inferior consideration."[41] Episcopacy derived its authority quite apart from the state. Its strength rested upon scripture, the practice of the Apostles, the testimony of the fathers and the whole history of the church.

His argument then moved to a more explicit consideration of the role of the state in the church. Here he demonstrated a position that, while associated with the Tractarians, was held by the orthodox, or old High Church party as well.[42] The church's claim simply did not rest upon the state, as it was "an everlasting claim." It could not be obviated by any action of the state, because God alone has ultimate authority over his church. Medley also declared that the state needs the church. That the state benefited from the union more than the church did had been asserted by High Churchmen since Hooker. The link between dissent and disloyalty had, of course, been made by many of the older High Church school in the past.[43] But, Medley sounded a note more clearly Tractarian in his insistence on the church's claims to independence from the state. That the chief benefit to the church was evangelical was argued by none other than Medley's friend Gladstone.[44] In the end, as Medley went on to say, all associations with the state could be stripped away and the church would remain, "holding fast the apostolic 'doctrine and fellowship, with breaking of bread and prayers' and adhering to the ancient discipline of bishops, priests and deacons."[45]

In his conclusion, Medley made clear that the real object of his discourse was not foreign Protestants or indeed, anyone outside of England, but those who dissented from the established church. He considered the church to be in a "critical position" for "every day shows that men are letting go their principles."[46] This led directly to "the evil of separation."[47] The fault for this lay with the Church of England itself, which had "suffered the rising generation to grow up ignorant" of the dangers of this evil. There was a practical remedy, which Medley provided in detail. Parents must begin to educate their children "in the reasons for adherence to the church," including not only the fundamental truths of the Gospel but lesser truths such as episcopal government.[48] The conductors of National and Sunday Schools ought to "inculcate in their proper place the principles of the Church whose ministers they are."[49] Above all, this must be done without an uncharitable or violent spirit, cooperating "in benevolent objects with those who dissent from us, where we can do so without a compromise of principle."[50]Although episcopacy was, for Medley, a matter of "discipline" and not of doctrine, it was nonetheless "agreeable to God's holy word, and to the customs of primitive church."[51] With regard to this he exhorted, "To principles let us hold fast."[52]

Five years after this tract, in which Medley aimed to express "moderate" church views, his tone had become considerably sharper. By 1840, much had changed. Hampden had been appointed Regius Professor over the strong objections of the Tractarians. The Tractarians had emerged as an identifiable party, one that was increasingly the object of criticism and abuse.[53] Froude's *Remains* had been published, provoking a still more violent storm of outrage against the Oxford Movement. A far more polarized atmosphere had arisen than that which existed in 1835.

In a sermon preached at Exeter, Medley was bold in his criticism of the established church and thus in his assertion of church independence from the state.[54] This sermon has been discussed already,[55] but it deserves some mention here. Medley named Calvin as responsible for many of the gross errors of the Puritans, including the denial of the apostolic succession.[56] The succession was listed by Medley as among the "most important doctrines of the gospel."[57] Aimed equally at Dissenters and Romanists, the sermon was a strong assertion of Anglican catholicity and independence.

By 1847, Medley had been bishop of Fredericton for two years. His tone had once again moderated, while still affirming the same principles as he held in 1835. "The Church is not an institution made by man. Christ was its founder: and all perfectly constituted Churches must trace their origin to him, and to his Apostles."[58] In the same year, Medley spoke at greater length on the matter in his first charge to the clergy of his diocese. For the first time, he spoke of the succession in relation to the validity of the sacraments: "unless our orders be valid, unless those who gave them to us, had the power to give them, our Ministerial acts must be invalidated."[59] A paragraph later he partially softened this statement, suggesting that those ministerial acts that were irregular, may nonetheless be "blessed even with larger measures of grace than a more regular ministry, but which there is no direct promise that he will bless?"[60] In this, he was making a partially conciliatory gesture toward Dissenters. But as much as he would have wished to be charitable in this direction, there was the danger of extending his argument too far. He went on to say that the truth of the succession was "one of the strongest arguments we have in a contest of argument with the Roman Catholic Body."[61]

This high view of episcopacy and the essential character of the apostolic succession led Medley to a greater criticism of the state. In particular he faulted the government of England for not providing bishops to its colonies, again alluding to the benefits that the state would have gained by doing so. "Bishops were looked on as likely to be incendiaries, and common disturbers, instead of what they would really have been, pillars of the connexion between America and the Mother Country."[62]

This high doctrine of episcopacy still retained a reformed Anglican character. Medley, for example, denied any "mechanical" view of the succession "unaccompanied by the proportions of Apostolic doctrine and practice."[63] He went further than that, saying,

> The Church guards us against another error, by her choice of the words used; [i.e., in the Ordinal] the error of the "opus operatum," as it is called; of supposing that by the mere act of consecration or ordination, consequent on the right intention of the giver, and independent of the will of the receiver, such gifts are bestowed. "Stir up the gift." Though these words relate to a past gift, they must, on every fresh action, be conditionally understood. For by some connection of our free-agency with the power and grace of God, which no man can explain, the possession and continuance of grace, in an adult, depends on our having the will to ask for it, and on our exerting that will with an earnest, hearty desire for its vouchsafement.[64]

Even here, though, Medley wanted to hold both sides together. While denying an *opus operatum* understanding of orders, he still affirmed the mystical transmission of spiritual gifts. To deny it was to fall prey to "that system of rationalism which refuses to believe whatever it cannot see, and which explains away the miracles of the Lord Himself."[65] This was simply one more "mystery of the faith" that could only be settled by "the text of Revelation."[66] If the bishops did not receive the same gifts that the Apostles received, Medley argued, how could the laity claim to receive those gifts received by the faithful in earlier ages?[67] In this case, the mystery operated like a sacrament, even if it did not strictly qualify as one. There was on the one hand the grace of God as the gift given. But this operated through the laying on of human hands. Again, the natural worked in concert with the divine.[68]

Ultimately Medley's understanding of the spiritual authority of the apostolic ministry and his growing disenchantment with establishment would intersect. This occurred most strikingly at the time of the Colenso controversy. By then Medley had no hesitation in expressing the independence of the church from the state. For example, speaking of the decision of the Judicial Committee that declared the coercive powers granted by the letters patent issued to colonial bishops null and void, he said in 1865, that the powers vested in the bishops of the church were those that "no Judicial Committee can deprive us of . . . [since] no such body was empowered to entrust [them] to us."[69] Consequently, the authority that a bishop held in the church was primarily spiritual and not founded upon statutes to begin with. The bishops acted as "trustees for the faith once delivered to the saints."[70] Moreover, the bishops themselves were not incapable of betraying the trust placed in their hands. Medley was as sharp in his criticism of Bishop Colenso[71] as he had been with the English bishops at the time of his defense of the Ritualists. Episcopal power was to be limited by the scriptures, by the Prayer Book and by the laity in synod.

By the end of his life Medley was able to say that the office of a bishop was better understood than when he was consecrated. In the past, "English statesmen seem to have thought of a bishop only as an officer of the State, a useful potentate to be respected, not a primitive bishop, mixing with the people of his charge, assisted and supported by his flock."[72] This image of a primitive bishop that so captured the imagination of the Tractarians was held by Medley as his ideal. He claimed "to join hands with a Clement, an Irenaeus, a Cyprian, an Augustine, a Leo in the West; with an Ignatius, a Chrysostom, a Basil in the East."[73] While there is no evidence that Medley was ever offered an English diocese, this may have been providential. It appears that the life of a missionary bishop suited Medley's spirit far more than a comfortable English diocese ever would have done.

Church and State

The corollary to Medley's understanding of episcopacy was his understanding of the relationship of the church to the state. This view was complicated by two factors. First, there is Medley's place on the High Church/Tractarian spectrum. While he was at many points an old High Church Tory, he also shared a measure of Froude's radicalism, especially in later years. However, Medley's position was not rooted in the romantic vision of Froude, but in hard-headed pragmatism. Secondly, there was his situation as a colonial bishop, with an ambiguous relationship to establishment. While external forces such as the Colenso affair undoubtedly affected Medley's position, it can be argued that his own inclination was ever more toward ecclesiastical independence, at least in the colonies.

Medley's attitude toward establishment manifested itself early in his career. For example, it was clearly evident in his speech before departing England for Canada in 1845.[74] But the ideas expressed on that occasion were not without precedent. In a sermon preached in 1840, he had expressed similar concerns. In a passage considering the difficulties then facing the Church of England, he suggested that problems that arose at the Reformation had not yet been addressed. In regard to discipline and order, he spoke of the church "laboring under the evils arising from a kind of connexion with the state, forced on her by unhappy circumstances, and which the difficulties and perils of each succeeding age have prevented her from amending."[75] He moved on in the same sermon to consider directly "the theory of an established Church." He asserted that the state had altogether failed in its obligations to the church. It was "more ready to confiscate what it has, than to add to it for the glory of God."[76] It had failed to provide new parishes where needed. He offered the example of Cornwall, observing that there were 206 churches in the time of Edward III. Since then, the population had grown fivefold, yet only about ten new churches had been added.[77] Not only that, but the state had prevented the church from administering its own proper discipline. The church could neither refuse communions nor burial without fearing sanctions from the state.[78]

Still, even at this point, Medley did not advocate disestablishment, but rather a reform of the relationship between the chuch and state. Medley still held out hope that it could be demonstrated "that the Church is the nation's best friend."[79] He saw that movement of which he was part as being even then in the process of bringing about this reform. That this was a popular movement, he was certain. He exulted, "The best and noblest spirits of the land are with us; the rising nobility, the youthful gentry, multitudes of the middle classes and the poor, and even many of those who, though they may be entangled by political embarrassments, must not be set down as the enemies of the Church. A sense of the necessity and value of unity is widely felt, is every day increasing."[80] The sense of dramatic irony in these words can hardly be overstated. The public outrage at *Tract 90* was just around the corner and Medley's own disillusionment with Newman, following his secession, had not yet occurred.[81]

It is interesting, given the above, that Medley's first published sermon in his new diocese was dedicated to the lieutenant governor, Sir William Colebrooke.[82] While there was, no doubt, some political wisdom in such a gesture, it was most likely motivated by Medley's close personal friendship with Colebrook. Primarily on the topic of "the Minister's duty and the Minister's accountableness," Medley nevertheless repeated part of his theme from his farewell address at Exeter. He declared that the church was being called "from earthly greatness and power, visible offices of authority in states and kingdoms, to its original separation from the world, to a life of suffering, unity and pureness."[83] Here the optimism of the earlier occasion with regard to the reforming of civil institutions, seemed to have faded. In fact, Medley recalled the state of the primitive church before "the Church was in possession of ample endowments, [before] the powers of the state cherished her in their bosom . . . In those days, the Church 'grew and prospered.' "[84] He was once again emphasizing the Romantic ideal notion of the church, separate from the world.

By the following year, Medley had been able to get a better sense of the constitutional state of the colonial church. In his sermon on the Reformation, he was able to speak quite specifically as to how the church in New Brunswick differed from that in England. In a lengthy appendix to the sermon he wrote, "We are further hampered by the anomalous connexion of our Church with the State." He then went on to trace the foundation of this relationship in English law. In every case, those characteristics which mark establishment were invisible or untenable in colonial New Brunswick. The Queen's representative, the lieutenant governor, was not required to be a member of the Church of England, the state did not maintain the church financially, and it was not even clear if English canon law was binding on colonial clergy.[85] Medley then turned his argument to those difficulties with establishment that particularly pertained to the colonial context. It is unclear at this point if he was aware that arguments similar to some of his own were being used with respect to the established church in England.[86] He may have had some anxiety as to the successor to his friend Colebrooke, for Sir Edmund Head, the new lieutenant governor, and Medley never enjoyed cordial relations, clashing over such issues as the right of presentation to benefices.[87]

Once again, as we have seen repeatedly with Medley, there was a practical basis for his concern about these constitutional matters. The growth and health of the church was being hindered by the perpetuation of this quasi-establishment.

> I only mention these things to show how much the undefined, anomalous state of our Church hampers us. Men's mind have been used to State-notions and State-assistance, and they are suddenly thrown into a new position, (without being positively assured of anything) and left to their own unaided resources, except so far as the voluntary charity of our English brethren steps in to help us. But unfortunately, the ancient notion clings to the mind when the reality is gone, and therefore, instead of helping themselves, many of us are trying to linger on in the dreamy security of an Establishment.[88]

These remarks become more striking, when one considers the sermon's dedication. Dedicated to the Chief Justice, Mr. (George Frederick) Street, it was preached to "The Honourable President and other Members of the Legislative Council, The Hon. The Speaker and the other Members of the House of Assembly, who [were] present at the delivery of this discourse." The sermon itself was a hearty defense of the Reformation and critique of the errors of Rome. Medley's protestant audience requested that it be published. When it appeared in print, however, it contained an appendix, with Medley's declaration that establishment was but a "dream." No doubt, many members of the government were less enthusiastic about this revised form of the sermon.

The idea that establishment, whatever its merits, was no longer a practical reality, became Medley's position for the rest of his life. He did later speak specifically about establishment's defects as well as its theoretical benefits. But the consideration of the benefits was for him purely academic. The colonial situation in New Brunswick had rendered impossible Hooker's vision of a state church. It is clear that even in the English context, establishment had ceased for Medley to be a desirable institution. However, there is no evidence that Medley either actively campaigned for English disestablishment or expressed public views on those who did. He did, though, express his opinion on Irish disestablishment in a private letter to Gladstone. He wanted to assure Gladstone of his "full belief in the righteousness & justice of your measure in respect to the Irish Church."[89] Medley went on to compare the church in New Brunswick to that in Ireland, noting its minority status among an Irish (and in New Brunswick, French) Catholic majority.[90]

Medley, having understood the limitations of establishment, needed to convince his clergy and he began that work in his first charge. The disruption in the relationship between the church and the state occurred by reason of the action of the state, Medley charged. In abandoning the "ancient theory of Establishment," it had chosen to recognize the religion of all the Queen's subjects, "without reference to the truth or error of any."[91] It is perhaps difficult for those who have only known a pluralistic society to empathize or even suppress wonder at Medley's position here. It must be remembered that he was not simply a reactionary or an intolerant bigot, as he would appear to contemporary eyes. He was born into a relationship of church and state where an explicit purpose of the civil government was to safeguard religious truth, not religious freedom. There existed an authoritative statement of the religious truth in the formularies of the Church of England. Religion was not believed to be external to the public interest, but central to it. Thus, it was the most natural thing in the world for Medley to have been disappointed in the state's refusal or failure to perform what he understood to be its constitutional duty.

Medley was not naively clinging to an old order. He recognized that he was in the midst of a dynamic social, political, and theological age. There is no indication that he believed the old order could be restored or that such a restoration should be attempted. In fact he was sharply critical of those who would romanticize the position that the church now occupied. He admonished his clergy, "No man who is placed in a situation of acknowledged difficulty, can be practically useful, who does not make himself master of his real position."[92] The importance of practicality reasserted itself here. While Medley recognized the changed relationship between the church and state, and even lamented the present circumstances in strong language, he did not think that there was any going back. Because of the state's indifference, there had resulted "an entire alteration in the relations of the church to the state, at home and abroad."[93] Medley did not see this as an unadulterated evil however. The removal of the crutch of the state had forced the church to recognize it must stand on its own.

Interestingly, at this point in his charge, Medley pointed to the Wesleyan revival as the last, best chance the church and state had to revitalize themselves. In the eighteenth century, the government had become "dead to a right sense of religious duty."[94] Without naming those who caused it, he said that "the people of England became awakened through God's mercy." Neither the church nor the state chose to give any direction to "this new and heavenborn impulse."

The result was a disastrous schism. Perhaps mindful of the dangers of associating himself too closely with the Tractarians, in this period of outrage over the stream of secessions to Rome, Medley was more circumspect in speaking of this later revival. He said only that "a proof has been given to the world that she [i.e., the church] is upheld not by human governments, but by God."[95]

In order for the church to seize any advantage from this new arrangement, it had to be realistic. He set before his clergy the reality of the actual place of the church in colonial society: "We cannot be said to belong to an Established Church, for there is nothing established."[96] He recited the list of advantages that establishment was purported to convey and noted that in each case those advantages were not present in their situation. He concluded wryly, "Something possibly of the odium of having been established we may retain, but that the name is of any practical service to us I have never been able to discover."[97]

Medley maintained that the damage to the state by the dissolution of their union was greater than that to the church. The church, in fact, was put in a position to exist in the apostolic purity that was its origin. Civil society would suffer, Medley argued, because of the "confusion" that resulted from the lack of any public religion. The "benefits of social order" that the state enjoyed by reason of its association with the church would soon disappear.[98] What had begun in the colonies must inevitably, he suggested, spread to England itself.

Having declared to his clergy what he took to be the unavoidable reality of their present situation, he proceeded to give them practical advice about functioning in this new (*de facto*, if not yet *de jure*) disestablished society, in which the church was in a minority position. "Our first business must be to persuade all men, even our enemies, of our sincerity: our next to be ready to learn something from everybody, and turn everything to account. In matters of lesser moment, let us lean to the merciful side, yet let us never be afraid to go right through with any great Christian principle."[99] We have here the tentative beginnings of a new relationship to a new type of society—one that Medley and his clergy had certainly never experienced. The modern, pluralistic, liberal democratic society was taking shape and Medley was at the center of one of its earliest English forms. He certainly recognized that he could not stem the tide of history, but he believed the church could respond positively to the changed circumstances in which it found itself.

It was not perhaps accidental in light of this that, as the years went by, Medley seemed to identify more and more with the Episcopal Church in America than with the church in England. In his next charge, delivered three years later, he returned to the question of church and state. He again placed the blame for the separation of America from England on the "obstinacy and folly" of the English establishment. Despite this separation, he looked to the United Sates and saw a church that exhibited "rapid progress, undoubted orthodoxy . . . learning and zeal."[100] This was considerably more complimentary language than he used to describe the Church of England at this time.

Medley pointed out that in the United States it was clear that the church must depend on its own means for financial support. On the other hand, he observed that the ambiguity of the colonial situation had crippled the church in New Brunswick. Although the church was nominally established, the full English system was never employed. The parochial system with its rates and tithes was never implemented. Because of the original support of the SPG, many inhabitants of colonies assumed that the clergy were simply paid by the government, a mistaken assumption, Medley said, "never to this hour eradicated."[101] As a consequence people in these situations had neglected to support their own clergy. This was part of that "odium" that attached itself to the presumed established character of the colonial church.

The Call for Synodical Government

It was not until his next triennial charge in 1853 that Medley first proposed a remedy to the difficult situation. The call for the revival of Convocation that had been suppressed since 1717 had been heard from many following the first Reform Bill of 1832, in which it became clear to many that Parliament was no longer the appropriate forum for the discussion of the business of the church. Following the Gorham Judgment, the Tractarian calls for the revival of Convocation had become more insistent.[102] According to Chadwick, although floated by many clergy, such proposals were opposed by "nearly all the laity and half the clergy."[103]Among the ordained opponents of Convocation were the two archbishops, who feared that it would simply be a forum for "schism and bitterness."[104] Among Convocation's supporters (significantly, for Medley), was W. E. Gladstone. Gladstone differed from the Tractarian leadership, inasmuch as he supported the inclusion of the laity in any such deliberative body.[105] Medley's old diocesan, Phillpotts of Exeter, had summoned the first diocesan synod in June of 1851.[106] Much discussion took place among High Churchmen and Tractarians as to the exact character of any new or revived deliberative body. Gladstone and Manning differed sharply over the merits of synods versus Convocation.[107] This was connected to the question of representation, that is, should the laity be included in such a body? The general Tractarian answer was no, as expressed by Keble (tentatively) and Pusey (forcefully).[108] R. I. Wilberforce went so far as to suggest the church would forfeit its claim to be Catholic if it accepted lay representation.[109]

Liddon recorded a letter from Keble to Pusey, telling of a conversation in which Medley's opinion on the matter had been solicited. Medley's biographer tells us that Medley, while visiting England in 1852 had visited Hursley.[110] Keble wrote to Pusey, "I had some talk with [Medley] about laymen in Synods, and found that he did not quite enter into our views. Still I think that *practically* we might agree. I think, though the Apostles would never have allowed laymen to sign Canons, they would not have minded them settling financial points, choosing officers, arranging districts and the like: and that is open to any Bishop, and if so, to any group of Bishops, to take them into his counsels to a great extent. With Medley all my arguments were the contrary way."[111] In fact, Medley was to side with Gladstone on the matter, more forcefully as the years went on. Medley wrote to him in February 1852 to express his support for a bill proposed by Gladstone concerning colonial bishops.[112] This would have had the effect of granting colonial bishops a certain independence and, by disestablishing the colonial churches, allowing the introduction of synodical government. As Gladstone recognized, for the colonial church, the connection to the state was "nothing but a source of weakness to the Church herself."[113] The words could have been Medley's. The atmosphere was still hot with anti-Roman sentiment following the "Papal Aggression" of 1850.[114] Medley wrote to tell Gladstone that despite his best efforts, the bill had failed to gain support in New Brunswick: "We have faired badly in this province respecting your Bill. The Exeter Hall party took infinite pains to circulate the most infamous slanders respecting you, your belief of Transubstantiation etc., and my cooperation with you in introducing *by this Bill*! all the errors of the Roman Church . . . it is horrible to see the clergy engaged in evil . . . lying and slandering."[115] Medley did not name the clergy guilty of these crimes, but his usual opponents were the strongly Evangelical clergy in Saint John. At this time, Medley would have had in mind the "Colonial Churches Bill," promoted by Bishop Wilberforce, intended to authorize colonial synods.[116]

While Medley argued for the restoration of Convocation, he intended that this would take an entirely different character from the Parliamentary institution that still existed in a purely formal way. "It is obvious that, to us, as colonial Churchmen, the Parliamentary feature of the English Convocation is of no further importance and interest than as an instructive record of the past."[117] Instead, he envisioned "Church Assemblies," such as had been called since the New Testament. He recalled "the first primitive council, of the four great councils of Nicaea, Constantinople, Ephesus and Chalcedon, who bequeathed us those Creeds which are the bulwarks of our faith."[118] Medley sought to buttress his argument by stating, "The leading statesmen in England declare that the colonial Church is not an established Church."[119] The assembly that Medley advocated would resemble the existing Convocation scarcely more than in name only. He believed that he, as bishop and successor to the apostles, was able to call such an assembly in his diocese. For models, one turned first to scripture and then to the fathers.[120]

This assembly would have sharply limited power, for "the record of our faith has come down to us: we have only to hand it on unimpaired."[121] Medley drew a distinction between the loyalty owed to the Sovereign and that owed to the Imperial Parliament. He argued that if any resort to the civil power was required it should be to the Colonial Parliament alone. Having traveled this far down the road, it was only natural that Medley should offer the Episcopal Church in America as an example. While not a republican (Medley made clear his loyalty to the Crown), he nevertheless saw in the church assemblies in the United States a model for study, at least.

Medley broached the topic of a "Synod or Convention" again in 1856, at his next triennial visitation.[122] The degree of hostility apparently generated by his remarks at the last visitation prompted him to "admit the uselessness of any such assembly, unless it were adopted with the general consent of the Church."[123] He was not prepared to force a synod on a reluctant diocese, but he tried again to explain its advantages. He wrote to Hawkins in 1856 to tell of the spirit of calm that seemed to have descended over the diocese after the controversies over the cathedral, the Gorham case and the "Papal Aggression" had died away. Speaking of his proposals for a diocesan synod, he related that, "The Diocese is at present quiet and free from any ecclesiastical troubles and our people are afraid of agitating the subject from an apprehension that it might lead to division and strife. I have made up my mind to act with the clergy and laity as far as possible and to introduce no new plan or system contrary to their known wishes."[124] As if foretelling the decision of the Judicial Committee of the Privy Council in the Colenso case he said, "Our Church though amply supplied with standards of doctrine, is ill furnished with discipline."[125] He envisioned that a diocesan synod would correct this by establishing a "code of Church law."[126]

Medley responded to the objections of those who feared that a synodical government would remove the protection that the laity enjoyed by virtue of parliamentary government. The concern that synods would be forums for the exercise of episcopal caprice was expressed in Low Church opposition to an episcopal veto in synod.[127] In Nova Scotia, opponents linked the synodical proposal explicitly to Tractarianism: "The introduction of this change is at this period particularly dangerous when Tractarianism in the form of a concealed enemy is laboring indefatigably to undermine the Church, and we know the formation of Colonial Synods to be a Tractarian measure."[128] Bishop Binney of Nova Scotia had referred to these opponents as those who were "frightened by a shadow or a name."[129]

In response to such objections, Medley argued that no measure could be passed that would not receive the assent of laity, clergy, and bishop. Although the bishop would therefore have a right of veto, he could not unilaterally enact any measure.[130] He went on to give other examples of the useful areas in which a synod might be employed, such as "regulating the temporal affairs of the Church, and in devising such prudent measures as may promote its enlargement and prosperity."[131] Still, the authority of synods would not extend to doctrinal matters. At this point there was the possibility of the "practical agreement" that Keble envisaged. While Medley supported lay representation, it was premised upon the limited power of the synod itself.

The practical difficulties of the ambiguous state of the colonial church prompted Medley to take up the question of establishment again in his next charge. The church was under financial pressure due in part to the decreased levels of support from the SPG.[132] Voluntary donations had not made up the shortfall. Many people, considering that the church was established, labored under the misapprehension that "somehow or other, Government takes care of the Church and the Clergy."[133] The very notion of establishment was thus a millstone about the church's neck.

Medley's realization of the radically different cultural circumstances of a North American church was resisted by many other Canadian prelates, who preferred to fight a rearguard action against the growing separation from the English model. The most vocal and significant of these actions was that led by Bishop John Strachan of Ontario against the secularization of the "Clergy Reserves."[134] These were tracts of land set aside for the benefit of the church. When Presbyterians claimed a share of these lands a major political controversy was set off in Canada. The former metropolitan of the Anglican

Church of Canada, Phillip Carrington, described Strachan as "a political Don Quixote, a knight errant for the old alliance of church and State."[135] Strachan was not alone in seeking to preserve the privileges of the Church. He was supported by the High Church Bishop Mountain of Quebec and Bishop Bethune of Toronto.[136] The conservative bishops believed that cutting the ties of establishment would simultaneously cut off the link to the Church of England.[137]

Bishop Strachan had begun calling for the establishment of synods as early as 1831.[138] After meeting with initial obstacles in forming synods, Strachan, along Mountain, established "Church Societies," which would allow the gathering of clergy to discuss matters of diocesan governance and finance.[139] Such a society had been established in New Brunswick by Bishop Inglis of Nova Scotia in 1836.[140] It was not until 1851 that five Canadian bishops—Strachan, Mountain, Fulford, Feild, and Medley—met in Quebec and drafted a recommendation to hold diocesan synods with lay representation.[141]

While the move toward synods of clergy and laity was generally positively received by Canadian churchmen, there was strong lay resistance in the diocese of Fredericton.[142] While the dioceses of Toronto and Nova Scotia held their first synods in 1856, followed by Huron in 1858, and Quebec and Montreal in 1859, New Brunswick hesitated. The resistance to synodical government in New Brunswick came from the same Evangelical faction that had opposed Medley from the beginning.

Medley took up the question of church and state directly in a sermon remarkable for both its content and its context. Preached in Christ Church Cathedral, Fredericton, in 1860, it was delivered on the occasion of the visit of the Prince of Wales, who was present for the service. The members of the provincial legislature and the other members of government were there as well. It is easy to imagine the consternation that must have been present in many (if not all) of the assembled members of the government. Given the bishop's publicly expressed views on establishment as well as his habitual bluntness, they might well have anticipated some significant departure from the polite platitudes that would normally comprise a sermon on such a royal visit. This anxiety was no doubt heightened when Medley began,

> Pardon me, my brethren, if the subject be not what you may have expected. You may have thought that I should hasten to express (as well my feeble abilities would allow) the language of congratulation and loyalty, and that I should be the mouthpiece of those feelings which not only exist but overflow in all your hearts. If I adopt a different course, it is not that

> I do not share with you the common joy. I rejoice with you heartily and loyally; but I have a higher duty to discharge. Can I, dare I, forget that you are all, from the highest to the lowest, immortal souls? Sinners redeemed by the blood of a common Saviour, Christians united by a common hope, placed for a few moments under my special care?[143]

His theme for the sermon was the insignificance of earthly power and attainment compared with the eternal salvation of our souls. "Earthly potentates" were dismissively compared with "the throne of God, seated in judgement." Medley had many times over the years expressed his admiration for Wesley's renewing zeal. This sermon reflected some of the same evangelical fervor. Medley imagined that day when "[we] stand with all our imperfections and sins, *alone with God—alone with God*! O merciful Father, what a sight will this be of our selves and of Thee! How will our poor feeble knees tremble at this interview! And on what can the best and holiest of us cast ourselves but on Thy mercy and the merits of our redeemer for salvation!"[144] It was man's radical equality before God that Medley wanted to stress. On a day when the cathedral was filled to overflowing,[145] with all the attendant displays of pomp and ceremony that one would expect on such an occasion, he wanted to emphasize that whether we were "subjects or rulers . . . electors or elected . . . rich or poor" we were in the end "those for whom Christ died, and for whom he intercedes and reigns in glory."[146] He did not discount the blessings that had come with a stable civil power: "How diligently should we guard and preserve the integrity of our limited monarchy, the wise balance of our respective Estates, the just and merciful administration of our laws, and the various safeguards of our freedom with which a gracious Providence has endowed us."[147] Medley was a loyal subject of the Crown and there was never an indication of anything contrary to that. He was at pains to make all earthly attachments subservient to religious responsibilities.

The relatively positive representation of the balanced relationship between the civil and spiritual powers presented in the sermon before the Prince of Wales would be called into question again with the events of the coming decade. The SPG had decided to alter its policies with regard to financial aid promised to missionaries sent out to the colonies many years earlier. Medley responded harshly to this.[148] There were at work here a number of factors. For one, Medley was frustrated that the earnest efforts of the colonial church appeared to have gone unrecognized. As he pointed out, during the previous twenty years, the number of clergy in the province had doubled and the contributions to the Diocesan Church Society (which helped to fund aided parishes) had increased sixfold.[149] It was not as if the diocese had not labored to pull its own weight. Secondly, there was an awakened sense of the chauvinism of the Church of England. Despite the efforts of recent years to extend the Gospel beyond its shores, Medley questioned the real commitment of his countrymen to any work outside their own realm. We cannot but help remember Medley's enthusiastic words before he departed England, giving thanks for the church having at last realized its responsibilities in the mission field.[150] His experiences in New Brunswick caused him to doubt the depth of the support, at least among the leaders of church and state. There was, below the surface, frustration at the continued bondage of the colonial church. He saw the injustice in decisions being made by those stuck in "profound ignorance" about the church they were governing.

All of this frustration was brought to a head with the Colenso affair.[151] Medley addressed the matter directly, telling his clergy that the decision of the Privy Council, distasteful though it was, should come as no surprise, as he had been informed years ago "by high legal authorities in this province," that he ought not to believe that his letters patent had given him any such "coercive jurisdiction."[152] After a swipe at Justice Lushington,[153] Medley said that "such a decision, however, does not, as it appears to me, deprive us of any power that is especially important."[154] His view of the spiritual independence of the church was unsettled by the decision. "We never sought the power [i.e., coercive jurisdiction]. It was voluntarily offered; and now we are told, that when it was offered, it was not in the Sovereign's power to give it."[155] It was unfortunate, Medley added, that "some timorous and mistrustful persons, forgetful of God's good providence," had rushed to the conclusion "that the powers of the colonial Episcopate are all swept away."[156] As far as Medley was concerned, the oaths of obedience to the bishop that the clergy took at their ordination, as well as their other oaths and subscriptions, were "a contract which the clergy have voluntarily entered into, and [could not] conscientiously be set aside."[157] Ultimately, he reminded them, the judgment was a legal and not a theological opinion. Although the presiding judge, Medley said, seemed to have a "theological bias," the judgment itself was restricted to jurisdiction, not doctrine. In the end, as he had always maintained, "the strength of the Church lies not in courts of law."[158]

This lengthy discussion of the Colenso case led to a reconsideration of the question of colonial church government in general. The Colenso affair only strengthened his conviction "that reliance on English Lawyers and statesmen, is resting on a broken reed."[159] He now arrived at the practical resolution of the difficulties, which he first raised nearly a decade ago. "Some Synodical assembly seems almost necessary, if any discipline is to be exercised."[160] The Colenso decision and recent canonical amendments in England[161] had called into question whether virtually any legal direction from England was necessarily binding on the colonial church. Under the circumstances, "It seems the most idle dream that ever entered into any man's mind, to lean on the old theory of our Established Church, and to resort for help to English Statesmen and English Lawyers."[162] For some years, Medley had concentrated his arguments concerning the church and state towards pointing out the different circumstances of the colonial church and how establishment did not function effectively in the colonies.[163] Here he returned to a more general Tractarian anti-Erastianism. "England herself seems to be undergoing a wonderful revolution in religious matters, and the connection between the State and the Church is seen to be loosening every year. Why then should we cling to ancient traditions which cannot have place in this new society in which our lot is cast, instead of endeavouring manfully to help ourselves."[164] This was his most explicit declaration to date that the problem was not just with the indeterminate character of colonial establishment, but with the very intermingling of civil and ecclesiastical authority. Before he had argued only that the relationship was malfunctioning and could be reformed. But here he seemed conscious of the dawning of a new age, not only in the colonies but in society in general.

In the end, Medley affirmed his intention to continue his work in the diocese, "with a Synod or without a Synod." He desired that there be one, but that question now rested "upon you [i.e., the clergy] and upon the laity of the diocese." To the printed charge, there was attached an appendix prepared by Chief Justice Robert Parker, of the Provincial bench. This contained an extract from the Colenso judgment as well as a history of the church/state relationship in New Brunswick from its founding to the present.

After ten years of arguing and cajoling, Medley finally had his way. Clergy and laity of the diocese assembled in July of 1866 to consider formally the establishment of a diocesan synod.[165] At that meeting Medley recalled Gladstone's Colonial Church Bill, which would have "enabled us to have Synodical action, had we been so minded." As Medley wrote to Gladstone on the previous occasion, that bill was overwhelmingly opposed within his diocese.[166] Medley suggested that he was not so committed to the idea of synods at that time and "was just as well pleased to let the Synod alone."[167] Now, contrary to what he suggested in his 1865 charge, "the position of the colonial Church is wholly changed." Since that time legal opinion on the case had suggested that the ramifications of the judgments of the Privy Council were much wider than earlier believed. That is, "that no legal Diocese were created by these Letters Patent in the Colonies to which the questions had reference; secondly, that the Letters Patent created no legal identity between the Episcopal Church presided over by the nominated Bishops, and the United Churches of England and Ireland; thirdly that the letters Patent did not introduce into those Colonies any part of the Ecclesiastical law of England; and fourthly, they conferred on the Bishops no legal jurisdiction or power whatsoever, and added nothing to any authority which the Bishops might have by law acquired."[168]

Whether this interpretation of the Privy Council's decision was correct as to the extent of that decision is not the point at issue. Medley and others took it to be a correct interpretation and acted accordingly.[169] He exclaimed, "What a position is this to place the Bishop in! The bishop has been stripped of all powers of discipline, no matter how egregious the crime."[170] He then appealed to those Evangelicals who supposed that he and others who advocated synodical government were using it as a ruse to introduce Romish ritual and other novelties. Thus suspecting the motives, they argued that the civil power existed to restrain criminal clergy and that should be sufficient. Medley replied that there were other offenses that a clergyman might commit, to which they too would object, e.g., "He may set up an image of the Virgin Mary and kneel down before it, and offer up public prayers to it—and who is to bring him to book?"[171] Medley cited Colenso as one who had made such a public breach of faith. The absence of a synod prevented any effective action from being taken against him.

Medley looked to the United States for example. He introduced a new element into his position by suggesting, "We see in the United States an active flourishing Episcopal Church. We know that democracy is jealous and exacting enough not to make autocrats of bishops."[172] Appeals to the democratic spirit were new for Medley and certainly abhorrent to the Tractarianism of Keble and Pusey. To allow popular representation into synods would lead ultimately, Pusey felt, "to the destruction of the Faith."[173] Medley pressed on, arguing that synods had proven to be valuable institutions in the United Sates and also elsewhere in Canada.[174]

He next pointed to the real effect that the Privy Council judgment was having upon the church. Recent changes had been made in the declaration made by ministers prior to ordination. Agreed upon by Convocation and passed by Parliament, at no time were the colonies consulted. Not only that, but they were not notified afterward of the change. This bore out practically what the Colenso decision had established theoretically, that the colonial Church was "no longer in the eye of the law, identified with the Church in England."[175] To take the matter up before the colonial legislature was not an acceptable alternative, for that pluralistic body was "not an assembly fitted to discuss such questions, nor indeed desirous to entertain them."[176]

Medley turned to consider the laity. He envisaged them as an important part of this synod. They would benefit by its establishment, gaining a voice in church questions. Prior to this time, they had been consulted only "to collect money, and to dispose of money." Finally, a synod would bring a "spiritual" element to the meetings. Medley concluded, "My reasons are all based on the decisions of the highest court of judicature in England, and on the growing conviction that a Church which is no longer legally identified with the Parent Church, which has no settled rules, and whose Bishop is in an undetermined, anomalous position, can have no weight in the community and is in a very unsafe state."[177] The consequence was that the colonial church must begin to think and act independently, "especially as our brethren around us on every side have concluded that the only effectual method of help is Synodical action." He noted that the movement was growing everywhere that colonial churches were of such a size as to make such action viable.

Medley's biographer tells us that following this address the delegates present unanimously approved the establishment of a diocesan synod.[178] A committee was formed to draft a constitution for the body and a declaration of principles. The Provincial Legislature subsequently granted a charter incorporating the Diocesan Synod of Fredericton and later, with the Church of England Act, formally codified the canon laws of the diocese and gave sanction to all other ordinances passed by the synod in accordance with the act.[179]

There remained opposition to synod from some Evangelical parishes, who had not attended the meeting in 1866, thereby making the unanimity of the synod's approval somewhat misleading. At the first meeting of the synod, some half dozen parishes were absent, chiefly owning to their fears that the bishop's veto power contained the "germ of papacy."[180] This opposition was to continue for some years. Medley would write to a friend in Ontario in 1869: "The difficulties we have in getting a Synod underway at all are enormous—from the ignorance and intolerable suspicion of our Churchmen, and these difficulties are daily aggravated by the unfair conduct of some of the clergy. It sometimes seems to me that we have the lowest type of Churchmen in the world. No dissenting sect seems so radical and so careless of its real spiritual interests."[181] Over a period of years, with the death of some strong opponents, such as the Reverend Mr. Gray of Saint John, and the coming of Confederation to Canada in 1867, fears of the consequences of independent government were gradually overcome. By the mid-1870s all the parishes in the diocese had joined the synod. Medley thus encouraged those present to "endeavor to win to your side" those who were absent.

1867 also saw the first Lambeth Conference. Despite the conference coming out of a Canadian proposal,[182] Medley was among those bishops of the Anglican Communion who did not attend. Of Medley's several reasons for not attending, among the most weighty was his objection to the exclusion of laity from the conference. It had long been Medley's position that the laity were proper members of the councils of the church. He would make this point in person at the second Lambeth Conference in 1878. He was also reluctant to travel to England to have affairs determined for his own colonial diocese. That seemed to represent the English paternalism, of which he was increasingly less patient.

As for the bishop of Natal, this was still a live issue for Medley and most other conservative churchmen. As Stephenson records, while some bishops shared Medley's view that the Colenso matter ought to have been part of the agenda, still others only agreed to attend if it were not discussed.[183] In the end, through the efforts of Selwyn and others, it was pushed onto the agenda and discussed at length. An unofficial declaration, signed by fifty-six out of a possible seventy-three bishops, concurred with Gray's excommunication of Colenso.[184]

Medley's 1868 charge dealt at length with synodical government and the Colenso affair. Reprinted in London and Oxford, a notice by "J. Wilkinson, Broughton Gifford" was attached as a preface: "I am desired by the Bishop to say, that though his Lordship did not attend the Lambeth Conference, yet that he fully concurs in the desirableness of summoning such an assembly, as a measure not only justifiable, but wise and provident, while at the same time he could have wished for a more definite arrangement of subjects ripe for discussion."[185] Referring at the outset to the "perilous crisis through which our Church is now passing,"[186] Medley went on to observe, "The whole theory of Tudor government has melted away."[187] He suggested that providence had been responsible "for three centuries plainly teaching us that the strength of our Church does not lie in its connection with the State."[188] But he went on to speak more directly of the end of establishment, his most forceful and systematic attack on establishment to date. The best days of establishment had passed, not only in the colonies, but in England itself. In the case of New

Brunswick, such passing was now considered by Medley to be an unequivocal good: "I would not wish it otherwise; for what can be a more invidious and dangerous position, than to be a Church of a small minority, caressed and pampered, and perhaps corrupted by State patronage, whilst all our fellow Christians, equally worthy of assistance with ourselves, are willingly giving their hard-earned money to the building of their churches and schools, and to the support of their clergy, and are denied other assistance or favor."[189] He declared that "whenever a Church is rooted in the affections of its people" it ought to be master of its own spiritual ship. The clear implication was that a time of testing was at hand that would reveal whether the English Church's people held sincere affection for their church.

While Medley was addressing the situation in his own diocese, it is clear that the very conception of establishment was on his mind. A free church "rooted in the affections of its people" seems to have been his ideal. That the legislature should deal with all religious bodies on the same footing, Medley "would not wish otherwise."[190] He recognized that the zeitgeist had changed and acknowledged that the sermons of Andrewes, Sanderson, and others, valuable as they were in many ways, could no longer be applied to the relations between church and state.[191] The "feelings and habits" of people had changed.[192] New wine could not be poured into old bottles. Medley was consciously pursuing a new polity that would serve a new age of the church and society. As he suggested before, this new spirit was not to be opposed but recognized as the providential hand of God. One might as well try and stop the course of a river as to retreat into a reactionary conservatism.[193] Medley was not alone in these sentiments among Canadian bishops. His two neighboring prelates, Fulford of Montreal and Binney of Nova Scotia, possessed High Church credentials and yet recognized that the Canadian situation could not be dealt with by simply applying English models.[194]

On the eve of the first session of the new diocesan synod,[195] Medley offered another argument in support of the value of synodical government. He again reassured the clergy that episcopal tyranny would be the least likely outcome of synods. Independent government would not sever the tie that existed with the Church of England. Even in England, it was clear that the Church "will, probably, in a few years, be less closely connected with the State than she is now."[196] He suggested that though this was inevitable, that did not imply that it would be unfavorable. Here he pointed to the Episcopal Church in America as being robust without any state attachment.

Medley ended by speaking about episcopal election. It was the

American custom and had become the practice elsewhere in Canada. He suggested that the clergy might well wish to consider it. He noted that he might not be around to see the event, but it should be so arranged that the election take place "decently and in order."[197]

Having experienced his first synod, Medley was more convinced than ever of their value by the time of his 1871 charge. He observed that synodical government was then the norm throughout North America, Australia, and New Zealand. In fact, "wherever the Church is free, numerous, and intelligent, this appears to be the form of self-government universally chosen."[198] A feature of these synods was the active participation of the laity. Medley argued that there must be a balance of clergy and laity to avoid domination by either group.[199] This constitution would also allow the synod to be mindful of the progress of secular learning. He suggested that "a Synod will do well and wisely not to reject those changes which the general progress of mankind, and the Providential course of the world, have rendered necessary—changes in the form, not in the essence of the truth."[200] In general terms, he conceived the synod to be a conservative body:

> In Synod, we neither meet to found a Church nor to settle the Canon of Holy Scripture, nor to frame an ecclesiastical Constitution, nor to separate ourselves from the Catholic believers before us, nor to begin to form a liturgy. We set out with these broad foundations laid already; on these we are to build, and in accordance with them we can alone prove our title to be wise builders . . . [Synod] must, if its work is intended to last, retain a strong conservative element in its constitution, requiring that essential changes should never be made without careful deliberation and the concurrence of all orders concerned in the change; and that when made, they should not be made in the interests of a party, nor for the purpose of crushing an adversary, nor should they place us in an antagonistic position to the decisions of the Catholic Church in all ages.[201]

The ambivalence that Medley demonstrated in several places was here present also. There was the typical Victorian confidence in the "general progress of mankind." This was connected with his sense of providence moving through history. The synod, which was to acknowledge this providential course, was also to understand that these changes would touch only on the "form," not the "essence" of the truth.

Although the Canadian Church was not to become independent until 1893, Medley already saw a *de facto* independence in operation. The English government had paid such scanty attention to the colonial church, that its "connection with England [was] severed, apparently without regret."[202] Changes had been made to the lectionary and the ordinal without consultation with or even subsequent notice to the colonial church. Since the colonial church had not sought this new relationship, Medley argued, "If it should come to pass that we should thus become an independent branch of the Church, in full Communion with the Church of England, as we did not seek such a position, we must accept it when it comes, as part of the Providential ordering of Him who knows best for us."[203]

He was confident that should this be the case the church would have nothing to fear. He spoke in a classic High Church manner, maintaining, "We have within us all the elements of a New Testament Church; a faith built on Christ our cornerstone, and in fundamentals derived from primitive Christianity; an Episcopate, apostolically descended; Presbyters and deacons rightly ordained; and a body of faithful Laity."[204] By this time, Medley had dropped all notion of a beneficial union between church and state. He recognized that the changes in society had made the old polity untenable in the colonies and practically so in England itself. But this was an opportunity to restore that primitive character to the church that Medley so desired in the episcopacy. Clearly though, it was important to Medley to say that this revolution had been forced upon the church and not pursued by it. His repeated recourse to providence served to underline that there was not any willful overturning of the established order.

Having come to a full sense of an independent and free church, Medley could no longer disguise his admiration for the Episcopal Church in the United States and for America in general. It had shaken off the bonds of colonialism and "grasped the reins of Empire." He admired that development by which America "in the true spirit of English freedom, 'gives place by subjection, no, not for an hour' to the exclusive supremacy of English domination."[205] Clearly, more than a quarter century of being a colonial bishop and observing the high-handed and paternalistic treatment of his church at the hands of the Imperial Parliament had left its mark on Medley. While he may have protested that the free and independent constitution, which appeared to be the future of the church in Canada, had been forced unbidden upon it, there can be no doubt that he welcomed the opportunity for the Anglican Church in Canada to leave the nursery of colonial subjection and finally become a mature Christian church.

In the latter years of Medley's episcopate, there was a noticeable lessening of the fiery zeal that characterized these years of constitutional struggle. He was able to look back on the time when "it was taken for granted, that the whole strength of the Church lay in its being an Established Church; a Church firmly bound to the State by golden fetters."[206] At the same time the recovery of Catholic forms of worship had been a kind of "second reformation." He asked, "Have we lost anything by the changes? Nay, are we not infinite gainers? Have we not been taught no longer to lean on the promises of statesmen, but on the strong arm of the Saviour standing on the right hand of God to succour us?"[207] The second Reformation had taken place and Medley was able to look back as one of those who helped bring it about. A new understanding of the church was gradually replacing the one that he had grown up with. Medley had a conception of a voluntary society, united by love. This was expressed with evangelical fervor in several places. For example, "Only, amidst all differences, in the midst of all dangers, if Jesus our Saviour loved His own to the end, if our Lord loves us in spite of our manifold sins and defects, we may surely love one another. That very word Synod is a word that pleads for love. It belongs to "one on the way," as the primitive Christians were called. And the preposition before the word, signifies that we walk together in this way, that is in truth and in love."[208] Intolerance and narrowness concerning *adiaphora* could no longer be part of the modern church.

While Medley attended the second Lambeth Conference some of his concerns from the previous Lambeth remained. Desirous of a "definite and practical" agenda, he maintained, "It will be readily admitted that it would be useless to bring a large body of Bishops from great distances to Lambeth for the mere purpose of social and agreeable discourse."[209] After cautioning Archbishop Tait not "to expect that one uniform and unyielding rule can be successfully applied to the administration of every diocese throughout the world," Medley, with his usual forthrightness, went on to suggest a number of topics for discussion at the conference. Among them were "The government of the Church. How to best choose Bishops in unestablished Churches . . . How to best promote learning among the clergy . . . How to best promote attachment to the Prayer Book among the laity."[210] While he did not mention the Ritualists or the PWRA in these suggestions, he intervened and spoke at length on the question when it arose in the course of proceedings, as we have seen.[211]

One of his more significant speeches at this second Lambeth conference concerned the constitution of church councils. In Medley's opinion, the resolutions of this conference could not be binding, "because the Bishops of the Church are not the whole Church." That is, they could not govern "without the assent of the Priests and laity."[212] "According to my view of the Church, although the Bishops occupy an important place in the Church and are in one sense its governing body, yet the presbyters are in another sense the governing body and the laity are a most essential component of the Church. . . . Until we have their assent, we will never have that consent which was given in the first Council of Jerusalem, "It seems good to the Holy Ghost and to us." I do not believe that the Church is properly represented till it has its Bishops, its Presbyters and its laymen together."[213] Medley thus held consistently to the position that he expressed in his conversations with Keble more than a quarter century previously.[214]

While Medley displayed democratic leanings[215] with regard to church government, these were only with regard to the church as *self-governing*. As long as the church was entangled with the state, significant problems would remain. He asserted that the church should not be judged on questions of faith and discipline, by persons who are not members of the church, i.e., by the Privy Council or civil courts.[216] His allusion to the Ritualist controversy illustrates how Medley's opposition to the PWRA did not simply arise from any personal love of ritual. Instead, the PWRA ran contrary to that conception of the church as the free, mystical Body of Christ, which transcended civil boundaries.

While in England in 1878, Medley also preached in Exeter Cathedral on the anniversary of the SPG and SPCK. Over the years Medley had an ambiguous relationship with those organizations, especially the SPG. While appreciative of its early support of the diocese, he was also harshly critical of its withdrawal of aid to the older missionaries. He believed that the SPG had a responsibility to support them as they had initially promised. Later, of course, Medley came to see continued external support of the diocese as crippling its own growth toward maturity.

On this occasion however, Medley chose to speak on the missionary responsibilities of the church. His sermon was an inspirational call to consider those members of society, those "other little ships" who were often neglected—the poor, the suffering, "for whom few human beings care."[217] He also reminded his listeners that there were entire churches around the world that stood as "other little ships" with regard to the Church of England. They too, deserved consideration. In the end it was not state connections that must be looked to but their true identity as members of the Catholic church down through history. While the church for many years following the Reformation was insular, now "the trump of God has sounded to awake a sleeping Church."[218] and the English Church had recognized that its faith extended beyond national boundaries. Recounting the various fields in which, with the assistance of the SPG and SPCK the church had entered into missionary work, Medley found yet again that the Church had been recalled to its true Apostolic nature.

In his final years Medley was able to recognize that the separation of the church from the state was not without its difficulties. With the church exercising diminished powers of influence in the state, the government would increasingly legislate without regard to the Church's interest. Such was the case, for example, with the controversy concerning the "Deceased Wife's Sister Bill." Introduced in 1880, this aroused a storm of controversy among conservative High Churchmen.[219] Medley devoted nearly half of his 1880 charge to the subject, condemning the proposed legislation in the strongest possible language. In the end, he advocated civil disobedience. If clergy were asked to perform such marriages they should decline, regardless of the civil legality of such a union.[220] Not surprisingly, for Medley, the law of God was prior to the law of Parliament.

Medley's last charge, delivered in 1886 at the age of eighty-two (he was too infirm to deliver one in 1889 or 1892), began by reminding his clergy of the true character of the church:

> The Church was never founded by a party in the State. It never throve on politics, and it was never in a less hopeful condition than when its richest benefices were the ill-earned reward of active and unscrupulous political partizans. My hope for the Church in Canada, of which we are members and ministers, is not that we are so numerous as to control the State; nor that we are so rich as to dispense with the contributions of our members; but that, being (as without arrogance we may consider ourselves) a branch of that Church which came to us from the ages past, which no storms of persecution have destroyed, and none of the manifold changes of the world have shaken, we still hope to hand down to our children the truth of God, which is indestructible.[221]

Little had changed over the course of fifty years in his conception of the church as a spiritual society. It was not to function apart from society but to be leaven in the loaf.

We have come almost full circle at this point. In one of his first publications, *The Advantages of Open Seats*, Medley had already sketched out this "spiritual kingdom, which is found in the New Testament."[222] People were not born equal into the natural or civil worlds. "Not only their stations, but their capacities and powers are unequal and various, even from their mother's womb."[223] The church functioned quite differently. There, "'rich and poor meet together' on some principle of equality [and] all ranks and degrees of men have a common Saviour, a universal redemption, a common salvation proposed to all on the same terms."[224] In fact, he went so far as to say, "The principle of spiritual equality between rich and poor is the very principle of Christianity itself."[225] The church had sinned terribly by trading this high calling for the order of the civil world. That is what the battle over rented pews versus free seats was all about.

For Medley, the spiritual part of the equation was always prior. Whether considering aesthetics, the sacraments or the relation of church to the state, he always gave pride of place to the religious argument as against the secular. This is hardly surprising in a bishop. What makes Medley interesting is the effort that he expended in carving out a place for the secular and natural within his religious consideration. In regard to faith, he struggled to allow for reason to operate. In the consideration of the sacraments, he sought to find an adequate inclusion of human subjectivity in the face of the objectivity of sacramental grace. In advocating a new constitution for church government, he argued for a lay (and hence secular) perspective within synods.

Conclusion

John Medley: A Tractarian Patriarch?

No matter what else has been written about John Medley over the past century, it has always been the assumption that John Medley was a Tractarian. The Evangelicals of New Brunswick in Medley's day were, in regard to the Tractarians, not unlike the McCarthyites with regard to communists: they looked for one under every bed. With little evidence that he was a Tractarian, they labeled him as one from his first day in the diocese. The partisan press of the day was so acutely sensitive to Tractarian influences that it took little persuasion to convince them that an Oxford man such as Medley, who had served under Phillpotts, regarded by them (erroneously) as one of the foremost "Puseyites," who advocated ecclesiological principles and had published books on such doctrines as the apostolic succession, must be a Tractarian himself. Building a Gothic cathedral only added grist to the mill. One opponent, looking on the cathedral walls as they were under construction had remarked, "And so we went onwards to Rome."[1]

It was not only Medley's opponents who advanced the view that the bishop was a Tractarian. W. O. Raymond, writing a biographical article on the bishop who had ordained him, and for whom he had enormous respect, said, "The Church of England in the Diocese of Fredericton learned to know the spirit of the original Oxford Movement, better than any history could teach it, in one who reflected what was best in it."[2] It ought to be kept in mind that for Raymond "the Oxford or High Church movements" were apparently interchangeable terms.[3] Medley's close friend and biographer W. Q. Ketchum was more circumspect in describing Medley's relation to the Tractarians. In fact, as a party, they are never directly mentioned in his book. As close as he comes is a passing reference, remarkable for its delicacy: "[Medley] came into note as an accomplished scholar in a marked period—when the greatest minds of the present century were beginning to employ their powers in a movement which was to exercise such a vast influence in the future work of the Anglican Communion. With these great men, Dr. Medley was in many ways a co-worker. He was the intimate friend of John Keble."[4] With this, Ketchum moves on, never to mention the Tractarians or Medley's connection with Pusey and Keble again. This omission was a particular irritant to Mrs. Medley, who wished to have her husband's role in that famous movement publicized.

Contemporary scholars have been unambiguous in their identification of Medley with Tractarianism. In his seminal article on Medley, E. R. Fairweather applied the label of "Tractarian Patriarch" and this has been the accepted view of Medley ever since. Fairweather wrote, "Quite obviously, the immediate inspiration for Medley's patient and devoted labours and broad sense of his responsibilities was the Tractarian vision of the Anglican Church."[5] Medley's advocacy of the *via media* is among the evidence put forward in support of this position. His close association with the ritualist Church of the Advent in Boston, and his own defense of the Ritualists are also pointed to.[6] But "the heart of Medley's Tractarian outlook and policy was, of course, the idea of the Church as a supernatural society, essentially independent of the state, calling men to a transcendent holiness, proclaiming a divine message in its doctrine and ministering divine grace in its sacraments, acting by the authority of Christ himself, visibly mediated through the apostolic succession of its bishops."[7] Fairweather furnished quotations from Medley's works in which the bishop seemed to concur with this view of the Tractarians as the sole revivers of an otherwise lost Catholic inheritance. However, much of what Fairweather attributed to the "Tractarian outlook" could also be applied to many High Churchmen who predated the Tractarians.

Still, scholars following Fairweather have repeated the same assertions about Medley and the Tractarians. Thus, Lyman Harding states simply, "Medley's theological views were unquestionably Tractarian."[8] He adds that Medley was one of those who found haven in the diocese of Henry Phillpotts, "the sole episcopal champion of the Tractarian movement."[9] These views are echoed in Harding's later book, which incorporated the earlier article.[10] Christopher Headon bolstered the argument for Medley's Tractarianism in his 1975 thesis, including Medley as among the first generation of Tractarians to have the oversight of dioceses.[11] In a subsequent article he identified Medley as one of those "Tractarian minded men," who were "particularly dissatisfied" with "old-fashioned high churchmanship."[12] Gregg Finley added his name to the list of those affirming Medley's Tractarianism with his thesis, subsequent book, and several articles.[13]

Two questions present themselves if we are to consider Medley in the light of the foregoing assessments. The first concerns our understanding of the place of the Tractarians themselves. Clearly, the position held by the Medley scholars named is representative of a historiographical perspective that is no longer tenable. The view of the Tractarians as the discoverers of a lost catholic inheritance, promoted by Tractarian hagiography, has been decisively refuted by Peter Nockles and other recent scholars.[14] Quite simply the Tractarians were not the only nineteenth-century defenders of the apostolic succession, baptismal regeneration, sacramental worship, or the spiritual independence of the church. The old High Churchmen had held to these positions in one form or another since the non-jurors (or earlier) and they continued to be an active force well into the Victorian era.[15] They were not all "high and dry" as their detractors charged and many were keenly interested in church reform and revival.[16] Interestingly, an anonymous correspondent in 1881, writing to a New Brunswick newspaper, criticized the Ritualists by pointing out that they had departed from the principles and practices of the "old High Church party of the Church of England." This party, the writer went on to say, had existed "since James I, while the Ritualists are of recent origin."[17]

Given the revised understanding of the place of the Tractarians we have now and the rehabilitation of the place of the old High Churchmen, the second question to be considered is whether Medley was in fact a Tractarian at all. This question is far from easy to answer. As we have seen, Medley himself occasionally seemed to accept and promote the mythology that saw the Tractarians as the sole guardians of the catholic tradition of the Church. However, we might extend a caution about placing too much weight on a single sermon, from which Fairweather extracted the quotation above. It was preached in defense of the Ritualists and sought to put them and their Tractarian colleagues in the best possible light. Medley might not have been averse to polishing the Tractarians' accomplishments for this end. Even if one were to allow that Medley did in fact obscure the distinction between the High Church and Tractarian parties, the problem still remains as to how best to classify Medley himself. For all of the attribution of Tractarian tendencies to Medley, by both friend and foe, he was curiously silent on the matter himself. In refusing to apply the Tractarian label to Medley, Ketchum, his biographer and close friend, may just have been following the bishop's own reluctance.

While the *prima facie* case for Medley's Tractarianism appears strong, there are counterarguments of significant weight. For example, he made Evangelicals, like Gray, canons of his cathedral, even though they denied the apostolic succession, eucharistic presence, and baptismal regeneration. He recognized others who were equally fervent in their Low Church feelings, such as Armstrong, who was made commissary of the diocese. Throughout his tenure in New Brunswick Medley never advocated any liturgical expression that was not consistent with natural interpretation of the Prayer Book. Beyond placing candles on the altar of the cathedral and the introduction of daily services, there is no evidence that Medley practiced any advanced ritual himself. He defended the Reformation and criticized, in measured tones, the Roman Catholic Church until his dying day. As far as we know, he never referred to a cleric as "Father," never spoke of hearing a confession, and remained on good terms with a host of political figures from the lieutenant governors of the province to Gladstone. In short, based upon his own practices, there is little to suggest that he was a Tractarian rather than an old High Churchman. He was regarded by many of his contemporaries as the former. When in London he preached at All Saints' Margaret Street and St. Peter's London Docks, where Charles Lowder presented him with a chalice.[18] Closer to home, as well as preaching at the American Tractarian shrine, the Church of the Advent, he preached for Father Woods at the ritualist St. John the Evangelist Church in Montreal.[19]

In short, there are many apparent contradictions in Medley's thought that cause difficulties in categorizing him. First, he argued in favor of the apostolic succession, and generally for a "high view" of episcopacy. Then, he came to support lay membership in church councils and synodical election of bishops. He argued for the prominence of the eucharist as the central form of worship on Sundays. At the same time he held a mildly receptionist view of the eucharistic presence. He was no advanced Ritualist, yet he defended those who were. At times he appeared as the perfect model of a nineteenth-century Romantic churchman. At other times, he was a hard-headed son of the Enlightenment, able to view the rich heritage of Christian tradition with cold dispassion: "We do not pretend that the Fathers were infallible: the age of blind and superstitious veneration for their writings has long since passed away."[20]

Without a doubt Medley was strongly influenced by the Oxford Movement and his association with its principal figures. He was also influenced by Romanticism, to which he gave expression through his participation in the Gothic Revival. The possible Low Church influences of his childhood and the Evangelical orientation of Wadham College while he was a student were, no doubt, also factors. Finally, he was influenced by a Victorian spirit of utility, which had its roots in the Enlightenment. Together with whatever unknown influences may have acted upon him in his formative years, these various strands combined with other contingent factors to form his character. It is not surprising that in such a dynamic age, with such powerful cultural and philosophical forces at work, Medley might hold at once positions that appear to be in opposition to one another.

The conventional analysis of these seeming contradictions would suggest that Medley was an odd, somewhat eclectic aberration from the true Tractarian model. Perhaps an alternate explanation is possible. Frances Knight suggests that, "it might be a flawed notion to suppose that churchmanship can be labelled and pinned down by an historian. The reality of human experience is more complicated."[21] In light of this, maybe it is truer to say that the truly aberrant character is the person who conforms rigidly to a particular ideology, so as to become its personification.[22] Especially in regard to an area as complicated and personal as faith, surely the more common pattern is to find in people a mixture of positions. Throughout his life, Medley never claimed membership in any party. Guided by a confidence in the veracity of scripture, the faithfulness of the Book of Common Prayer to that record and the witness of the church down through the ages, Medley fashioned a theological and devotional position for himself, as millions have done, before and since.

Medley's Legacy

The diocese that John Medley left at his death in 1892 was very different from the one he had found forty-seven years earlier. There were many changes that were no doubt forced by economic and larger cultural circumstances. It is indisputable that many of the changes that took place were the direct result of intentional action by the first bishop of Fredericton. When he arrived in New Brunswick in 1845 the opinion that external forms could be vehicles for divine grace was very much in question. Even stained glass windows were distrusted and the mere questioning of liturgical practices was subject to suspicion. By the end of his long episcopate Gothic churches dominated the diocese, regular celebrations of holy communion were common, and while a diversity of churchmanship continued in the diocese, the High Church orientation was predominant.[23]

Beyond this, Medley supervised the creation of an entirely new model of the Church in his diocese. He arrived in New Brunswick in 1845 as the first bishop of the established church in that colony. At the time his new diocese was largely dependent upon England for money, ministers, and spiritual direction. Over the next five decades, Canada made the transition from colony to independently governed nation. Parallel to this, the Church of England there developed into an independent branch of what would become the worldwide Anglican communion. Just a year after Medley's death the Anglican Church of Canada would come into being, formalizing the independence that had been a *de facto* reality for many years, thanks to the efforts of John Medley and others like him.

In Medley's own life and theology we see the movement to a new understanding of the church mirrored and its reasons revealed. He was a staunchly conservative individual, who over a long episcopate came to realize that the goals of empire and the church could not be identified without damage to the church. This departure from traditional Toryism was, in some measure, due to the radical political aspects of Tractarianism. For the Tractarians, the church's legitimacy was found in the historic episcopate and not in the state. This could certainly account for Medley's enthusiasm for the Episcopal Church in the United States. While the Loyalist members of his own diocese might have had reservations about the churchmen to the south, who had forsaken the Crown and dared to establish a church sundered from any such attachment, Medley did not share this view. Just six years into his career as bishop of Fredericton he traveled to Boston in order to raise funds to complete his cathedral. In a sermon preached at the Tractarian Church of the Advent he described a conception of the Church of England that pointed to the future Anglican Communion. This was a church no longer united by political ties, instead associated by spiritual ties rooted in the episcopate.

> At no very distant period the little sea-girt isle of England had no Congregations of the faithful in her communion beyond her own narrow shores. Now, nearly one hundred Bishops belong to her communion. All the great points of the world are being taken up, and secured for the Kingdom of Christ. In Southern and in Western Africa, in the East and West Indies, in the great continents of America and Australasia, and even in China, Bishops are placed. Wherever there is a Bishop, there is not only a centre of unity, but a rallying point for action. The Bishop, by God's ordinance, stands not alone. He has in himself the power to send, to increase, to multiply. By these few loaves and fishes, these fragments of his saving mercy, the Great Bishop of souls still feeds his scattered flock, and everywhere augments his fold. Where there is a Bishop, there is a Cathedral Church, the mother-Church of the diocese, Jerusalem and her daughters. . . . When the word of God was confined to a single Church, and that Church shut up in Palestine, no sounds of health and salvation were heard in these distant and benighted parts of the world. But now, in the East and West, in the North and South, the high praises of our God are sung. No day declines, no interval of night succeeds, without hymns of thanksgiving. When we retire to rest, the opposite nations of the globe begin their

> matin-chant; and when they sing their even-song, our early prayer awakes. . . . Our united Church, therefore, can no longer be called barren. God hath visited her; the Most High hath made her a fruitful mother of children. We deny not to other churches, the Latin and the Greek, their apostolical foundation, their proper mission in their several spheres. Only we maintain and cherish our own.[24]

This vision of a great spiritual body, transcending borders and political structures, rooted in the Apostles and flowing down through the ages, was consistent with the argument made years earlier in his book on the apostolic succession and was entirely in keeping with Tractarian orthodoxy.

Medley ultimately repudiated the Romanticism of the Tractarians, even if he always maintained a place for their aesthetic ideals. In this same sermon preached at the Church of the Advent, he decried the "anarchy, rationalism, and infidelity" that seemed to be the hallmarks of the modern age. This pessimistic view, which expressed itself in a Romantic vision of the church as a pure vessel set apart from society,[25] eventually was transformed into a more confident and optimistic vision of the church, one in which the church was not a refuge from modernity but a dynamic body, capable of responding to modernity and adapting itself to new forms. While partially proceeding from theoretical considerations, such as a revised view of the relationship between God's providence and the "spirit of the age," Medley's change of approach and emphasis was, for the most part, a consequence of his deeply practical personality. In the end Medley sought for a synthesis of theory and practice and in this quest he was at least partially successful.

From a philosophical and theological standpoint, Medley was a somewhat enigmatic man. Just as his churchmanship resists narrow labeling, so too his intellectual influences are hard to neatly categorize. In sermons and charges he explicitly endorsed aspects of the thought of Newton, Bacon, and Mill, among others, as well as demonstrating some familiarity with the thought of the Enlightenment and German Idealism. While Mill's philosophical position was, no doubt, abhorrent to Medley in many respects, he spoke favorably of the general "utilitarian tendency" that Mill advocated. But he accepted the Romantic critique of "rationalism," while rejecting the pantheism, detachment from reason, and emotionalism prevalent in Romanticism. Although he never mentioned Kant, his emphasis upon moral considerations and his neglect of speculative philosophy, particularly metaphysics, indicates a Kantian tendency in his thought. This tendency, common to the age, was shared by many of the Tractarians.[26]

Ultimately we are led to see that Medley's intellectual eclecticism served his fundamental practicality. This was not simply because of the practical nature of a diocesan bishop's work. Even prior to his consecration he had argued for the priority of practical considerations even in such a seemingly aesthetic arena as architecture. This practicality was not merely naive, as if Medley were ignorant of the importance of theoretical or philosophical considerations. Instead, he appears to have deliberately chosen to pursue a sort of pious pragmatism, to have made a conscious choice to direct his theological and philosophical explorations toward the practical ends of the church. Medley thought of the faith as a received and known entity. Thus, what remained for human agency was the practical utilization and explication of that faith.

Certainly this pragmatism was demonstrated in Medley's approach to controversy. He had ample opportunity to become a controversialist after the pattern of his old friend Henry Phillpotts. The Evangelical party in New Brunswick baited him from the beginning and persecuted numerous priests suspected of Tractarian leanings. Medley neither engaged in public debate, nor attempted to force High Church doctrines on recalcitrant people, either clergy or laity. Baptismal regeneration was explicitly rejected by clergy such as Gray of Saint John, yet Medley made no attempt to censure them, nor to refuse to license clergy who agreed with this and other Low Church points. He did recruit clergy who shared his High Church perspective, but made no efforts to block the election of Low Church clergy by Evangelical parishes. This patient approach, constantly stressing toleration, proved to be ultimately successful as the Evangelical animus was worn down over the years and vicious party strife substantially eroded within the New Brunswick church.

Medley's Romanticism, which found in an idealized picture of the early church a model of ecclesiastical independence, was balanced by a resolute pragmatism, which did not shrink from abolishing old structures in order to construct a new polity able to meet the realities of the Victorian colonial situation. Those who have been eager to see Medley as simply a Tractarian or as an exponent of the imperial ideal have overlooked this progressive aspect of his thought. While he admired the American Church on Tractarian grounds as an example of "a primitive Church" unsullied by participation with secular governments, he was also inclined to support it as a model of a modern, educated, and voluntary religious body, able to function in a new North American society.

This ambiguity is perhaps best seen in the way that Medley exercised his episcopal office. Possessed with a confidence in the apostolic succession and a sure sense that he could freely act in the best interests of his diocese, nevertheless he seldom exercised unilateral power. Particularly in his later ideas regarding church councils and government, he recognized that any expressions of abstract authority would not suffice in a contemporary context. For example, in his view participation by the laity would be necessary in order to make any decision from a Lambeth Conference binding on the church. While both Catholic and Protestant nineteenth-century reactions against "rationalism" took the form of assertions of authority,[27] Medley believed that educated and open debate was the best hope for responding to new challenges to the faith.

John Medley managed to create a diocese in the wilderness, build a hundred churches in that diocese, and create an accompanying climate of Christian devotion and service. Over a nearly half century episcopate, he resisted the slide into bitterness that might have been the outcome of one who watched his old world crumble. Instead, he continually stressed to his clergy the need to stay current with secular studies, so that their message could be presented in ways that were intelligible to their contemporaries. He refused to spend his days tied up in courts or endless controversy. He won over most of his Evangelical enemies, while encouraging High Church principles to the end.

Ultimately, many of Medley's own positions were destined to be a part of history. Neo-Gothic churches are no longer built in his diocese. Utilitarian, "horizontal design" structures speak more to a contemporary spirituality. His rigor concerning baptism, preparation for the Eucharist, the rules of marriage and countless other practices are now regarded as narrow and archaic. His expectations for the level of theological scholarship of parochial clergy have been replaced with a greater concern for practical, professional skills.

Do we then consider our study of Medley to be merely of antiquarian interest? Or, are there lessons to be learned that have contemporary application? Certainly the conception of nature as a vehicle for the divine is an essential Christian understanding that requires renewal in every age. To attempt to hold the natural and divine together in their individual integrity is part of the Chalcedonian orthodoxy that, if misunderstood, leads to significant distortions in practical Christianity. Medley strove against both denying the natural in a too immediate appropriation of the divine, or allowing the divine to be lost in the natural. He attempted this mediation in music, architecture, liturgy, preaching, and the sacraments.

To attempt to find contemporary forms that express eternal spiritual truths is surely our struggle as much as it was his. On the cusp of a new age, Medley attempted to translate ancient forms into this new milieu. He faced the loss of the privileged position of the Church of England in society and recognized that from that point on, the formal authority of the church in society would be much restricted. He saw too that membership would be entirely voluntary and the structures of the church would have at least partially democratic forms. While retaining a firm confidence in the eternal truth of the Gospel and the calling of the church, Medley knew that it was impossible to stem the tide of the modern world. If the church was to retain its evangelical calling it would need to understand the new culture in which it found itself. Indeed, the church would need to understand that wherever it found itself, the culture would be unique. The Church of England could not be a garment with one size fitting all. It would have to be tailored and adapted in its form. To engage in this process while retaining "the faith once delivered to the saints" is the challenge of the contemporary church as much as it was John Medley's.

In John Medley's life we are able to observe the beginning of the end of the Church of England extended throughout the world as a representative of the British Empire, a relatively brief and ultimately failed experiment. In its place we see the beginning of the idea of the Anglican Church—an institution that has its roots in England, but is successful just to the extent that it has been able to turn away from those roots and adapt itself to local circumstances. The transitional church of Medley's day, still clinging to the vestiges of establishment, has been replaced today, in former colonial settings, with a truly international and denominational body. In his own diocese, the Anglican Church has become simply one of many Protestant groups, fighting to retain its members at the dawn of a new millennium.

Ultimately, the final judgment of Medley's theology and its effectiveness must remain in reserve. He and his Tractarian colleagues desired a church free from state interference. They believed that such a church alone could maintain the purity of the apostolic Body of Christ. This independent body, which they so desired, and which came into existence initially outside of England, is not yet able to be assessed in terms of its long-term viability. In Medley's vision these various national churches would be bound together by the common historic faith and episcopate as well as a common liturgy and devotional life. Now that much of this commonality has all but disappeared in worldwide Anglicanism, its claim to be a Catholic church is far from being as clear now as it was to the Tractarians. There is now no common Anglican theology, or common form of liturgy throughout the communion. There has not emerged an administrative or authoritative structure capable of resolving divisions over doctrine and practice. The historic episcopate seems to be one of the last common threads binding the fabric together. Recent divisions in the Anglican communion over matters of doctrine and morality have pointed to the tenuous nature of its unity.

Having achieved the Tractarian goal of independence, the Church of England, now transformed into the Anglican Communion, has yet to discover an undisputed foundation for its unity. The very independence that the Tractarians saw as vital to the church's spiritual integrity seemingly precludes the possibility of Anglicanism being a single church, in anything but name only. Yet this need not be interpreted as an utter failing. While the Tractarian vision of a church unified in its conformity to ancient doctrinal and devotional forms has proven to be a Romantic fantasy, it is possible that something has been gained in the invention of the messy and divided organization that is the Anglican Church. Perhaps the church ought not to rely on mere authority to legitimize itself in society. The fissures and uncertainties that mark contemporary Anglicanism may be necessary concomitants of a church that engages modern society and takes its claims seriously. Established churches are clearly impossible in liberal democracies. The church must instead convince individual people of its value in their lives.

John Medley believed that the newly emerging church needed to adapt itself to society while remaining true to its doctrinal foundation. He did not believe that administrative structures alone either within the church or external to it would be sufficient to guarantee its survival or integrity. If he was correct in this judgment the Anglican Communion will need to discover some common doctrinal ground to preserve it or even justify its continued existence.

Notes

Introduction

1. T. Mozley, *Reminiscences* (London: Longmans 1882), pp. 1–3.

2. Ibid., p. 9.

3. For a trenchant account of Mozley's strengths and failings as an historian of the Tractarian Movement, see O. Chadwick, *The Spirit of the Oxford Movement* (Cambridge: Cambridge University Press, 1990), Chapter 7.

4. To understand the considerable scope of Tractarian studies, one simply has to look at the voluminous bibliography of literature (over four thousand entries) assembled by the Reverend Lawrence Crumb in *The Oxford Movement and its Leaders: A Bibliography of Secondary and Lesser Primary Sources* (Metuchin, 1988). A *Supplement* (1993) has been published and he is at present working on another supplement.

5. W. Q. Ketchum, *The Life and Work of the Most Reverend John Medley, D.D.* (Saint John: J. & A. McMillan, 1893).

6. As a result, Medley's widow, Margaret, was dissatisfied with Ketchum's work, complaining that it portrayed her late husband as a simple colonial missionary and failed to identify Medley's significant role in the Oxford Movement. Her opinion is revealed in a private letter to Medley's friend, Sir George Parkin. Margaret Medley to G. Parkin, August 10, 1893, NAC, MG 30 D44, vol. 8.

7. W. O. Raymond, "John Medley," in *Leaders of the Canadian Church*, ed. Bertal Heeney (Toronto: Musson, 1918), pp. 99–134.

8. M. H. Blom, T. E. Blom, eds. *Canada Home: Juliana Horatia Ewing's Fredericton Letters 1867–1869* (Vancouver: University of British Columbia, Press 1983). Juliana Ewing went on to become a celebrated children's author. See *DNB*.

9. Eugene R. Fairweather, *The Oxford Movement* (New York: Oxford University Press, 1964).

10. Eugene R. Fairweather, "A Tractarian Patriarch: John Medley of Fredericton," *CJT* 6 (1962) pp. 208–11; "John Medley on Irish Church Disestablishment: An Unpublished Letter," *CJT* 7 (1961): 198–200; "John Medley as Defender of 'Ritualism': An Unpublished Correspondence," *CJT* (1962): 208–11.

11. This title is claimed by others. In the preface to his book *Alexander Forbes of Brechin: The First Tractarian Bishop* (Oxford: Clarendon Press, 1995), Rowan Strong adds the qualifier that Forbes was "the first Tractarian Bishop in the United Kingdom" (p. vii).

12. Fairweather, "Tractarian Patriarch," p. 15 n.

13. Ibid., p. 24

14. The Ritualists were actually distinct from the Tractarians, although the two movements were related. More will be said about the Ritualists in chapters 5 and 6.

15. Lyman Harding, "John by Divine Permission: John Medley and the Church in New Brunswick," *JCCHS* 8 (1966): 76–87.

16. D. S. Richardson, "Christ Church Cathedral, Fredericton, New Brunswick" M.A. thesis, Yale University 1966).

17. Christopher Neal Headon, "The Influence of the Oxford Movement Upon the Church of England in Eastern and Central Canada, 1840–1900" (Ph.D. diss., McGill University, 1974).

18. See also two articles by Christopher Headon: "An Unpublished Correspondence between John Medley and E. B. Pusey," *JCCHS* 16 (1974): 72–74; and "Developments in Canadian Anglican Worship in Eastern and Central Canada 1840–1868," *JCCHS* 17 (1975): 26–36.

19. Bob Watson, *Christ Church Cathedral A History and Christ Church (Parish) Church, Fredericton: A History* (Fredericton: The Fredericton Historical Research Project 1983).

20. Robert L. Watson, *Christ Church Cathedral, Fredericton: A History* (Fredericton: Unipress, 1984).

21. Timothy Gene Cooper, "Church Music in Nineteenth Century Canada as Represented by the Compositions of John Medley" (Ph.D. diss., University of Georgia, 1989).

22. For example see D. F. Cook, "A Survey of Hymnody in the Church of England in Eastern Canada to 1909," *JCCHS* (1965): 36–61.

23. Gregg Finley, "New Brunswick's Gothic Revival: John Medley and the Aesthetics of Anglican Worship" (Ph.D. diss., University of New Brunswick, 1989).

24. Gregg Finley and Lynn Wigginton, *On Earth as it is Heaven* (Fredericton: Goose Lane, 1995).

25. Gregg Finley, "'Habits of Reverence and Awe': Bishop John Medley and the Promise of Ecclesiology," *JCCHS* (1993): 3–22; "The Gothic Revival and the Victorian Church in New Brunswick," *Material History Review* 32 (1990): 1–16; "Stained Glass and Stone Tracery: The Gothic Revival and the Shaping of Canadian Sensibilities," *British Journal of Canadian Studies* 5 (1990): 78–98.

26. Philip Carrington, *The Anglican Church in Canada* (Toronto: Collins, 1963); Thomas Millman and A. R. Kelly, *Atlantic Canada to 1900: A History of the Anglican Church* (Toronto: Anglican Book Centre 1983); Judson D. Purdy, "The Church of England in New Brunswick During the Colonial Era 1783–1860" (M.A. thesis, University of New Brunswick, 1954).

27. For instance, Medley is not even mentioned by Owen Chadwick in *The Victorian Church*, 2 vols. (London: A & C Black, 1966 and 1970) or by Geoffrey Rowell in *The Vision Glorious* (Oxford: Oxford University Press, 1983), despite the fact that both authors devote some attention to colonial and missionary bishops.

28. See below, chapter 1, where their correspondence is described. A collection of letters from Medley to Pusey is preserved at PH.

29. See chapter 1, where this relationship is described.

30. Ibid.

31. Medley also knew Charles Marriott, A. P. Forbes, J. T. Coleridge, Isaac Williams, and R. W. Church.

32. He worked with Bishop Henry Phillpotts and S. S. Wesley, for instance.

33. Medley, of course, knew all of the major figures in nineteenth-century Canadian Anglicanism such as Bishops Mountain, Fulford, Binney, and Strachan. He was well acquainted with J. M. Neale as wells as the great Victorian architects William Butterfield and Frank Wills. He also knew successive archbishops of Canterbury, was a friend of George Selwyn, the pioneering missionary bishop of New Zealand, and many other leading ecclesiastical figures.

34. Medley's relationship with Gladstone will be discussed below in chapter 6. Part of Medley's correspondence with Gladstone is preserved at the BL.

35. See chapter 2 for Medley's meeting with Ruskin.

36. Quoted in a letter from Lord Chief Justice Coleridge to Mrs. Medley, after the bishop's death, in W. Q. Ketchum, *Life of Medley*, p. 302.

37. John Medley, *The Episcopal Form of Church Government* (London: John W. Parker, 1835).

38. In the end this did not happen. Whatever the case may be, there is no indication by Medley that Keble was involved with any corrections or otherwise participated in the production of the final work. Nor do we have any indication why the tract was published separately and not as part of the *Tracts for the Times.* See *The Letters and Diaries of John Henry Newman*, ed. Thomas Gornall, (Oxford: Clarendon Press, 1981), 5: 10–11.

39. Medley contributed translations and the index to a volume of Chrysostom's homilies. "Homilies of St. John Chrysostom" in *A Library of the Fathers* (Oxford, 1838). Newman suggests in a diary entry that Medley might edit them.

40. John Medley, *Elementary Remarks on Church Architecture* (Exeter: P. A. Hannaford 1841).

41. A firsthand account of this founding was given almost half a century later by the then aged former curate, the Reverend J. L. Fulford. A typescript of Fulford's handwritten original is preserved in PANB. For more on Medley's involvement with these societies see Finley, *New Brunswick's Gothic Revival* and Phoebe Stanton's *The Gothic Revival and American Church Architecture: An Episode in Taste, 1840–56* (Baltimore: Johns Hopkins University Press, 1968). More about Medley's involvement in local church architecture is given by Martin Cherry "Patronage, the Anglican Church and the Local Architect in Victorian England," in *The Victorian Church: Architecture and Society*, ed. Chris Brooks and Andrew Saint (Manchester: Manchester University Press, 1995), pp. 173–91.

42. For a fuller account of this see Finley, *New Brunswick's Gothic Revival.*

43. John Medley, *The Advantages of Open Seats* (Oxford: I Shrimpton, 1843).

44. E. B. Pusey described Medley's "impressive" preaching to J. H. Newman. See *The Letters and Diaries of John Henry Newman*, vol. 71, ed. Gerard Tracey (Oxford: Clarendon Press, 1995), letter of E. B. Pusey to J. H. Newman, August 27, 1839.

45. Before he left England there appeared a published volume: John Medley, *Sermons Published at the request of Many of His Late Parishioners* (London: Rivingtons, 1845).

46. *Life of Medley*, p. 218 and 233–36. Medley did not attend the first Lambeth conference in 1867. Correspondence between Medley and Archbishop Longley reveals the reasons for his absence. With a characteristically blunt tone, Medley cited four reasons why he did not intend to accept the Archbishop's invitation to the Conference: it was scheduled at an inconvenient time since he had confirmations arranged for the same date as the meetings; no agenda had been given, thus raising the question of whether the long absence form his diocese would be justified; he believed that the difficulties of the colonial Church were best addressed by the whole diocese, Clergy and lay, in that diocese; and, since the single most pressing matter, that of the bishop of Natal, was not to be discussed, he was disinclined to attend.

47. See Ketchum, *Life of Medley*, pp. 301–2. See also Ruth Teale, "Dr. Pusey and the Church Overseas," in *Pusey Rediscovered*, ed. Perry Butler (London: SPCK, 1983) p. 204, for a list of those colonial and missionary bishops who accepted translation back to England.

48. Romanticism has relatively specific meanings in literature and music. However, in referring to the Romantic Movement, this thesis will employ the term in its broader sense. That is, reference will be made to that general movement in European

culture that included developments in literature, art and architecture, philosophy, and other aspects of culture. Understood in this broader sense, Romanticism is somewhat amorphous, but some definition is possible. At the very least, it involves a reaction against reason and an assertion of "feeling" in its place. This is linked to an exaltation of nature and the "natural man." For more on this see the useful introduction by Stephen Prickett in *The Romantics*, ed. Stephen Prickett (London: Methuen, 1981), pp. 1–14.

49. Peter Nockles, *The Oxford Movement in Context: Anglican High Churchmanship 1760–1857* (Cambridge: Cambridge University Press, 1994).

50. See the Introduction to Rowell's *Vision Glorious*. This point has also been explored by Wayne Hankey, "The Way Forward in Theology," *150th Anniversary of the Oxford Movement: The Way Forward* (Charlottetown: St. Peter's Publications, 1983), 24–53. See also Robert Crouse, "'Deepened by the Study of the Fathers,' The Oxford Movement, Dr. Pusey and Patristic Scholarship," *Dionysius* 7 (1983): 137–48.

51. See below, p. 109 where reference is made to E. B. Pusey's *An Historical Enquiry into the Probable Causes of the Rationalist Character Lately Predominant in the Theology of Germany* (London: Rivingtons 1828).

52. Rowell, *Vision Glorious*, pp. 52–54.

53. The relation of the Tractarians to Romanticism has long been accepted. Sheridan Gilley outlines its genesis in "The Church of England in the Nineteenth Century," *A History of Religion in Britain: Practice and Belief for the Pre-Roman Times to the Present*, ed. Sheridan Gilley and W. J. Sheils (Oxford: Blackwell, 1994), 296–97; see also, Nigel Yates, *The Oxford Movement and Anglican Ritualism* (London: Chameleon Press, 1983), pp. 8–9, where he speaks about "popular medievalism," also his more recent *Anglican Ritualism in Victorian Britain 1830–1910* (Oxford: Oxford University Press, 1999), especially chapter 2; and, Geoffrey Rowell, "'Church Principles' and 'Protestant Kempism', Some Theological forerunners of the Tractarians," in *Newman From Oxford to the People* (Leominster: Gracewing, 1996), p. 18.

54. Finlay, *New Brunswick's Gothic Revival*, pp. 54–98.

55. See A. Addison, *Romanticism and the Gothic Revival* (New York: Gordian Press, 1967).

56. For example, an account of the anti-Enlightenment tendency of S. T. Coleridge's position and Coleridge's theological influence on Newman is given by Douglas Hedley in "Participation in the Divine Life: Coleridge, the vision of God and the thought of John Henry Newman" in *Newman, From Oxford to the People*, pp. 238–51.

57. For an outline of Tractarian attitudes toward the Reformation see Nockles, *The Oxford Movement in Context*, pp. 122–27. Also see Peter Toon, *Evangelical Theology: A Response to Tractarianism* (Atlanta: John Knox Press, 1979); and, William J. Baker, "Hurrell Froude and the Reformers," *Journal of Ecclesiastical History* 21, no. 3 (1970): 243–59.

58. Medley, *1850 Charge.*, p. 52.

59. See Nockles, *The Oxford Movement in Context*, p. 221–3, for an account of the dissatisfaction of many of the Tractarians with the Book of Common Prayer.

60. Such as in his sermon before Provincial Synod, preached at the age of seventy-three. See below, where this sermon is discussed in chapters 5 and 6.

61. For a refutation of this charge see Nockles, *The Oxford Movement in Context*, pp. 44–103.

62. For example see John Medley, *A Charge Delivered in Christ Church Cathedral, July 4th 1871* (Fredericton: H. A. Cropley) where Medley makes clear his views on the spiritual power of the Episcopal Church in the United States and also asserts that the American empire is as great as the British, pp. 18–19.

63. See Lyman Harding, *Citizens with the Saints: A Brief History of Anglicanism in New Brunswick* (Fredericton: The Diocesan Synod of Fredericton, 1994), p. 33.

64. In a letter to Sir George Parkin, August 10, 1893, (NAC, MG 30 D44, vol. 8, 2339–40), Margaret Medley details the various writers to whom she has made her late husband's letters and papers available.

65. Ibid.

66. In a letter to Sir George Parkin, Edward Medley refers to his possession of correspondence between his father and E. B. Pusey (NAC, MG 30, D44, vol. 21, folio 6053).

67. None of the provincial or diocesan archives in neighboring Newfoundland, Nova Scotia, or Quebec contain any Medley letters, although the papers of the Anglican bishops who were Medley's peers in the ecclesiastical province of Canada are preserved.

Chapter 1. Medley's Life

1. It is unclear why Ketchum omitted this material. There were letters from all of these men available to him, but he chose not to use them. Mrs. Medley had at least "thirty or more (letters) of Keble's, about 20 of Pusey's, some from Isaac Williams, Dean Church and others." This, she relates in a letter to Sir George Parkin (August 10, 1893) NAC, MG 30 D44, vol. 8.

2. A copy of this certificate is kept at the Devon record office. The Provincial Archives of New Brunswick (PANB) also has a copy. His father's occupation is omitted.

3. The successive wardens are listed on plaques hanging around the church below the gallery.

4. Ketchum, *Life of Medley*, p. 43.

5. See H. P. Liddon, *Life of Edward Bouverie Pusey*, 4 vols. (London: Longmans, 1893), 1:2.

6. Ibid.

7. This information was provided after Medley's death by Margaret Medley to W. Q. Ketchum, his biographer, *Life of Medley*, p. 44.

8. Ibid., *Life of Medley*, p. 45.

9. The Lt. Gov. at this time was the Honorable A. H. Gordon (always addressed simply as "Mr. Gordon" by Medley). He and Gordon were friends, sharing a common interest in the church and an inclination towards High Churchmanship.

10. PANB, RS 347, F7636. Letter of John Medley to A. H. Gordon, December 5, 1860.

11. See entry in *ODCC*.

12. For other High Church and Tractarian objections to the practices of the Bible Society see C. Brad Faught, *The Oxford Movement: A Thematic History of the Tractarians and their Times* (University Park: Pennsylvania State University Press, 2003) p. 51.

13. See W. R. Ward, *Victorian Oxford* (London: Frank Cass, 1965), for numerous references to Wadham's Evangelicalism.

14. See entry for Wren in *DNB*.

15. A life size painting of Bishop Medley used to hang in the hall of Wadham. It has, in recent years, been on loan to the diocese of Fredericton and can be seen in the cathedral.

16. A copy of Medley's Oxford examination certificate, dated May 10, 1826, is preserved in PANB (MC223, DB-1–6A3). It is signed by "Car. T. Longley."

17. *DNB.*

18. A copy of a certificate is preserved at PANB. It reads, "I certify that John Medley of Wadham College, in this University, attended my lectures in the year 1827, Charles Lloyd, Regius Professor of Divinity."

19. Peter Nockles refers to Oakeley's *Historical Notes on the Tractarian Movement* (London, 1865), pp. 12–14. Lloyd has received his own study by W. J. Baker, *Beyond Port and Prejudice: Charles Lloyd of Oxford* (Orono: University of Maine, 1981).

20. See Charles Lloyd, *ODCC*. See also Sheridan Gilley, *Newman and his Age* (London: Dartman, Longman and Todd 1990), p. 48.

21. Lloyd may well have had other effects on Medley's intellectual development. Medley was never afraid of critical inquiry and later in life at least exhibited a great interest in German biblical scholarship. It was Lloyd, after all, who had encouraged Pusey, as a young man, to go to Germany. Newman described Lloyd thus: "he had more liking for exegetical criticism, historical research, and controversy, than for dogma or philosophy." As quoted by Albrecht Geck, "The Concept of History in E. B. Pusey's First Enquiry into German Theology and its German Background," *Journal of Theological Studies* 38, pt. 2 (1987): 393.

22. PH, Letters of John Medley to E. B. Pusey.

23. *Letters and Diaries of John Henry Newman*, vol. 7, letter of E. B. Pusey to J. H. Newman, August 27, 1839.

24. Ibid., p. 193, "breakfasted with Acland to meet Mr Medley." Sir Thomas Dyke Acland and other members of his family were lifelong friends of Medley's. Acland was at this time M.P. for North Devon.

25. *Letters and Diaries of John Henry Newman*, vol. 5, p. 3.

26. Ibid., index, p. 416.

27. J. T. Coleridge, *A Memoir of the Rev. John Keble, M.A.* (Oxford and London: James Parker, 1874), p. 29.

28. To the end of the poem for Trinity XXI, Keble appends two stanzas, "To the Red Breast." These, along with an expression used in Keble's own poem are "borrowed from a friend." (John Keble, *The Christian Year* (Oxford: James Parker, 1866), p. 251. Coleridge, p. 31, identifies the friend as G. J. Cornish.

29. Medley and G. K. Cornish were the coeditors of a volume of Chrysostom's homilies.

30. This information was obtained on the World Wide Web at www.familysearch.org. The date of the marriage was July 10, 1826.

31. See *DNB.*

32. For more on Phillpotts, see below.

33. Ketchum suggested he became prebendary in 1838. However, Exeter Cathedral archives indicate it was not until 1843.

34. See Ketchum, *Life of Medley*, p. 328.

35. *Diaries and Letters of John Henry Newman*, Vol. VII, p. 131. In a letter to Newman dated August 27, 1839, Pusey writes, "I preached for Medley at Exeter and so heard another of his sermons; they are very clear, plain-spoken and impressive."

36. These are kept at Pusey House and have been published in part by C. F. Headon, "An Unpublished Correspondence." They are grouped together and cataloged in Pusey's letters as vol. 29/1.

37. See below, pp. 79–82, where this aspect of the letter is further discussed.

38. See Liddon, *Life of Pusey*, 2: 81–113, for an account of her illness and death and the profound effect it had on Pusey.

39. PH, Letters of Medley to Pusey, December 21, 1840. Unfortunately, we do not know what passage of Chrysostom Medley was referring to.

40. PH, Medley to Pusey, May 1841.

41. Ibid.

42. See Liddon, *Life of Pusey*, 2: 98. Keble counseled Pusey against this sort of claiming of personal responsibility for terrible events, even the suffering of others. Pusey had evidently expressed thoughts similar to Medley's.

43. Medley was always to retain some sense of God's direct correction of human sin. More than thirty years later he will still have the same inclinations, viewing the terrible fire that destroyed much of the port city of Saint John as a corrective "visitation." See *A Sermon Preached on Occasion of Saint John Fire, St. James Day 1877* (Saint John, 1877).

44. Liddon, *Life of Pusey*, 2: 107–9.

45. Many of the leading figures in the Tractarian movement or connected with it suffered similar personal tragedies around the same time. David Newsome, in *The Parting of Friends* (London: John Murray, 1966), details the personal tragedies suffered by, among others, Henry Manning, and Robert and Samuel Wilberforce.

46. Probably "I Believe in the Communion of Saints," which was later reprinted in: John Medley, *Sermons.* This sermon, preached following his wife's death begins: "I address you, my brethren and sisters in Christ our Lord, looking up to God for his help, but from the midst of no ordinary trial. Yet, painful as it is to speak to you at all, I can no longer hold my peace, though 'my sorrow is stirred'" (p. 424).

47. PH, Letter of Medley to Pusey, June 7, 1841.

48. PH, Letter of Medley to Pusey, July 12, 1841.

49. A pamphlet, describing the tour, was published, *A Report containing information obtained during a tour made by the Revd. G. Martin and the Revd J. Medley at the desire of the Exeter Diocesan Board of Education* (Exeter, 1840). This is cataloged as pamphlet #2795 at PH.

50. This monument was placed in the chancel of St. Thomas' Church, Exeter. The *DNB* records that Bacon was also the creator of several monuments at Westminster Abbey and St. Paul's Cathedral. For more on this, see below, p. 153.

51. PH, Letter of Medley to Pusey, July 13, 1841.

52. PH, Letter of Medley to Pusey, July 16, 1841.

53. The reference is to Isaac Williams. He had been nominated for the Poetry Professorship, following Keble's resignation. The resulting contest became a political struggle between the Tractarians and their opponents. See Liddon, *Life of Pusey*, 2: 260–68. We know too that Medley and Williams corresponded with each other. See letter of Margaret Medley to Sir George Parkin, NAC, MG 30 D44, 8: 234.

54. Why Medley did this is unknown. We have no other indication that he was dissatisfied with Oxford or Wadham.

55. PH, letter of Medley to Pusey, January 7, 1842.

56. On May 14, 1843, Pusey had delivered a sermon entitled "The Holy Eucharist, A Comfort to the Penitent." It served as the opportunity that many were waiting for to attack the Tractarians. It was charged that the sermon taught erroneous doctrines concerning the Lord's Supper. It was condemned and Pusey was banned from preaching in the university for two years. Liddon recounts the entire episode in *Life of Pusey*, 2: 306–69.

57. See Liddon, *Life of Pusey*, vol. 2, pp. 339–44.

58. For a more detailed account of the theological implications of Pusey's sermon see Alf Härdelin, *The Tractarian Understanding of the Eucharist* (Uppsala, 1965), pp. 212–15.

59. Ketchum, *Life of Medley*, p. 59.
60. PH, letter of Medley to Pusey, May 1, 1844.
61. Whether no more letters were written after this time, or whether they were written and have been subsequently lost is unknown. We do know that more letters than those we have at present between Medley and Pusey were written at some time. Margaret Medley remarks in later years about possessing "about 20 of Pusey's." See letter of Margaret Medley to Sir George Parkin, NAC, MG 30 D44, 8: 2339.
62. See details on Medley's appointment below.
63. See Ketchum, *Life of Medley*, pp. 38–42.
64. An outline of the history of the Church of England In North America (and elsewhere overseas) is given by W. M. Jacob, *The Making of the Anglican Church Worldwide* (London: SPCK, 1997), chapter 2.
65. See for example, Nockles, *The Oxford Movement in Context*, where he quotes Jones of Nayland in support of this view. Medley himself argued this in his first visitation charge. *A Charge Delivered at his Primary Visitation held in Christ Church Cathedral, Fredericton, August 24th 1847 by John, Bishop of Fredericton* (Fredericton: John Simpson), pp. 21–22. This argument has been mentioned in virtually every account of the colonial North American episcopate. For example, a review of literature prior to 1992 can be seen in Frederick V Mills "The Colonial Anglican Episcopate: A Historiographical Review" in *Anglican and Episcopal History* 61 (Sept. 1992): 325–46. Henry Roper has dealt with the Canadian history in "The Anglican Episcopate in Canada: An Historical Perspective" in *Anglican and Episcopal History* 57 (Sept. 1988): 255–71. A more extensive account of the colonial episcopate has been given by Peter Doll in *Imperial Anglicanism in North America, 1745–1795* (D.Phil. thesis, University of Oxford, 1989) and his subsequent book, *Revolution, Religion, and National Identity: Imperial Anglicanism in British North America, 1745–1795* (New Jersey: Fairleigh Dickinson University Press, 2000). See also, R. N. Hebb *The Church of England in Loyalist New Brunswick, 1783–1825* (New Jersey: Fairleigh Dickinson University Press, 2004).
66. The broad outlines of early New Brunswick history as sketched here are well known. The standard text for New Brunswick history is W. S. MacNutt, *New Brunswick: A History 1784–1867* (Toronto: Macmillan, 1963). For a recent, detailed account of the relationship of the English church and the French inhabitants of Eastern Canada, see Doll's *Revolution, Religion, and National Identity*.
67. See Harding, *Citizens with the Saints*, pp. 7–8 for the first English services in New Brunswick.
68. Scott W. See, in *Riots in New Brunswick: Orange Nativism and Social Violence in the 1840's* (Toronto: University of Toronto Press, 1993) gives a brief account of the Pre-Loyalist demographic character of New Brunswick, especially in chapter 1.
69. Among studies of the Loyalists in New Brunswick see E. C. Wright, *The Loyalists of New Brunswick* (Fredericton: 1955) and more recently D. G. Bell, *Early Loyalist Saint John* (Fredericton: New Ireland Press, 1983).
70. See Purdy, *The Church of England*, pp. 7–9.
71. See D. G. Bell, "Charles Inglis and the Anglican Clergy of Loyalist Nova Scotia," *Nova Scotia Historical Review* 7, no. 1 (1987), p. 26. Prof. Bell points out that it is somewhat unfair to judge Inglis by the standard of later activist bishops like Medley, p. 27. For more on Inglis see J. Fingard, *The Anglican Design in Loyalist Nova Scotia, 1783–1816* (London: Published for the Church Historical Society by S.P.C.K., 1972); more recently, see Brian Cuthbertson, *The First Bishop* (Halifax: Waegwoltic Press, 1987).
72. Harding, "John, By Divine Permission," p. 77.

73. While conceding that the Loyalists "were for the most part vigorous and determined men," he notes that their traditions seemed "to be all of the Georgian, none of them of a primitive and catholic, character." *A Charge to the Clergy of the Diocese of Fredericton, Delivered at his eighth Triennial Visitation in the Church of St. Paul's Portland, Saint John, June 30th, 1868* (London: Macmillan), p. 23.

74. The Reverend Ross Hebb, in doctoral research for the University of Wales, has uncovered sermons from some of the Loyalist clergy wherein, for example, the doctrines of the eucharistic presence and the apostolic succession figure prominently.

75. Harding, *Citizens with the Saints*, p. 14.

76. Ibid., p. 12.

77. Saint John *Courier*, March 20, 1824, as quoted in Ketchum, p. 38.

78. See MacNutt, *New Brunswick*, 89–90. He records that there was little opposition when, by Act of Legislation in 1786, the laws of Nova Scotia were applied to New Brunswick. The Loyalists who were nominally adherents of the Church of England, in many cases were actually Congregationalists, Presbyterians or members of several dissenting sects. In addition, of course, there was the large French Roman Catholic majority who had predated the arrival of the Loyalists. Purdy, *The Church of England*, chapter 2, provides greater details of the various divisions in the province before Medley's arrival.

79. Ketchum, *Life of Medley*, p. 60.

80. Harding, *John, By Divine Permission*, p. 79.

81. This claim appears in her article, "Dr. Pusey and the Church Overseas," p. 192. However, subsequent research has been unable to locate the supporting document.

82. Ketchum, *Life of Medley*, p. 61.

83. This letter is reprinted in full in Ketchum, *Life of Medley*, p. 61.

84. *Annals*, p. 61.

85. See Arthur Burns, *The Diocesan Revival in The Church of England, c. 1800–1870* (Oxford: Clarendon Press, 1999), p. 203.

86. BL, MS Eng. Letters, 135, folio 140.

87. Ibid., f. 141. W. O. Raymond, "John Medley," confirms that Medley was never robust. See p. 112.

88. Letter of Coleridge to Keble of July 11, 1844, BL, MS Eng. Lett., 135, ff 123–24.

89. This Fund was initiated by Bp. Blomfield of London in 1841. In 1843 the Colonial Bishoprics Committee Fund appropriated £20,000 to the establishment of a new diocese. See Harding, *John, By Divine Permission*, pp. 78–79.

90. BL, MS Eng, Lett. 135, folio 146.

91. Ibid., f. 155.

92. Ketchum, *Life of Medley*, p. 62.

93. Ketchum, *Life of Medley*, p. 59.

94. Ibid.

95. PANB, Fulford manuscript, p. 5.

96. Ibid.

97. See above.

98. Of Bishop Kaye, Medley speaks admiringly later, calling him "a prelate to whom the world is largely indebted," Medley, *1847 Charge*, p. 17.

99. Yates, *Anglican Ritualism in Victorian Britain*, pp. 172–94.

100. See Yates, *Anglican Ritualism in Victorian Britain*, pp. 38, 50, and 138. For example, Mant shared with Medley an abhorrence of "the wickedness of distinguishing in the house of God between rich and poor." See Yates, *Anglican Ritualism*, p. 138.

101. See Burns, *The Diocesan Revival*, pp. 138–43.
102. Norman Sykes, in G. C. B. Davies, *Henry Phillpotts, Bishop of Exeter 1778–1869* (London: S.P.C.K., 1954), p. 7.
103. Desmond Bowen, *The Idea of the Victorian Church* (Montreal: McGill, 1968), p. 98.
104. See entry in *The Concise Dictionary of National Biography* (Oxford, Oxford University Press, 1983).
105. See entry in *ODCC.*
106. Nockles, *The Oxford Movement*, esp. pp.101–2 and 138–40.
107. Arthur Burns, *The Diocesan Revival*, pp. 138–43.
108. Although with Selwyn there almost certainly was correspondence, given his personal friendship with Medley.
109. Medley, *A Charge Delivered in Trinity Church, St. John, to the Clergy of the Diocese of Fredericton, by John, Bishop of Fredericton and Metropolitan of Canada, at His Triennial Visitation, St. Peter's Day, 1886* (Saint John: Ellis, Robertson & Co.), p. 8.
110. See the catalog of the Medley Library, Christ Church Cathedral, Fredericton.
111. See *Annals*, 3 October 1874.
112. For more on Hamilton see Chadwick, *The Victorian Church*, pp.468–69; and, Yates, *Anglican Ritualism in Victorian Britain*, pp. 184 *ff.*
113. See Strong, *Forbes of Brechin.*
114. Ibid., pp. 24–46.
115. Ibid., 47–52.
116. Ibid., p. 69.
117. See Strong, *Forbes of Brechin*, chapter 4.
118. Ibid., see pp. 183–84.
119. Ibid., p. 232.
120. Ibid., p. 51.
121. Ibid., p. 52.
122. Ibid., p. 53.
123. Ibid., pp. 56–57.

Chapter 2. John Fredericton

1. See Headon, *The Influence of the Oxford Movement*, p. 2.
2. Ibid.
3. See C. N. Headon, *The Influence of the Oxford Movement;* see also his "Developments in Canadian Anglican Worship," pp. 26–36.
4. Jacob Mountain was bishop of Quebec from 1793 to 1825. For more on his life see T. Millman, *Jacob Mountain, First Lord Bishop of Quebec, A Study in Church and State, 1793–1825* (Toronto: University of Toronto Press, 1947); also see Carrington, *The Anglican Church*, for numerous references.
5. Headon, *The Influence of the Oxford Movement*, p. 11.
6. George Mountain became bishop of Montreal in 1835 and of Quebec in 1836. See Carrington, *The Anglican Church*, for the outline of George Mountain's career. There are also two nineteenth-century biographies: A. W. Mountain (George Mountain's son), *A Memoir of George Jehoshaphat Mountain, D.D., D.C.L., late Bishop of Quebec* (Montreal: J. Lovell; London: S. Low, Son & Marston, 1866), and Fennings Taylor, *The Last Three Bishops Appointed by the Crown for the Anglican Church in Canada* (Montreal: J. Lovell, 1870).

7. Taylor, *The Last Three Bishops*, p. 162, as quoted by Headon, *The Influence of the Oxford Movement*, p. 13.

8. Headon, *The Influence of the Oxford Movement*, pp. 12–13.

9. Ibid.

10. A nineteenth-century biography of Feild exists, H.W. Tucker's *Memoir of the Life and Episcopate of Edward Feild, D.D., Bishop of Newfoundland, 1844–1876* (London: W. W. Gardner, 1879). More recently studies of Feild have been produced by Frederick Jones, *Bishop Feild: A Study in Politics and Religion in Nineteenth Century Newfoundland* (Ph.D. diss., University of Cambridge, 1971); *Edward Feild, Bishop of Newfoundland, 1844–1876* (St. John's: Newfoundland Historical Society, 1976.); "The Making of a Colonial Bishop: Feild of Newfoundland" in *JCCHS* 15 (March 1973): 2–12; and, "The Early Opposition to Bishop Feild of Newfoundland," *JCCHS* 16 (June 1974): 30–40. See also Edgar House, *Edward Feild: the man and his legacy* (St. John's, Nfld.: Jesperson Press, 1987); and Edward Lear, *Edward Feild (1801–1876) Ecclesiastic and Educator: His Influence on the Development of Denominational Education in Newfoundland* (M.Ed. thesis, Bishop's University, Lennoxville, Que., 1986).

11. See Jones, *Bishop Feild*, p. 13

12. Ibid., p. 14

13. Ibid.

14. Ibid., p. 22.

15. Jones, *Edward Feild*, p. 11. This seemingly harsh judgment is nevertheless confirmed by other Feild biographers, such as Lear and House.

16. Ibid., p. 12.

17. See Headon, *The Influence of the Oxford Movement*, p. 49. For more on Binney see also Carrington, *The Anglican Church*; Glen Kent, "The Right Reverend Hibbert Binney, Colonial Tractarian Bishop of Nova Scotia 1851–1887" (M.A. thesis, University of New Brunswick, 1969); and C. H. Mockridge, *The Bishops of the Church of England in Canada and Newfoundland* (Toronto: F. N. W. Brown), 1896.

18. Headon, *The Influence of the Oxford Movement*, p., 50.

19. Ibid., p. 130.

20. Hibbert Binney, *A Charge Delivered to the Clergy of the Diocese of Nova Scotia at the Vitiation Held in the Cathedral Church of St. Paul, Halifax, on the 11th* Day of October, 1854 (Halifax: Wm. Gossip, 1854) p. 24.

21. Ibid., pp. 131–32.

22. See Mockridge, *The Bishops of the Church of England in Canada*, p. 143.

23. See Kent, *The Right Reverend Hibbert Binney*, p. 188.

24. See O. R. Osmond, "The Churchmanship of John Strachan," *JCCHS* 16 (September 1974): 46–59. See also Headon, *The Influence of the Oxford Movement*, pp. 54–57.

25. For evidence of Fulford's High Church and Tractarian Sympathies see Headon, *The Influence of the Oxford Movement*, pp. 47–49; and, T. R. Millman, "A Sketch of the Life of Francis Fulford," in *JCCHS* 17 (December 1975): 82–93, especially pp.85–86.

26. See Clive Clapson, "John Travers Lewis: An Irish High Churchman in Canada West," *JCCHS* 22 (October 1980): 17–31.

27. Apart from his family and their governess, Medley was not accompanied by any entourage, or even new clergy for his diocese.

28. They were married 4 May 1864 in Westend by Southhampton, Hampshire. This information was obtained at www.familysearch.org.

29. They were married 2 January 1864 at Whangarei, Auckland, New Zealand. This information was obtained at www.familysearch.org.

30. These figures are from the Canada Census for 1861. Although censuses had been prepared in earlier years this was the first one that provided detailed religious data. This information is also quoted in Finley, *New Brunswick's Gothic Revival*, pp. 103–4.

31. See the 1891 census, which records Roman Catholics as 37 percent and Anglicans as 13.4 percent. There were 42,776 Anglicans in 1861 and 43,095 in 1891. The population of the province had swollen by 25 percent over the same period.

32. MacNutt, *New Brunswick*, p. 277.

33. Ibid., p. 278.

34. See *Riots in New Brunswick*, p. 17.

35. For more on nineteenth century Irish immigration to New Brunswick see P. M. Toner, *New Ireland Remembered: Historical Essays on the Irish in New Brunswick*, 2nd ed. (Fredericton: New Ireland Press, 1989); see also See, *Riots in New Brunswick*, chapter 3.

36. See MacNutt, *New Brunswick*, pp. 302–4.

37. See *Riots in New Brunswick*, p. 35.

38. Ibid, p. 9.

39. See *Riots in New Brunswick*, where these events are detailed.

40. The Woodstock riot of 1847 saw over three hundred Orangemen engage an equal number of Catholics, leaving at least ten dead. A dozen more were killed in another large battle in Saint John two years later. For more on these and other significant violent confrontations see See, *Riots in New Brunswick*, chapters 5–8.

41. See below, chapter 3.

42. Medley, *1850 Charge*, ibid., p. 12.

43. Ibid., pp. 12–13.

44. An account of the anti-Catholic vitriol and the various fevered conspiracy theories that peppered New Brunswick's Protestant controlled press is given in See, *Riots in New Brunswick*, chapter 3.

45. Medley, *1850 Charge*, p. 13.

46. Ibid.

47. This story is told by W. O. Raymond, "John Medley," pp. 131–2.

48. Ketchum, *Life of Medley*, p. 109.

49. See below, chapter 3.

50. This is recounted in Finley, *New Brunswick's Gothic Revival*, p. 272.

51. Accounts of such subscriptions crop up regularly in the *Annals*.

52. See Finley, *New Brunswick's Gothic Revival*, for an account of these models.

53. An account of this is contained in *The Ecclesiologist* (1853), p. 296, and quoted by Finley, *New Brunswick's Gothic Revival*, p. 191.

54. Watson, *Christ Church (Parish) Church*, p. 16 suggests that Medley was assisted in this undertaking by Lieutenant Governor Colebrooke, among others.

55. See Finley, *New Brunswick's Gothic Revival*, p. 277.

56. This document is preserved in PANB. It will henceforth be referred to as *Annals* and references will be made to the date of the written entry.

57. Ibid.

58. Among other notable Loyalists, Benedict Arnold was a member of Trinity's congregation at one point. Ross Hebb, in *The Church of England in Loyalist New Brunswick*, p. 100, describes the congregation's early resistance to even modest High Church architectural innovations.

59. PANB, Vestry Records of Trinity Church, Saint John, MC-223. The address presented to Medley is contained in minutes of a meeting held on June 9, 1845, the same day that the address was presented to Medley in Saint John.

60. The local papers were regular currents of news, both civil and ecclesiastical, from England. As we will see below, the Tractarians, and those associated with them, were notorious among the Evangelical party in Saint John.

61. This will be discussed in detail in chapter 6.

62. Ibid.

63. See Headon, *The Influence of the Oxford Movement*, p. 110.

64. Fredericton is about sixty miles north of Saint John.

65. An account of this day is given in the *Annals* as well as by Ketchum, *Life of Medley*, p. 63.

66. Medley, in a letter to the SPG, as quoted by Ketchum, *Life of Medley*, p. 63.

67. These were, in many cases, simply parishes in name—that is, civil divisions, without functioning church life.

68. Ketchum, *Life of Medley*, p. 29.

69. Ibid., p. 56. Medley provided these figures in the speech he gave on the eve on his departure for New Brunswick in May of 1845.

70. John Medley, *A Statement Respecting the Condition and Wants of his Diocese by the Bishop of Fredericton* (London: J. Masters, 1848), p. 2.

71. Ibid., p. 28.

72. *Life of Medley*, p. 28.

73. Ibid., p. 29.

74. This is quoted in Ketchum, *Life of Medley*, p. 29

75. RH, SPG letters, Medley to Hawkins, November 14, 1856.

76. Medley, *1865 Charge*, p. 7.

77. To this day the diocese of Fredericton operates without any real endowment, apart from a few small trust funds. While a few, mostly urban, New Brunswick parishes possess modest endowments, the diocese operates on a year-by-year basis. The salary of the bishop, the costs of diocesan administration and programs, and the support of aided parishes (which comprise a quarter of the diocese's eighty parishes) are entirely dependent upon monthly payments from each parish.

78. See Ketchum, *Life of Medley*, pp. 32–34, for an account of the formation of the Diocesan Church Society. The (mildly) High Church clergy of the Fredericton area were supportive of it and the Rector of Christ Church, Fredericton, Archdeacon George Coster, was its first president. For a variety of reasons, some of which were rooted in party spirit, many of the clergy of Saint John refused to join the Society. See also Finley, *New Brunswick's Gothic Revival*, pp. 120–22; T. R. Millman & A. R. Kelley, *Atlantic Canada to 1900*, pp. 76–77; and Fairweather, *A Tractarian Patriarch*, p. 17.

79. This is an extract from part of a letter printed in Ketchum, p. 35. See also Headon, *The Influence of the Oxford Movement*, pp. 106–7.

80. W. O. Raymond, *John Medley*, pp. 119–20.

81. Ibid., p. 120.

82. So Medley writes in a letter to Ernest Hawkins, secretary of the SPG. This letter, dated June 26, 1845, is quoted in C. F. Headon, "Developments in Canadian Anglican Worship," p. 28.

83. See Finley, *New Brunswick's Gothic Revival*, pp. 155–56.

84. Ibid., p. 157.

85. Saint John *Courier*, June 28, 1845 as quoted by Richardson, *Christ Church Cathedral*, p. 59.

86. PANB, Trinity Church vestry minutes, for July 15, 1845.

87. Ibid., July 23, 1845.

88. Ibid.

89. Ibid, November 11, 1845.
90. PANB, Christ Church Fredericton, vestry minutes, January 12, 1846.
91. Ibid., January 1842, minutes of the annual meeting.
92. Ketchum, *Life of Medley*, p. 65.
93. Ibid.
94. "I fear Greeks, even when bearing gifts." Ibid.
95. For example, Exeter.
96. This letter is one of eighteen Medley letters at UKC, The Rowley Collection of letters of the Anglican Bishops of Canada, ANG 43, folder number 4.
97. One well known story recounts an occasion on which the young bishop was asked by a prominent Churchman his opinion upon a recently constructed church. Looking at the Georgian structure, Medley remarked to the proud and expectant inquirer, "Sir, when you build a church, build a church, but when you build a barn, build a barn." This story appears in Raymond's "John Medley," p. 121 and is repeated by (among others) Finley in *On Earth as it is in Heaven*, p. 74.
98. Medley, 1851 SPG report. This is quoted in Finley, *On Earth as it is in Heaven*, pp. 69–70.
99. *The Church Witness* is preserved in PANB. Its masthead declared that it was "Established for the advocacy of the TRUE PRINCIPLES of the Church of England and Ireland."
100. Finley, *New Brunswick's Gothic Revival*, p. 144.
101. *Church Witness*, October 16, 1850.
102. Ibid.
103. Ibid., July 30, 1850; August 20, 1851; October 10, 1851, for instance.
104. See below, chapter 6.
105. See the *Church Witness*, especially Gray's editorial for July 30, 1851.
106. See above pp. 49–50.
107. Ibid., November 17, 1852.
108. Ibid.
109. *The Courier*, April 3, April 10, April 24 and May 1, as quoted by Finley, *New Brunswick's Gothic Revival*, p. 133.
110. *The Loyalist*, June 11, 1847, as quoted by Finley, p. 132.
111. See Finley, *New Brunswick's Gothic Revival*, pp. 236–79 for an account of Hudson's architectural influence on the diocese.
112. *The Gleaner and Northumberland Schediasma*, Chatham. N. B. Medley's letter was published along with other related correspondence on June 6, 1846.
113. Ibid.
114. *The Gleaner*, August 8, 1846.
115. Medley warned his clergy about the error of Newman's "doctrine" on this point. See below, pp. 84–88.
116. Ibid.
117. Fulford of Montreal, while generally sympathetic to Tractarian principles, similarly distanced himself from any explicit defense of them, lest he be thought a "party man." See Headon, *The Influence of the Oxford Movement*, p. 122. So too, Hibbert Binney in Nova Scotia made pains to avoid any positions that would be explicitly those of the Tractarian party. Ibid., p. 130.
118. Ibid.
119. For a detailed account of this see Watson, *Christ Church Cathedral*. Chapter 4 below will provide more on St. Anne's.
120. RH, SPG letters, Medley to Hawkins, vol. 2, February 14, 1855.
121. *Annals*, August 4 to September 7, 1846.

122. Ibid.

123. This story, contained in Charles Medley's annual report to the SPG, is recounted by Ketchum, *Life of Medley*, pp. 131–32.

124. Harding, *Citizens with the Saints*, p. 21.

125. *Annals*, December 20, 1885.

126. See Harding, *Citizens with the Saints*, p. 38.

127. Harding, *Citizens*, Ibid., p. 38. An M.A. thesis on Kingdon, written from a hostile Evangelical perspective was prepared by Lee Potter, "The Episcopate of Hollingworth Tully Kingdon, Second Lord Bishop of Fredericton" (M.A. thesis, University of New Brunswick, 1970).

128. For more on Webb see *ODCC* and *DNB.* Also, see Peter Anson, in *Fashions in Church Furnishings 1840–1940* (London: Studio Vista, 1965), pp. 203–4 for a brief account of St. Andrew's, Wells St., under Webb.

129. See E. R. Fairweather, "A Milestone in Canadian Theology: Bishop Kingdon's *God Incarnate*" *Canadian Journal of Theology* 4 (April 1958).

130. See Harding, *Citizens*, pp. 37–38.

131. Medley, *The Advantages of Open Seats*, p. 3.

132. Harding, *John by Divine Permission*, p. 82.

133. Headon, *The Influence of the Oxford Movement*, pp. 114–15.

134. *Life of Medley*, p. 279.

135. This letter is reprinted by Ketchum, *Life of Medley*, p. 331.

136. Ibid.

137. RH, SPG letters, Kingdon to Tucker, July 3, 1891.

138. *Annals*, January 27, 1879.

139. Sir Henry Acland (1815–1900) was the son of Sir Thomas Acland (1787–1871). Thomas had been M.P. for Devon and a lifelong friend of the Coleridges and Kebles. He was a supporter of the Tractarians and friend of Medley. Henry, in turn, was also interested in church matters, especially Ecclesiology, as a friend of John Ruskin. See *DNB* entries on the Aclands.

140. While Medley preached for Lowder and, according to the *Annals*, received a gift of a gold chalice from him, we have no indication that they had any closer relationship. In a letter to his sister, recorded by Maria Trench, Lowder remarks, concerning Medley's visit: "The Bishop of Fredericton, a very nice old man, Dr. Medley, preached during the festival." This hardly suggests any great intimacy between the two. See *Charles Lowder* (London: Kegan Paul, 1881).

141. All of this information is contained in the *Annals*.

142. BL, Gladstone Papers, vol. 370, MS 44455, f. 322. A letter from Medley to Gladstone dated December 14, 1877, indicates Medley's "greatest pleasure to comply with your kind request."

143. BL, Gladstone Papers, vol. 372, MS 44786, f. 61. Letter from Medley to Gladstone dates July 23, 1878.

144. See Morley, *Life of Gladstone* (Toronto: Morang, 1903), 3:259.

145. See H. C. G. Matthew, *Gladstone 1875–1898*, pp. 11, 67, 237, 300, and 317.

146. Ibid., p. 281.

147. BL, Gladstone Papers, vol. 701, MS 44786, f. 61. For more on Gladstone's relationship with Ruskin, see Michael Wheeler "Gladstone and Ruskin," in *Gladstone*, ed. Peter J. Jagger (London: The Hambledon Press, 1998) pp. 177–96.

148. See *Annals.* See also R. J. E. Boggis, *A History of St. Augustine's College, Canterbury* (Canterbury: Cross & Jackman, 1907), pp. 70, 74, where Medley's attendance at the inauguration of St. Augustine's in 1848 is mentioned.

149. See *Annals.*

150. Ketchum, *Life of Medley*, p. 278.
151. *Annals*.
152. This last account was given by Margaret Medley and recorded by Ketchum, *Life of Medley*, p. 295.
153. See Ketchum, *Life of Medley*, p. 302.
154. Ibid., p. 319. This association with American High Churchmen had begin early in Medley's episcopate. Medley traveled to Boston to preach at the Church of the Advent in 1851. See *Two Discourses Preached in the Church of the Advent, Boston on Sunday, October 19, 1851* (Boston: Charles Stimpson, 1851). In return, the Rector of the Church of the Advent, Horatio Southgate, was Medley's choice to preach at the consecration of Christ Church Cathedral. See *A Sermon preached at the Consecration of Christ Church Cathedral, Fredericton, N.B* by The Right Reverend Horatio Southgate, D.D. Late Missionary Bishop at Constantinople, and Rector of the Church of the Advent, Boston, Mass. (Boston: Ticknor, Reed, and Fields, 1853).
155. Ibid., p. 307.
156. Heeney, "John Medley," p. 127.
157. The *Annals* record each church consecrated.
158. For an account of the socioeconomic character of nineteenth-century New Brunswick, see W. S. MacNutt, *New Brunswick, A History*.
159. The agonizing process and the many individual hardships that this caused are made clear during the course of Medley's correspondence to the SPG.
160. PANB, Diocese of Fredericton, Synod Journal for 1871.
161. *RH*, 1846 SPG report.
162. *Annals*, August 23, 1848. For more on Coleridge, see *DNB*. See also Boggis, *A History of St. Augustine's College*, pp. 168–70.
163. Boggis, *A History of St. Augustine's College*, lists seventeen students of St. Augustine's as sailing for Fredericton, pp. 312–27. It is interesting that during the episcopate of Medley's successor, H. T. Kingdon, no additional St. Augustine's alumni joined the diocese.
164. For example see the letters of John Medley to F. W. Vroom, copies of which are preserved at PANB, MC223, DB-1–4J.
165. Medley to Vroom, November 10, 1879.
166. Blom and Blom, *Canada Home*, pp. 32–35. Among note papers found in the books of Medley's library were numerous German vocabulary sheets he had written out to study. See PANB, MC223, DB-1–4I.
167. John Medley, *The Book of Job, Translated from the Hebrew Text, with an Introduction, A Summary of Each Chapter, and Brief Notes in Explanation of Obscure Passages* (St. John: J. & A. McMillan).
168. To be discussed in detail below in chapter 4.
169. Timothy Gene Cooper, *Church Music in Nineteenth-Century Canada*, p. 77.
170. Ibid.
171. Ibid., pp. 76–77.
172. Ketchum prints a number of letters from former members of Medley's choir, who wrote after his death to recount anecdotes and happy memories of their time with the bishop, *Life of Medley*, pp. 323–30.
173. Medley also served as his own dean, leading the daily offices personally and being the principal celebrant and preacher on most Sundays.
174. For a mention of the resistance to Medley's musical innovations see D. F. Cook, "A Survey of Hymnody," p. 48.
175. *Annals*, 23 April, 1890.
176. See Nockles, *The Oxford Movement in Context*, pp. 79–85. He describes

Froude's disestablishmentarian tendency and its effect on Keble, among others. However, none of the principal Tractarians, apart from Froude, publicly and explicitly denounced establishment.

177. Ibid., p. 62. Nockles goes on to persuasively demonstrate the older High Church recognition of the church's spiritual independence. See pp. 63–67.

178. The tendency was for diocesan meetings to declare themselves as "synods" even prior to enabling state legislation. For example, such a organization took place in Toronto in 1851 and was not legally recognized until an act allowing synodical government was passed in 1857. In Nova Scotia, the first synodical meeting took place in 1856, in Quebec in 1859 and in the diocese of Ontario in 1862. See Carrington, *The Anglican Church*, chapters 8–9 for the history of this development; also Ross Hebb, in an unpublished paper delivered at the Church History Conference of the ecclesiastical province of Canada, *The Establishment of Synodical Government in Maritime Canada: 1850–1871* (Halifax, July 8, 1993).

179. John William Colenso (1814–1883) was appointed the first bishop of Natal in southern Africa. A biblical scholar, he authored a critical introduction to the Pentateuch that challenged Mosaic authorship. He was subsequently deposed by his metropolitan, Robert Gray of Cape Town. He did not deny the specific charge, but that Gray had jurisdiction over him. (ODCC) For more on Colenso see Chadwick, *The Victorian Church*, 2:90–97; Peter Hinchliff, *John William Colenso, Bishop of Natal* (London: Nelson, 1964); Jeff Guy, *The Heretic: a Study of the Life of John William Colenso, 1814–1883* (Johannesburg: Ravan Press, 1983). For a recent, (and more positive) account of Colenso, see Gerald Parsons, "Rethinking the Missionary Position: Bishop Colenso of Natal," in John Wolffe, ed., *Religion in Victorian Britain*, vol. 5, *Culture & Empire* (Manchester: Manchester University Press, 1997).

180. Hinchliff, *John William Colenso*, p. 153.

181. Chadwick, *The Victorian Church*, 2:93.

182. *Annals*, July 15, 1866. At a meeting of clerical and lay delegates to the Diocesan Church Society, the desirability of a synod was affirmed and a committee formed to make preparations. The following year, Synod met and a constitution was passed. The development of synodical government is dealt with in detail in chapter 6 below.

183. Details in his obituary, which Medley had affixed to the *Annals*, October 12, 1878.

184. See Burns, *The Diocesan Revival*, for the revival of ruridecanal institutions in the Victorian Church of England, chapter 4.

185. *Annals*, June 11, 1847.

186. *Annals*, June 29, 1874. See also the Synod Journal for that year.

187. A brief account of this process is given by Harding, *Citizens with the Saints*, p. 32.

Chapter 3. Medley's Intellectual Context

1. Frances Knight provides another illustration of the contradictory positions that one might reasonably expect to find in people, when they are studied in sufficient detail to see them as more than cardboard stereotypes. She describes two Victorian clergymen, Francis Massingberd and John Rashdall, who might easily have been taken as representatives of Tractarianism and Evangelicalism, respectively. Upon closer examination, their actual positions were much broader than any such simple characterization could encompass. See *The Nineteenth Century Church and English Society* (Cambridge: Cambridge University Press, 1995), p. 210.

2. Fairweather, "A Tractarian Patriarch."

3. Finley, *New Brunswick's Gothic Revival*, p. 286 and 297.

4. This argument has been made by Gregg Finley in *New Brunswick's Gothic Revival*. Finley's thesis about Medley's place in Canadian cultural history turns upon seeing Medley as simultaneously a representative of the Romantic movement and British Imperialism. In fact, it is far from clear that he was either, in any simple sense.

5. In support of this assertion see Agnes Addison, *Romanticism and the Gothic Revival.* She traces the development of the Gothic movement and offers circumstantial evidence for its connection to Romanticism. Gregg Finley takes up Addison's argument in his thesis. However, Finley too closely identifies the Gothic Revival with the Tractarian Movement. See *New Brunswick's Gothic Revival*, p. 49. Although related, the two movements ought not to be simply equated.

6. For a recent account of the relationship between Tractarianism, ritualism, and the Ecclesiological movement see Yates, *Anglican Ritualism in Victorian Britain*, pp. 48 *ff.*

7. Sheridan Gilley, "John Keble and the Victorian Churching of Romanticism," in *An Infinite Complexity: Essays in Romanticism*, ed. J. R. Watson (Edinburgh: Edinburgh University Press, 1983), p. 232.

8. Ibid., p. 236.

9. Pusey, *Parochial Sermons*, 1: viii, as quoted by Nockles, *The Oxford Movement*, p. 201.

10. Crouse, "Deepened by the Study of the Fathers," pp. 144–47.

11. J. S. Mill, *Dissertations I*, quoted by Crouse, "Deepened by the Study of the Fathers," pp. 143–44.

12. For more on Coleridge's relationship to the Enlightenment and his subsequent influences on the Tractarians, especially Newman, see Hedley, "Participation in the Divine Life."

13. Crouse, "Deepened by the Study of the Fathers," p. 147.

14. Nockles, *The Oxford Movement*, p. 203.

15. Ibid.

16. For Liddon's account of this see *Life of Pusey*, I, 146–77. This has been more recently explored by David Forrester in *Young Doctor Pusey* (London: Mowbray, 1989).

17. See R. D. Crouse, "Deepened by the Study of the Fathers," pp. 137–48. Here he argues that Tractarianism generally should "be seen, not as an isolated phenomenon, but within the broad context of a movement of antirationalism, or neo-pietism, widespread in early nineteenth century Europe; a movement that in protestant Germany (largely through the influence of Pusey's special friends) involved a revival of pietism and Lutheran orthodoxy, and in France, and in catholic Germany, as well as in England, inspired a new religious interest in Christian antiquity" (p. 144).

18. Johann Neander (1789–1850) was a Jewish-born church historian who, after studying under Schleiermacher, converted to Christianity. He wrote a critical response to D. F. Strauss's *Leben Jesu*, that most rationalistic of early nineteenth century Christian works. See *ODCC.*

19. F. A. G. Tholuck (1799–1877) was influenced by Neander and became a dedicated opponent of rationalism. See *ODCC.*

20. F. D. E. Schleiermacher (1768–1834) was the most influential member of this school of theologians. He is usually associated with the Romantic movement in Germany.

21. As quoted by W. J. Hankey in "Making Theology Practical," p. 89. Prof. Hankey offers a useful and critical account of the relation of the Tractarians, such as

Pusey, to the overall revolt against the Enlightenment. He includes the Roman Catholic response as expressed in Pope Leo XIII's promotion of Thomas Aquinas as a defense against this "evil teaching" (p. 90).

22. Liddon, *Life of Pusey*, 1: 84–85.

23. W. J. Hankey in "Making Theology Practical: Thomas Aquinas and the Nineteenth Century Religious Revival," *Dionysius* 9 (December 1985), p. 89.

24. Ibid., p. 124.

25. Ibid.

26. See Rowell, *The Vision Glorious*, pp. 11–14.

27. Ibid., p. 247.

28. John Medley, *Episcopal Form,* p. 22.

29. John Medley, *How are the Mighty Fallen* (Exeter: P. A. Hannaford; also London: Rivingtons and Longmans; and Oxford: Parker, 1840), p. 17.

30. Ibid., p. 20.

31. Ibid.

32. Ibid.

33. Ibid., p. 21.

34. The early Evangelical roots of several Tractarian figures are well known. For example, on Newman's background see Sheridan Gilley, *Newman and his Age,* part 1; see also Rowell, *The Vision Glorious*, pp. 44ff. On Newman's own account see *Apologia Pro Vita Sua* (New York: W. W. Norton, 1968), chapter I.

35. Medley, *How are the Mighty Fallen*, p. 21.

36. Ibid., p. 9.

37. PH, Letters of John Medley to E. B. Pusey (Pus. 29/1). This letter is undated, but another hand has added 1840 to the top of the page. Parts of this correspondence were printed, without commentary, by Christopher Headon in "An Unpublished Correspondence," pp. 72–74. The rest of this letter is discussed above, p. 28.

38. London: S. Manship, 1697.

39. Ibid.

40. See entries in the *ODCC* and *DNB.*

41. Quoted in John Hoyles, *The Waning of the Renaissance 1640–1740* (The Hague: Martinus Nijhoff, 1971) p. 6.

42. Ibid., Norris, *Reason and Faith*, preface.

43. For more on Toland see *DNB; ODCC;* R. E. Sullivan, *John Toland and the Deist Controversy: A Study in Adaptations* (Cambridge: Harvard University Press, 1982); and S. H. Daniel, *John Toland: His Method, Manners and Mind* (Kingston: McGill-Queen's University Press, 1984). Toland dismissed the realm of the mysterious as medieval superstition, arguing that "there is nothing in the Gospel; contrary to reason, nor above it" (from the subtitle to the work).

44. For example, other replies to Toland were written by Peter Browne, *A letter in answer to a book entituled, Christianity not Mysterious* (London: North, 1697); Jean Gailhard, *The blasphemous Socinian heresie disproved and confuted . . . with animadversions upon a late book called, Christianity not Mysterious* (London: Wellington, 1697); Edward Stillingfleet, *The Bishop of Worcester's answer to Mr. Locke's letter, . . . with a postscript in answer to some reflections made on that treatise in a late Socinian pamphlet* (London: Henry Mortlock, 1697); Thomas Beverly, *Christianity, the great mystery: in answer to a late treatise, Christianity not mysterious* (London: W. Marshal, 1696).

45. Norris, *Reason and Faith*, p. 7. He makes clear (p. 16) that he is not attempting to prove the particular doctrines of the Trinity or Incarnation, but only that they *may* be believed.

46. Ibid., p. 10. Norris employs Descartes on this point, quoting from his *Meditations on First Philosophy.*

47. Ibid., p. 11.

48. Ibid., p. 14.

49. Ibid.

50. Ibid., pp. 116–17. Medley was not alone in his admiration for Norris. Richard Acworth in *The Philosophy of John Norris of Bemerton* (New York: Georg Olms, 1979), p. 348, points out that his work had been commended by Daniel Waterland and William van Mildert.

51. Ibid., p. 12.

52. Norris, *Reason and Faith*, as quoted by David A. Pailin, "Rational Religion in England from Herbert of Cherbury to William Paley," in Gilley and Sheils, *A History of Religion in Britain*, p. 217.

53. Medley, *How are the Mighty Fallen*, p. 29

54. Ibid.

55. Ibid., p. 35.

56. Ibid., p. 36.

57. For an account of the Tractarian approach to Patristic study see R. D. Crouse, "Devout Perusal: The Tractarian Revival of Patristic studies," in E. A. Livingstone, ed., *Studia Patristica,* vol. 18 (Kalamazoo and Louvain, 1990), pp 328–34. "Tractarian patristic scholarship was strongly practical, and certainly not disinterested. It was 'devout perusal' in the service of faith and piety, and not much concerned with criticism." p. 331. See also Nockles, *The Oxford Movement*, p. 205.

58. Ibid., p. 12.

59. Ibid. See below, where Medley's understanding of architecture will be discussed in detail in chapter 4.

60. Medley, *Elementary Remarks*, p. 39.

61. On Pusey's sense of his own utter depravity, and by extension, the depravity of human nature, see Gabriel O'Donnell "The Spirituality of E. B. Pusey," in *Pusey Rediscovered*, pp. 231–54. For an even darker account of Pusey's spiritual perspective see David Forrester's *Young Doctor Pusey* (London: Mowbray, 1989).

62. John Medley, *Two Ordination Sermons Preached in Christ Church Cathedral* (Fredericton: J. Simpson, 1846).

63. Francis Bacon, *Advancement of Human Learning*, as quoted in Medley, *Two Ordination Sermons*, p. 16.

64. Ibid., Medley, *Two Ordination Sermons*, p. 16.

65. Ibid., p. 17.

66. Ibid.

67. Ibid.

68. Medley's library, held at Christ Church Cathedral, bears out this observation. There is a substantial collection of chiefly German conservative critical scholarship represented on its shelves. This is mostly in translation. Medley did not take up the study of German until he was over sixty. A full catalog of the Medley library has been produced by Eric Swannick and Mark Lewis.

69. Blom and Blom, *Canada Home,* p. 31.

70. John Medley, *The Reformation, its Nature, its Necessity and its Benefits* (Fredericton: James P. A. Phillips, 1847), pp. 19–20.

71. Medley also associated this view of the Articles with Ward, as we saw above, p. 63.

72. Ibid., 11. Medley says that "persecution for religion is a religious crime, and a political blunder." He goes to argue that the advent of universal toleration is a good thing, unless "we confound toleration with scepticism."

73. Ibid., p. 10.

74. John Henry Newman published *An Essay on the Development of Christian Doctrine* in 1845, immediately following his joining the Roman Catholic Church, although the book had been written while he was still an Anglican. He argues there for an evolutionary development of the Christian doctrine: "Unless some special ground of exception can be assigned, it is as evident that Christianity, as a doctrine and worship, will develop in the minds of recipients, as that it conforms in other respects, in its general propagation or its political framework, to the general methods by which the course of things is carried forward" (New York: Image Books, 1960), p. 79. For a full bibliography of literature on this work see Crumb, *The Oxford Movement*.

75. Ibid., Medley, *The Reformation*, p. 11.

76. See above, p. 30. Even as early as the summer of 1845, Medley had indicated his disapproval of Newman's views.

77. See above, p. 30.

78. Medley, *The Reformation*, p. 1.

79. Ibid., p. 28.

80. Ibid., pp. 28–29.

81. This was to be in addition to the "Bray Library" that was already in the Diocese, located at Trinity Church Saint John. These libraries, the idea of Thomas Bray, founder of the SPCK and the SPG were established in many colonial dioceses and parishes. Interestingly, A. P. Forbes embarked on a similar project to establish a diocesan library early on in his episcopate. See Strong, *Forbes of Brechin*, p. 80.

82. John Medley, *1850 Charge* (Saint John: W. L. Avery, 1850), p. 8.

83. Ibid, p. 9.

84. Ibid., p. 11.

85. Ibid.

86. Ibid., p. 20.

87. Ibid., p. 18. This concern had been shared with Pusey in a letter some years earlier. See above, Chapter 1.

88. Ibid., p. 25.

89. See chapter 5.

90. Robert Crouse, "Christology from Chalcedon to Anselm," in *Who do you say that I am: The Person and Mission of Jesus Christ* (Charlottetown: St. Peter Publications, 1998), p. 77, makes the point that for Anselm and medieval theology generally the Chalcedonian Christological definition was paradigmatic of the entire relation of nature to the divine. That is, nature exists in union with the divine, while maintaining its own integrity. Or as Aquinas famously expresses the relationship "*gratia non tollat natura, sed perficiat*" (S.Th. I, 1, 8 *ad* 2).

91. Ibid., p. 13.

92. John Medley, *Faint, Yet Pursuing: An Ordination Sermon Preached in the Cathedral of Christ Church, Fredericton* (Fredericton: J. Simpson, 1856), p. 6.

93. In his support of the English Reformation he makes this clear. His sermon on the Reformation, which we looked at above, and to which we will return below, strongly criticizes the medieval Roman Church for its "errors and superstitions."

94. John Medley, *A Charge to the clergy of the diocese, at his fourth triennial visitation holden in Christ Church Cathedral, Fredericton, 1856* (Fredericton, N.B.: J. Simpson), p. 59.

95. John Medley, *A Charge delivered in Christ Church Cathedral, Fredericton, September 13th, 1865, at the Triennial Visitation by John, Bishop of Fredericton* (Saint John: Wm. M. Wright), p. 14.

96. One of the principal causes of Gray's censure of Colenso concerned his claimed demonstration of the factual (and chronological) inconsistencies of Genesis.
97. Medley, *1865 Charge*, p. 15. Charles Darwin had published *The Origin of Species* in 1859.
98. Ibid.
99. John Medley, *The Book of Job*.
100. Ibid., p. ix.
101. Among his sources Medley names Schultens, Rosenmüller, Goode, Lee, Driver, Canon Barry, and the bishop of Lincoln (Christopher Wordsworth).
102. Medley, *The Book of Job*, p. x.
103. In this, Medley was more optimistic than, for example, his contemporary, A. P. Forbes of Brechin. While cautiously approving of science in some fields, Forbes was extremely wary of its value to biblical studies. See Strong, *Forbes of Brechin*, pp. 187–89
104. Medley, *1865 Charge*, p. 18.
105. Ibid.
106. For more on the Gorham case see below, pp. 114–15.
107. Medley, *1865 Charge*, p. 18.
108. Ibid., p. 24.
109. John Medley, *The Mission of the Comforter* (Fredericton: Henry A. Cropley, 1867), p. 8.
110. Ibid., p. 15. In affirming that man requires divine aid to do any good work, Medley was simply affirming the Anglican formularies. See Article XIII "Works done before the grace of Christ, and the inspiration of his Spirit, are not pleasant to God, forasmuch as they spring not of faith in Jesus Christ, neither do they make men meet to receive grace, or (as the School-authors say) deserve grace of congruity: yea rather, for that they are not done as God hath willed and commanded them to be done, we doubt not but that they have the nature of sin."
111. Ibid., p. 16.
112. Ibid., p. 18.
113. John Medley, *1868 Charge*, p. 10.
114. Ibid.
115. Ibid., pp. 10–11.
116. Ibid., p. 12.
117. In fact, quite the contrary is true. Near the end of his life, in 1887, Medley recalled the deplorable state of the Church fifty years previous and expressed great satisfaction at the progress made. See below, conclusion.
118. John Medley, *1871 Charge*, p. 6.
119. In a sermon preached in 1877 before the Provincial Synod, he asked "how far has the spirit of the age insensibly led us all away from the Apostolic standard?" (Montreal: Lovell, 1877), p. 7. Yet, even here, he did not advocate legislation to correct perceived errors in religious doctrine or practice. The answer was to be found in "sound knowledge" for "the power of truth is stronger than the force of law." (ibid., p. 11).
120. Ibid., p. 8.
121. Ibid.
122. John Medley, *1886 Charge*, p. 7.

Chapter 4. Medley the Ecclesiologist

1. See entry in *ODCC*. A full history of the group is given by James F. White, *The Cambridge Movement: The Ecclesiologists and the Gothic Revival* (Cambridge; Cambridge University Press, 1962)

2. White, *The Cambridge Movement,* pp. 38–39.

3. Ibid., p. 25.

4. For a history of the Gothic Revival prior to the Camden Society see Addison, *Romanticism and the Gothic Revival,* especially chapters 2 and 3. More recently, Nigel Yates has detailed the origins of Victorian ritualism and the interrelation of Tractarianism, ritualism, and ecclesiology in *Anglican Ritualism in Victorian Britain,* esp. chapter 2. See also Nigel Yates, *Buildings, Faith and Worship: The Liturgical Arrangement of Anglican Churches 1600–1900* (Oxford: Clarendon Press, 1991), pp. 115–9 for pre-Camdenite and pre-Tractarian ecclesiological development.

5. See Yates, *Anglican Ritualism*, p. 50.

6. For an account of Victorian Church societies, see Burns, *The Diocesan Revivial,* pp. 115–30.

7. See White, *The Cambridge Movement*, p. 44 for a list of other Ecclesiological societies.

8. See Chris Brooks, "Building the Rural Church: Money Power and the Country Parish" in *The Victorian Church: Architecture and Society* (Manchester: Manchester University Press, 1995), p. 63. Brooks suggests that the Exeter society was the first such organization at a diocesan level.

9. Ibid. Cherry lists Viscount Courtenay, Earl Egremont, and Lord Clinton as among the influential early members. See p. 179.

10. See Cherry, "Patronage and the local architect" in *The Victorian Church*, p. 179.

11. Brooks, "Patronage," p. 176.

12. Ibid., pp. 180–81.

13. Ibid.

14. Ibid., p. 179.

15. See above chapter 1, where Medley's former curate furnished evidence of Medley's role in the founding. This was verified by the Annual Report of the society for 1845, when, on the occasion of Medley's having resigned in order to take up the See of Fredericton, a tribute to him recorded his seminal role in the organization.

16. Finley says that Medley's architectural interest had begun at Wadham, but supplies no evidence of this. Detailed studies of Medley's architectural contributions have been carried out. The works of Gregg Finley and Douglas Richardson, mentioned above, are fully devoted to Medley and the churches he built. Stanton's *The Gothic Revival* contains lengthy examinations of two of Medley's New Brunswick churches.

17. Agnes Addison suggests that the name "Ecclesiologist" as well as "ecclesiology" were inventions of the Camden Society. White provides evidence that the terms had been used, albeit with a different meaning a few years before the Camden society appropriated it and gave to it its more conventional sense. See *Romanticism and the Gothic Revival,* p. 68. See also J. F. White, *The Cambridge Movement*, p. 48. A more recent account of the role of ecclesiology in the Victorian Church is given by Nigel Yates, *Buildings, Faith and Worship*, chapter 8.

18. John Medley, *Elementary Remarks on Church Architecture*. The *Ecclesiologist* declared that it could recommend the work "most safely." See Cherry, "Patronage," in *The Victorian Church*, p. 181.

19. See Stanton, *The Gothic Revival*, p. 128.

20. Ibid. One of these articles was an architectural study of Exeter Cathedral.

21. Medley, *Elementary Remarks*, pp. 11–12.

22. See Finley and Wigginton, *On Earth as it is in Heaven*, pp. 69–74. For a recent scholarly account of the state of church architecture on the eve of the ecclesio-

logical movement see Yates's two works, *Buildings, Faith and Worship* and *Anglican Ritualism in Victorian Britain*. Yates makes clear that the ecclesiologists' criticisms of the preceding architectural periods were far from dispassionate and, thus, not always accurate or fair.

23. Here Medley is referring to the system of "pews." In his day this meant boxed stalls, with doors that were often either rented or sold to prosperous families. They became the private preserve of their owners and were particular targets of the Tractarians and ecclesiologists.

24. Medley, *Elementary Remarks*, p. 37.

25. John Medley, *Open Seats*, p. 2.

26. Medley, *Elementary Remarks*, p. 39.

27. Medley, *Sermon at the Consecration*, p. 13.

28. John Medley, *The Advantage of Open Seats*. This was originally published in the first volume of the proceedings of the EDAS.

29. J. M. Neale, *A History of Pues* (Oxford: Parker, 1842). On the Ecclesiologists' opposition to pews (and galleries) see Nigel Yates, *Buildings, Faith and Worship*, pp. 159–60.

30. *Ecclesiologist* (June 1942), as quoted by Finley, *New Brunswick's Gothic Revival*, p. 92.

31. Ibid., Finley, p. 90.

32. PANB, Fulford manuscript, p. 3.

33. Medley, *The Advantages of Open Seats*, p. 13.

34. Medley, *Open Seats*, p. 4.

35. *New Brunswick's Gothic Revival*, pp. 94–95.

36. Medley, *Open Seats*, p. 4.

37. Ibid. p. 5.

38. John Keble, "No. 89," *The Tracts for the Times*, vol. 4, pp. 148 and 151. The source of this notion of the *verba visibilia* was Augustine's *De doctrina Christiana*, see 2: 5.

39. See also Gilley, "The Victorian Churching of Romanticism," p. 231.

40. See above, chapter 1.

41. *The Transactions of the Exeter Diocesan Architectural Society* appeared between 1843 and 1894. The Medley Library at Christ Church Cathedral, Fredericton preserves copies of them.

42. *First Annual Report of the Exeter Diocesan Architectural Society, read at the general meeting of the subscribers, April 7, 1842* (Exeter: P. A. Hannaford, 1843), p. 3.

43. Ibid., p. 8.

44. Ibid., pp. 8–9.

45. *Second Annual report of the Exeter Diocesan Architectural Society, read at the annual meeting, holden in the College Hall, April 6, 1843* (Exeter: P. A. Hannaford 1843), pp. 18–20.

46. Ibid, pp. 13–14.

47. See below, chapter 5.

48. *Annual Report of the Exeter Diocesan Architectural Society* (Exeter: P. A. Hannaford 1844), p. 5.

49. This compared with the Camden Society's membership of 750.

50. *Quarterly Report*, read July 24, 1845. Printed in the proceedings of the EDAS, p. 104.

51. Ibid., p. 105.

52. Ibid.

53. Ibid.

54. John Bacon Jr., the eminent sculptor, came out of retirement to execute his daughter's monument. An account of this impressive memorial has been written by C. L. Brooks and J. H. Cox, "John Bacon Junior and the Medley Memorial," *International Society for the Study of Church Monuments* 7(1982): 129–33.

55. Ibid., p. 128.

56. Ketchum, *Life of Medley*, p. 59.

57. *Ecclesiologist*, July 1842, as quoted by Stanton, p. 128.

58. PANB, Fulford manuscript, pp. 3–4.

59. This extract from *The Ecclesiologist's* review of the chapel is quoted by Martin Cherry, "Patronage" in *The Victorian Church*, p. 181.

60. Ibid.

61. For Victorian attitudes toward Georgian ecclesiastical architecture see Yates, *Buildings, Faith and Worship*, pp. 175–78.

62. Ibid., p. 64.

63. See an account of the state of pre-Medley New Brunswick ecclesiastical architecture in Finley, *New Brunswick's Gothic Revival*, p. 116–20; see also, Finley and Wigginton, *On Earth as it is in Heaven*, pp. 70–76.

64. Finley and Wigginton, *On Earth as it is in Heaven*, p. 70.

65. W. A. Spray, *David's Kingdom* (Chatham: St. Paul's Church Corporation, 1979), p. 20.

66. For more on the arrangements of Anglican churches in the eighteenth and early nineteenth century, including a defense against the commonly leveled charge of neglect, see Nigel Yates, *Buildings, Faith and Worship*, especially chapter 3.

67. Medley's architectural principles and achievements are comprehensively detailed in the various works by Gregg Finley.

68. RH, SPG letters, vol. 2, folios 119ff, letter dated August 2, 1851.

69. The development and significance of this wooden Gothic style is fully explored by Finley in *New Brunswick's Gothic Revival*. See also, D. S. Richardson, "Hyperborean Gothic; or Wilderness Ecclesiology and the Wood Churches of Edward Medley," *Architecture* 2 (1972): 42–74

70. See Paul Thompson, *William Butterfield* (London: Routledge and Kegan Paul, 1971), p. 346, where Edward Medley is mentioned as a pupil of Butterfield's.

71. Finley & Wigginton, *On Earth as it is in Heaven*, p. 136.

72. D. S. Richardson, "Hyperborean Gothic," p. 44.

73. Finley and Wigginton, *On Earth as it is in Heaven*, p. 136.

74. Ketchum, *Life of Medley*, p. 64.

75. *Annals.*

76. Ibid.

77. See Stanton, *The Gothic Revival*, p. 129.

78. PANB, Christ Church Parish vestry records. The vestry minutes for June 2, 1845, record that the address presented to Bishop Medley on his arrival assured him that their church would accommodate his need for a cathedral "until a more suitable building shall have been provided."

79. PANB, Christ Church vestry minutes for July 14, 1845.

80. Ibid., October 7, 1845.

81. Ketchum, *Life of Medley*, p. 67–74, gives an account of the occasion.

82. RH, SPG Letters, vol. 2, *ff.* 225–330, letter dated August 26, 1854. See also Bob Watson, *Christ Church (Parish) Church*, p. 18.

83. See Ketchum, *Life of Medley*, chapters 3 and 4, for an account of the archdeacon's devotion and faithful labours.

84. Richardson, *Christ Church Cathedral*, also recounts the history of relation

between the three Fredericton churches: Christ Church, the cathedral, and St. Anne's.

85. Medley's choice of Snettisham and its background is discussed by D. F. Richardson, *Christ Church Cathedral, Fredericton*, p. 41–43.

86. The *Ecclesiologist* lamented "that so well-meant, so noble an attempt at better things, should not embody all those characteristic features of an English cathedral, which modern research has already put us in possession of" (Feb. 1846, as quoted by Stanton, *The Gothic Revival*, 129.

87. Richardson's thesis is substantially concerned with the life and career of Frank Wills. Stanton as well chronicles Wills's subsequent work through North America. Wills was to go on to become the official architect of the New York Ecclesiological Society, mirroring the position held by the celebrated Gothic revival architect William Butterfield with the Cambridge Camden Society. Butterfield himself, the architect of such Tractarian strongholds as All Saints', Margaret Street, eventually contributed designs for much of the interior of the cathedral.

88. Stanton, *The Gothic Revival*, pp. 142–43. See also Bob Watson, *Christ Church Cathedral: A History*, pp. 21–24.

89. See Stanton pp. 142–43.

90. *Ecclesiologist*, June 1847, as quoted by Finley, *New Brunswick's Gothic Revival*, p. 155.

91. See the proceedings for the EDAS, 1847.

92. Stanton, *The Gothic Revival*, p. 130.

93. St. Anne's was consecrated March 14, 1847. An account of the service is found in the *Annals*.

94. *Annals*, 30 May 1846.

95. Medley and Wills collaborated on four more New Brunswick churches. See Finley and Wigginton, *On Earth as it is in Heaven*, p. 109.

96. For a more detailed study of St. Anne's chapel see Robert Watson, *Christ Church (Parish) Church*; and Stanton, *The Gothic Revival*, pp. 127–58.

97. Stanton, *The Gothic Revival*, p. 130. More about the character of St. Anne's will be given in chapter 4.

98. John Medley, *The Staff of Beauty and the Staff of Bands* (Saint John: Avery, 1847).

99. Ibid.

100. See Harding, *John, By Divine Permission*, p. 22.

101. John Medley, *1847 Charge*, p. 31.

102. Medley, *The Staff of Beauty*, pp. 5–6.

103. Ibid., p. 6.

104. Ibid., pp. 7–8.

105. Ibid., p. 9.

106. Ibid.

107. Ibid., p. 11.

108. On Keble's Romanticism see Rowell, *The Vision Glorious*, pp. 27–33. See also Sheridan Gilley, "John Keble and the Victorian Churching of Romanticism."

109. Medley, *Staff of Beauty*, pp. 11–12.

110. Ibid.

111. Ibid., p. 14.

112. Ibid.

113. Ibid., p. 15.

114. Ibid., p. 16.

115. John Medley, *1850 Charge*, p. 22.

116. Ibid., p. 45.
117. Ibid.
118. John Medley, *1853 Charge*, p. 5.
119. Ibid., p. 46.
120. Ibid. 47.
121. Due to cost, however, Medley was forced to build nearly all of his churches in New Brunswick out of wood.
122. Medley, *1853 Charge*, pp. 1–2.
123. *1853 Charge*, pp. 5–6.
124. Ibid., p. 11.
125. John Medley, *The Mission of the Comforter*, p. 7.
126. Ibid., p. 9.
127. See Finley, *New Brunswick's Gothic Revival*, pp. 190–94.
128. On June 20, 1877, a disastrous fire destroyed much of New Brunswick's leading commercial center, Saint John. Many churches were destroyed. Ketchum quotes a "moderate" estimate of the damages to the city as over $20,000,000—a colossal sum in the context of nineteenth-century New Brunswick. See *Life of Medley*, p. 177.
129. Ibid., pp. 310–12.
130. *Annals*, November 23, 1872.
131. Finley, *On Earth as it is in Heaven*, p. 176.
132. Finley and Wigginton, *On Earth as it is in Heaven*, p. 110.
133. Ibid., p. 201.
134. Ibid., p. 321.

Chapter 5. The Sacraments

1. Articles of Religion, XXV.
2. John Medley, *The Sermon at the Consecration of Thomas Frederick Davis, D.D. and Thomas Atkinson, D.D. to the Episcopate* (New York: Church Depository, 1853), p. 11.
3. Most notable among those thus affected by the Gorham affair was Henry Manning. An account of his reaction to the case and subsequent secession can be found in David Newsome, *The Parting of Friends,* chapter 8.
4. For more on the Gorham case see J. C. S. Nias, *Gorham and the Bishop of Exeter* (London: SPCK, 1951). Also, H. P. Liddon, *Life of Edward Bouverie Pusey,* 3: 201–56; F. W. Cornish, *The English Church in the Nineteenth Century* (New York: AMS, 1910) 319–36; David Newsome, *The Parting of Friends,* pp. 347–53; Owen Chadwick, *The Victorian Church,* Part I, 250–70; Desmond Bowen, *The Idea of the Victorian Church,* pp. 96–111.
5. PANB, *Church Witness*, Saint John, N.B.
6. Ibid., October 29, 1851.
7. Ibid., see, for example, October 10, 1850, October 30, 1850, August 6, 1851, August 20, 1851.
8. *Of the Laws of Ecclesiastical Polity*, book 5, xxi, 3.
9. Medley, *1850 Charge*. p. 22.
10. Ibid., p. 25.
11. Ibid.
12. Ibid.
13. Ibid.
14. Ibid., p. 26.

15. Ibid., p. 27.
16. Acts 3.
17. Ibid., p. 29.
18. Ibid., p. 30.
19. For more on the Savoy conference see Edward Cardwell, A *History of Conferences and Other Proceedings Connected with the Revision of the Book of Common Prayer* (Oxford: Oxford University Press, 1849), chapters 6 and 7.
20. Ibid., pp. 37–38.
21. Medley, *1850 Charge*, pp. 37–38.
22. Nockles points out that this position of Sumner, which appeared to support regeneration had previously caused him to offer a defense of his apparent inconsistency, *The Oxford Movement in Context*, p. 230.
23. Medley, *1850 Charge*, p. 40. Interestingly, Medley borrows the the phrase, "the stammering lips of ambiguous and uncertain formularies," from the introduction to Newman's *Tract 90*.
24. Chadwick, *The Victorian Church*, part 1, p. 262.
25. See Perry Butler, *Gladstone: Church State and Tractarianism* (Oxford: Clarendon Press, 1982) pp. 22–23.
26. Chadwick, *The Victorian Church*, part 1, p. 262.
27. See chapter 6 for an account of the development of Medley's views on disestablishment.
28. Ibid.
29. Medley, The *Mission of the Comforter*, p. 9.
30. Medley, *Reformation*, p. 8. Joseph Hall was bishop of Exeter and later Norwich in the seventeenth century. Although suspected by Laud of Calvinist sympathies, he is nevertheless quoted in many Tractarian *Catenae*.
31. While he always had some measure of criticism for the continental reformers, Medley was consistent over the years in his defense of the English Reformation.
32. Ibid., p. 13.
33. Ibid., pp. 13–14.
34. "The bread and wine are not changed in their substance from being the same with that which is found at ordinary table; but in respect of the sacred use whereunto they are consecrated, such a change is made that they differ as much from common bread and wine, as Heaven from earth. Neither are they to be accounted barely *significative*, but truly *exhibitive*, also of those Heavenly things whereto they have relation, as being appointed by God to be a means of conveying the same unto us, and putting us in actual possession thereof. So that in the use of this holy ordinance, as verily as a man, with his bodily hand and mouth, receiveth the same earthly creatures, so verily doth he with his spiritual hand and mouth, if any such he have, receive the body and blood of Christ, as this is that real and substantial presence which are affirmed to be in the inward part of this sacred action. The truth which must be held, is this, that we do not there receive only the benefits that flow from Christ, but the very body and blood of Christ, that is Christ himself crucified." For more on Ussher's position see R. B. Knox, *James Ussher, Archbishop of Armagh* (Cardiff: University of Wales Press, 1967). See p. 20 for Ussher's view of Calvin.
35. Nockles refers to the selective approach that the Tractarians took to scanning earlier periods of the church for witnesses, *The Oxford Movement in Context*, p. 4.
36. See Article XXVIII: "Transubstantiation (or the change of the substance of Bread and Wine) in the Supper of the Lord, cannot be proved by holy Writ; but is repugnant to the plain words of Scripture, overthroweth the nature of a Sacrament, and hath given occasion to many superstitions."

37. James Ussher, "A Sermon preached before the Common House of Parliament in St. Margaret's Church, at Westminster, the 18th of February, 1620," *Works* (Dublin: Hodges and Smith, 1847), vol. 2. For scholastic use of this terminology see, for example, Thomas Aquinas, *Summa Theologiae*, IIIa, qq. 60–65.

38. Ibid.

39. This is, of course, Newman's effort with regard to the Articles in *Tract 90*.

40. Medley, *Reformation*, p. 19.

41. Ibid., p. 14.

42. Medley had been bishop of Fredericton for two years.

43. It is on just this point that a clear divergence emerges between the Tractarians and "old High Churchmen." Nockles demonstrates this effectively in *The Oxford Movement in Context*, pp. 122–27. Sheridan Gilley lists W. E. Gladstone, Samuel Wilberforce, and Walter Hook as among other High Church contemporaries of Medley, "who retained a strong element of Protestantism in their Anglo-Catholicism." See Gilley, "The Ecclesiology of the Oxford Movement: A Reconsideration," in *Newman From Oxford to the People* (Leominster: Gracewing, 1996), p. 66.

44. John Medley, *1847 Charge*, pp. 10–11.

45. Ibid., p. 5.

46. Ibid., p. 39.

47. See entry for Cecil Wray in *Papers of British Churchmen* (London: Her Majesty's Stationary Office, 1987). Wray was himself a ritualist. During his time at St. Martin's, the church was known for its ritualism. For example see Anson, *Fashions in Church Furnishings*, p. 66, where he mentions that St. Martin's had an intoned service, surpliced choristers, encaustic tiles, and "even a cross and candlesticks on the 'considerably elevated altar.'" C. P. S. Clarke, *The Oxford Movement and After* (London: Mowbray & Co., 1932), p. 185, records that St. Martin's was the site of ritualist riots.

48. LPL, Letters to the Reverend Cecil Wray, M.A. MS 1604 f. 426. This letter is dated March 20, 1857.

49. This refers to one of the more famous controversies of the period. George Anthony Denison, Archdeacon of Taunton, was involved in legal action over his teaching of the real presence in the Eucharist. For more on Denison see Joyce Coombs, *George Anthony Denison: The Firebrand* (London: Church Literature Association Society of Saints Peter & Paul, 1984).

50. See L. E. Ellsworth, *Charles Lowder and the Ritualist Movement* (London: Darton, Longman and Todd, 1982). See also Rowell, *Vision Glorious*, p. 128; and Trench, *Charles Lowder*, p. 72.

51. This contrasts with, for example, the opinion of Keble, who believed that the Denison matter had raised questions "concerning the reality of our Communion with the Universal Church." Letter in Guardian, Nov. 22, 1854, p. 898, as quoted in H. P. Liddon, *Life of Edward Bouverie Pusey*, 3: 430.

52. Chadwick, *The Victorian Church*, part 1, p. 492.

53. Coombs gives an account of this affair and its aftermath in *George Anthony Denison*, pp.124–51. While tracing the events, she does not, regrettably, provide much insight as to the particulars of Denison's theological position. Liddon's evidence is more helpful on this latter point. See *Life of Pusey*, 3: 427–48.

54. For an account of these proceedings see Chadwick, *The Victorian Church*, part 1, 491–95. For more on Denison's character see Coombs, *George Anthony Denison*.

55. Medley to Wray, March 20, 1857.

56. See Coleridge, *Memoir of the Rev John Keble*, p. 423.

57. See Ellsworth, p. 18, where she quotes R. W. Church on the Lushington judgment, in which the court had ruled against most of the ritual practices at St. Barnabas's: "[The judgment has served] to close questions which at the least are open ones."

58. Nockles, *The Oxford Movement in Context,* pp. 235–48, gives a good summary of contemporary opinions of the real presence. He shows that not only were such High Churchmen as Phillpotts receptionists (of a sort), but also many of the Tractarians, including the early Newman and Pusey were, at best, unclear on the doctrine. Also, see the account of Keble's early receptionism given in Alf Härdelin, *The Tractarian Understanding of the Eucharist*, pp. 129–32. However, as Härdelin makes clear, Keble and Pusey both eventually came to an acceptance of the doctrine of the real presence. See also Härdelin, "The Sacraments in the Tractarian Spiritual Universe," in *Tradition Renewed*, ed. Geoffrey Rowell (Allison Park: Pickwick Publications, 1986), pp. 78–95.

59. John Medley, *The House of God, The Christian's Home* (Quebec: Lamoureux 1856) p. 3.

60. The difficult relation between these two churches and the move to separate them is detailed in Trench, *Charles Lowder,* 33–60. See also Ellsworth, *Charles Lowder*, chapter 3.

61. See chapter 5.

62. LPL, Ms 1604. Letters from John Medley to Cecil Wray, pp. 425–30.

63. Medley, *Mission of the Comforter,* p. 10.

64. Ibid., pp. 17–18.

65. This was written in a letter from Medley to the Reverend E. Hawkins, secretary of the SPG in 1845. It is quoted by Headon, *The Influence of the Oxford Movement*, p. 109

66. The six points were: the eastward position, eucharistic vestments, the mixed chalice, altar candles, unleavened bread, and incense. These were set out in a manifesto published by the Tractarian "English Church Union"; see *ODCC.*

67. Nigel Yates details the political difficulty that many English bishops faced with regard to the Ritualists, in walking "a fine line between legitimate indulgence and a desire to restrain clerical enthusiasm." See *Anglican Ritualism in Victorian Britain*, p. 177 ff.

68. *1847 Charge*, p. 11.

69. Nockles, *Oxford Movement in Context*, pp. 215–16. A more detailed account of the genesis and theological roots of the nineteenth-century Ritualists is given by Nigel Yates in *Anglican Ritualism in Victorian Britain.*

70. Finley, *New Brunswick's Gothic Revival*, pp. 54–98.

71. Medley, *1847 Charge*, p. 10.

72. See *ODCC* on the Ritual Commission and its role in examining church ritual.

73. John Medley, *1868 Charge,* p. 8.

74. Ibid., p. 10.

75. Ibid., pp. 10–11.

76. Ibid., p. 13.

77. Ibid., pp. 13–14.

78. Ibid., p. 15.

79. Ibid., pp. 18–19.

80. It wouldn't be until 1881, when the Mission Church of St. John the Baptist opened in Saint John, that the diocese would have a single advanced Ritualist church.

81. Ibid., p. 21.

82. Ibid.

83. See, for example, John Shelton Reed's account of Anglo-Catholic practices in London in the mid-1860s, in *Glorious Battle: The Cultural Politics of Victorian Anglo-Catholicism* (Nashville: Vanderbilt, 1996), chapter 3. If not common, at least frequent were examples of "processions with relics, and the stations of the cross, . . . Latin in worship and . . . [the] service of Benediction" (p. 61). Since these practices were highly publicized and the objects of popular controversy, it is hard to believe that Medley was unaware of the extent of Ritualist practice.

84. A copy of this service is preserved in the *Annals.*

85. Medley, *1871 Charge,* p. 23.

86. Ibid.

87. Ibid.

88. The PWRA was passed seven years after Confederation in Canada. Consequently, it had no legal effect there. It had already become clear, since the Colenso case, that colonial churches were essentially beyond the control (or protection) of English law. For more on the PWRA see J. Bentley, *Ritualism and Politics in Victorian Britain: The Attempt to Legislate for Belief* (Oxford: Oxford University Press, 1978), pp. 40–75; for a consideration of the PWRA in the wider context of Victorian Ritualism see N. Yates, *Anglican Ritualism in Victorian Britain,* pp. 235–76.

89. John Medley, *A Charge Delivered at St. Paul's Church, Portland on Tuesday June 30th 1874* (Saint John: Knodell, 1874), p. 11.

90. Ibid., pp. 11–12.

91. Ibid., p. 12. The association referred to here was almost certainly the Church Association, formed in 1865 to oppose the perceived Romanizing tendencies of the Ritualists.

92. For accounts of the outcome of the attempts to impose uniformity through legislation and prosecutions see Chadwick, *The Victorian Church,* Part 2, pp. 321–28; Bentley, *Ritualism and Politics,* chapter 4; and Reed, *Glorious Battle,* chapter 13.

93. Parts of this correspondence were published by Eugene Fairweather, "John Medley as Defender of Ritualism," no. 3, pp. 208–11.

94. See John Morley, *Life of Gladstone,* 2: 501ff.; also, David W. Bebbington, *William Ewart Gladstone, Faith and Politics in Victorian Britain* (Grand Rapids: Eerdmanns, 1993), p. 226.

95. BL, Gladstone Papers, Ms. Add. 44443, vol. 277, fol. 301f.

96. BL, Gladstone Papers, Ms. Add. 44444, vol. 359, fols. 191–93.

97. See Chadwick, *Victorian Church,* 2: 150.

98. BL, Gladstone Papers, Ms. Add. 44455, vol. 370, fol. 206f.

99. BL, Gladstone Papers, vol. 370, fol. 322.f.

100. John Medley, *A Sermon Preached before the Provincial Synod of Canada in Christ Church Cathedral, Montreal* (Montreal: Lovell , 1877), pp. 3–4.

101. Ibid., pp. 4–5. It is interesting that Medley at once denies that the Tractarians were Ritualists, while at the same time using the Tractarians as important figures for his defense of the Ritualists.

102. See below, chapter 6.

103. Ibid., pp. 5–6.

104. For a concise account of several of these proceedings see Bentley, *Ritualism and Politics,* chapter 5. An analysis of cases brought under the PWRA is also given by Yates, *Anglican Ritualism in Victorian Britain,* pp. 248–76.

105. Medley, *Sermon Preached Before Provincial Synod,* p. 7.

106. Ibid., p. 10.

107. Ibid., p. 11.

108. Ibid.

109. Ibid., pp. 11–12.
110. For instance, the PWRA.
111. Ibid., pp. 12–14.
112. Ibid.
113. Ibid.
114. Ibid., p. 14.
115. Ibid.
116. Finley makes the argument that Medley was a sort of salesman for the British Imperial *ethos*. He speaks of a perceived "sacred bond between the Church and British civilization," among some of Medley's associates and students, such as Sir George Parkin, the "prince of Imperialists and their first missionary," *New Brunswick's Gothic Revival*, pp. 286 and 297. The implication is that Medley shared this sentiment.
117. See below, chapter 6.
118. Ibid., *Sermon before Provincial Synod*, p. 14.
119. LPL, Reports of the second Lambeth Conference, 1878, 8: 146.
120. Ketchum, *Life of Medley*, p. 221.
121. LPL, Reports of the second Lambeth Conference, 1878, 9: 34.
122. Ibid., p. 135.
123. Ibid.
124. Ibid., p. 136.
125. Ketchum, *Life of Medley*, p. 221.
126. Bentley, *Ritualism and Politics*, pp. 112–14. For a partial defense of the PWRA's effectiveness, see Yates, *Anglican Ritualism in Victorian Britain*, pp. 275–76. He argues that the act itself did not fail insofar as it mostly accomplished its goal of suppressing particular instances of ritual excess. However, Yates agrees that it was largely ineffective in "[putting] a brake on ritual innovation," ibid., p. 277.
127. John Medley, *A Charge to the Clergy of the Diocese of Fredericton Delivered at his Visitation held on June 30th 1880* (Saint John: Daily News, 1880), p. 6.
128. John Medley, *1886 Charge*, p. 12.
129. Ibid.
130. John Medley, *The Sermon Preached in St. Luke's Pro-Cathedral, Halifax August 12th 1887, Being the Centenary of the Founding of the Colonial Episcopate* (Halifax: Gossip & Son, n.d.), p. 7.

Chapter 6. Authority

1. *The Episcopal Form of Church Government.*
2. Ketchum, *Life of Medley*, p. 48, identifies him as "S. T. Trist." This must refer to the Reverend S. P. J. Trist, who was, according to *The Clergy List for 1841* (London: C. Cox, 1841), "vicar of Veryan, near Tregony, Cornwall." He had been there since 1829.
3. Ibid. Medley, *Episcopal Form of Church Government*. p. 8.
4. Ibid.
5. Ibid.
6. Ibid., p. 9.
7. Ibid., p. 10.
8. Burns, *The Diocesan Revival*, p. 17, refutes this perception, referring to the "profusion of works treating apostolical succession published after 1800."
9. Ibid., pp. 10–11.

10. Ibid., pp. 11–12.

11. Ibid., p. 13.

12. Ibid. Also Medley, *Episcopal Form of Church Government*, p. 13.

13. Ibid., p. 14.

14. Ibid.

15. For example see the introduction by Joseph Butler, *The Analogy of Religion* (London: J. M. Dent, 1906).

16. Ibid., Medley, *Episcopal Form of Church Government*, pp. 16–17.

17. See Finley, *New Brunswick's Gothic Revival*, pp. 84–85. Also, see Chapter 5.

18. Medley, *Episcopal Form of Church Government*, p. 19.

19. Ibid., pp. 18–19.

20. Hooker, *Laws.* See particularly the argument of book 2.

21. Medley, *Episcopal Form of Church Government*, p. 19.

22. Ibid., p. 20.

23. "We do not presume to anathematize all who dissent from the Church of England, but we may fairly avail ourselves of the testimony of this great man, who declares that he was compelled by necessity to adopt the Presbyterian form, and that it was not his own free choice." See R. B. Knox, *James Ussher*, p. 125, for an earlier example of Calvin being used in support of episcopacy. Knox suggests that Ussher misrepresents Calvin's position in this matter.

24. Medley, *Episcopal Form of Church Government*, p. 21.

25. Ibid., p. 23.

26. Ibid., p. 22.

27. Ibid.

28. Ibid., p. 24.

29. Ibid.

30. Ibid., pp. 24–25.

31. Ibid., p. 28.

32. Medley is referring to the Lutheran Church historian Johann von Mosheim (1694–1755). The second-century church writer Hegesippus was a favorite of Medley's, used several times. Eusebius's testimony is in direct support of New Testament practice. Medley refutes those who use Cranmer in support of there being only two orders in the primitive church. He points to the introduction to the Ordinal: "It is evident unto all men, reading Holy Scripture and ancient authors, that from the apostles' time there have been these three of ministers—Bishops, priests and deacons . . ."

33. Medley, *Episcopal Form of Church Government*, pp. 33–39.

34. Ibid., p. 42.

35. Chadwick, *The Spirit of the Oxford Movement,* p. 29. See also Robert Crouse's article, "'Devout Perusal.'"

36. Medley, *Episcopal Form of Church Government*, p. 42.

37. Ibid.

38. Ibid., p. 43.

39. Ibid., p. 44.

40. Ibid., pp. 45–47.

41. Ibid., p. 53.

42. See Nockles, *The Oxford Movement in Context*, chapter 1.

43. Ibid.

44. Ibid., pp. 87–88.

45. Medley, *Episcopal Form*, p. 56.

46. Ibid.

47. Ibid., p. 57.

48. Ibid.
49. Ibid.
50. Ibid., p. 58.
51. Ibid., p. 59.
52. Ibid.
53. For example, Thomas Arnold had written his famous attack on "The Oxford Malignants." See Liddon, *Life of Pusey*, 1:381–84.
54. Medley, *How are the Mighty Fallen!* This sermon was also published in London and sold by Rivingtons, Longmans, and Parker. It can therefore be presumed to have had a wide readership.
55. See chapter 4.
56. Ibid., p. 26.
57. Ibid., p. 27.
58. John Medley, *The Reformation*, p. 8.
59. Medley, *1847 Charge*, p. 12.
60. Ibid.
61. Ibid.
62. Ibid., p. 22. Medley, in a footnote to the above passage, directs his reader to see, in support, "Archbishop Secker's remarks quoted in the Bishop of London's Sermon on the Consecration of four Bishops in Westminster Abbey." That the short-sighted nature of the English policy was responsible, at least in part, for the loss of the American colony, had been long argued by High Churchmen. Medley himself made this charge explicitly three years later, saying that America was lost precisely because of "our obstinacy and folly" in refusing to send spiritual help. See also Nockles, *The Oxford Movement*, p. 74.
63. Ibid., p. 8.
64. Medley, *Sermon at the Consecration of Thomas Frederick Davis*, p. 12.
65. Ibid., pp. 8–9.
66. Ibid., p. 9.
67. Ibid., p. 10.
68. Ibid.
69. Medley, *1865 Charge*, p. 11.
70. Ibid., p. 13.
71. See both his 1865 and 1868 *Charges*.
72. Medley, *The Sermon Preached in St. Luke's Pro-Cathedral Halifax*, p. 7.
73. Ibid., p. 8.
74. See chapter 2.
75. John Medley, *How are the Mighty Fallen!*, p. 17. Like Medley's tract on episcopacy, this was also reprinted and sold by Rivingtons and Longmans, London and Parker, Oxford. A copy of it is among a collection of pamphlets formerly belonging to Pusey, held at Pusey House Library. It is inscribed, in Medley's hand, "with kind regards."
76. Ibid., p. 22.
77. Ibid., p. 24.
78. Ibid., pp. 28–29.
79. Ibid., p. 36.
80. Ibid., pp. 26–27.
81. Although Newman was aware of Medley through Pusey and Keble, they had only just met six months prior to this sermon. See *The Letters and Diaries of John Henry Newman*, vol. 7, diary entry for December 14, 1839.
82. John Medley, *Two Ordination Sermons*. In fact, the dedication records that

the sermon was being published at the lieutenant governor's request and reads, "With every sentiment of respect and esteem, By his obliged and sincere friend and servant, John, Fredericton." Medley enjoyed close and cordial relations with many (although not all) of the lieutenant governors and other Imperial officers, with whom he associated in Fredericton. Purdy, *The Church of England in New Brunswick*, traced the relations of Medley with several of the leaders of the Provincial Government. Colebrooke was reform minded, actively promoting responsible government for New Brunswick. For more on Colebrooke, see MacNutt, *New Brunswick*, chapter 12.

83. Medley, *Two Ordination Sermons*, p. 8.

84. Ibid., p. 9.

85. John Medley, *The Reformation*, pp. 25–26.

86. See Chadwick, *The Victorian Church*, 2:427–39, for more on the movement in England for disestablishment.

87. See, Purdy *The Church of England in New Brunswick*, pp. 113 *ff.*

88. Medley, *The Reformation*, appendix, p. 26.

89. Having won the election of 1868 with his plan to disestablish the Irish Church, Gladstone proceeded in the following year to implement his policy.

90. This letter, preserved in the BL as Add. MS, 44420, fols. 120–23, was published with brief commentary by Eugene Fairweather, *CJT* 7: no. 3 (1961); 198–200.

91. Medley, *1847 Charge*, p. 9.

92. Ibid., p. 20.

93. Ibid., p. 22.

94. Ibid.

95. Ibid.

96. Ibid.

97. Ibid., p. 23.

98. Ibid.

99. Ibid., p. 29.

100. Medley, *1850 Charge*, p. 14.

101. Ibid., p. 53.

102. See Chadwick, *The Victorian Church*, part 1, pp. 262–64 and 309–24.

103. Ibid., p. 311.

104. Ibid.

105. See Morley, *Life of Gladstone,* 2: 162–63, where a letter explaining his position is reprinted.

106. Liddon, *Life of Pusey*, p. 343. For greater details surrounding the Exeter Synod see C. G. B. Davies, *Henry Phillpotts*, pp. 264–86. Medley would have assuredly been aware of this development. Also see Burns, *The Diocesan Revival*, chapter 9, for background about the move to diocesan conferences and eventually synods.

107. See V. Alan McClelland, "Gladstone and Manning: a Question of Authority," in *Gladstone, Religion and Politics*, ed. Peter J. Jagger.

108. See Liddon, *Life of Pusey*, pp. 341–51.

109. Ibid., p. 351.

110. Ketchum, *Life of Medley*, p. 115.

111. Quoted in Liddon, *Life of Pusey*, p. 352.

112. Medley had met the previous year in Montreal with other Canadian bishops. The minutes of this meetings include a call for diocesan synods, including the laity. See Phillip Carrington, *The Anglican Church,* p. 113.

113. Morley, *Life of Gladstone*, 1:361.

114. In September 1850, Pope Pius IX had declared Britain to be a province of the Roman Catholic Church and had created a hierarchy, complete with diocesan bish-

ops and an Archbishop. This reintroduction of the Roman system for the first time since the middle of the sixteenth century aroused a storm of public outrage and national paranoia. Lord John Russell added to the chaos by writing an incendiary response to the action, which linked the "Puseyites" to the Roman conspiracy. Given Newman's secession to Rome, and after the Gorham decision, the similar conversions of other high-profile Tractarians such as Manning, the public was more than ready to attack the "Puseyites." Legislation was introduced (the Ecclesiastical Titles Bill) that would prevent Roman Catholic bishops from holding any titles to English territories. Overwhelmingly popular with the public, it was nevertheless opposed in principle by Gladstone. See also Morley, *Life of Gladstone*, 1:408–15; and, Perry Butler, *Gladstone*, pp. 143–44.

115. BL, MS. 44374, f. 15, letter of Medley to Gladstone, February 10, 1852. "The Exeter Hall Party" was another term for the Evangelical party, named after a London building often used for Evangelical meetings. See *ODCC*. For more on the Exeter Hall meetings see Kenneth Hylson-Smith *Evangelicals in the Church of England, 1734–1984* (Edinburgh: T & T Clark, 1988), pp. 171–73.

116. Rowell, *Vision Glorious*, p. 163.

117. BL, MS. 44374, f. 16, letter of Medley to Gladstone, February 10, 1852.

118. Medley, *1853 Charge*, p. 14.

119. Ibid., p. 17. A footnote to this remark simply identifies the "leading statesmen" as Lord John Russell and Mr. Gladstone.

120. Ibid., p. 15.

121. Ibid.

122. Medley, *1856 Charge*, p. 54.

123. Ibid.

124. RH, SPG letters, July 10, 1856.

125. Medley, *1856 Charge*, p. 54.

126. Ibid., p. 55.

127. See Bentley Hicks, "Synodical Government with Canadian Anglicanism: Retrospective Implications," in *JCCHS* 33 (October 1991): 123–40. See especially pp. 129 ff, for a discussion of the place of the episcopal veto in the development of synodical government in the diocese of Quebec, adjacent to the diocese of Fredericton.

128. This comment is quoted by T. R. Millman in "Beginnings of the Synodical Movement in Colonial Anglican Churches with special reference to Canada," *JCCHS* 21 (1979): 3–19; see p. 15.

129. Binney, *1854 Charge*, p. 4.

130. Ibid., p. 56.

131. Ibid.

132. Medley, *1859 Charge*, p. 82.

133. Ibid. p. 79.

134. For more on Bishop Strachan and his political involvement see, David Flint, *John Strachan: Pastor and Politician* (Toronto: Oxford University Press, 1971); also, *John Strachan: Documents and Opinions*, a selection edited with an introduction by J. L. H. Henderson (Toronto: Maclelland and Stewart, 1969).

135. Carrington, p. 77. Chapter 5 contains an account of the Clergy Reserves controversy and the involvement of various Anglican prelates in it.

136. See Headon, *The Influence of the Oxford Movement*, pp. 33–36.

137. Ibid., p. 36. See also Faught, *The Oxford Movement*, p. 140.

138. See T. R. Millman, "Beginnings of the Synodical Movement," pp. 3–19.

139. Ibid., p. 6.

140. See Ketchum, *Life of Medley*, pp. 28–34 for an account of the origins of the New Brunswick Diocesan Church Society.
141. Millman, "Beginnings of the Synodical Movement," p. 8.
142. Ibid., p. 9.
143. John Medley, *A Sermon Preached Before His Royal Highness, The Prince of Wales on His Visit to Fredericton* (Fredericton: John Graham, 1860), p. 3.
144. Ibid., p. 5.
145. *Annals*, August 4, 1860.
146. Ibid., p. 7.
147. Ibid., p. 9.
148. See above, chapter 2, for an account of the SPG's changing financial relationship with the diocese of Fredericton.
149. Ibid.
150. See above, chapter 2.
151. See above, p. 198 n. 179.
152. Ibid., p. 147.
153. The Dean of Arches had rendered the decision on the case.
154. Medley, *1865 Charge*, p. 10.
155. Ibid., p. 11.
156. Ibid., p. 12.
157. Ibid. This is in reference to another celebrated case, *Long* v. *the Bishop of Capetown,* in which the Privy Council had ruled that the voluntary submission of a cleric to his Bishop, undertaken by the oath of obedience was binding irrespective of the Letters Patent. See the appendix, p. 30, to this charge for relevant references. For more on this see Hinchliff, *John William Colenso*, pp. 153–54.
158. Ibid., p. 18.
159. Ibid.
160. Ibid., p. 21.
161. Convocation had requested alteration of two canons. Permission had been granted, but the Lord Chancellor had determined that the alteration would not extend to the colonies. See Medley, *1865 Charge*, p. 21.
162. Ibid., pp. 21–22.
163. Interestingly, this same line was taken by Bishop Gray of Cape Town. See Rowell, *The Vision Glorious*, p. 170.
164. Medley, *1865 Charge*, p. 22.
165. An account of the move to synodical government in the Canadian Church is given by Carrington, *The Anglican Church*, chapter 9. Bishops in other Canadian dioceses had experienced, for the most part, less opposition than Medley and thus synods were established earlier in most of them.
166. See above, p. 154.
167. PANB, *An Address of the Lord Bishop of Fredericton At a Meeting of Clergy and Lay delegates, Convened by the Unanimous desire of the Clergy Present at the Late Visitation of this Diocese, and held at St. John, July 5th*, 1866. p. 1.
168. Ibid., p. 2.
169. Ross Hebb, in *The Establishment of Synodical Government in Maritime Canada*, p. 20, suggests that this interpretation of the decision was exaggerated and that the only effective force of the decision was to say that English ecclesiastical law did not apply in a colony with its own legislature. Nevertheless, Gray of Cape Town accepted the wider interpretation of the decision and took it to mean that "The privy Council had declared that the Church of England as by law established did not and could not exist in South Africa." This enabled "Gray to create an independent, unes-

tablished province in South Africa, with a synodical government, its own courts, and a workable system of church discipline, which would be based, so far as the civil courts were concerned, on the constitution of a voluntary association." (Hinchliff, *John William Colenso*, pp. 155–56.)

170. PANB, *Address of the Lord Bishop of Fredericton*, p. 3.

171. Ibid.

172. Ibid.

173. See Liddon, *Life of Pusey*, 3:346.

174. PANB, *Address of the Lord Bishop of Fredericton*, p. 4. Within the past decade, all other Canadian dioceses had established synods.

175. Ibid., pp. 4–5.

176. Ibid., p. 5.

177. Ibid., p. 8.

178. Ketchum, *Life of Medley*, p. 143.

179. Ibid.

180. *The Church Witness and Monitor*, July 7, 1869.

181. UKC, Rowley Collection of Letters of Canadian Bishops, John Medley to the Reverend P. W. Loosemore, March 24, 1869.

182. For the Canadian role in bringing about the first Lambeth Conference see A. M. G. Stephenson, *The First Lambeth Conference* (London: SPCK, 1967), pp. 150–76. For a more recent account see W. M. Jacob, *The Making of the Anglican Church Worldwide* (London: SPCK, 1997), chapter 5.

183. Stephenson, *The First Lambeth Conference*, p. 267 and p. 269.

184. Ibid., pp. 120–49 and pp. 267–79.

185. Medley, *1868 Charge.* This was certainly a less tart explanation of Medley's absence than that communicated to Longley. It is unclear if this more eirenic tone was Medley's own, or the result of a diplomatic representation by Mr. Wilkinson.

186. Ibid., p. 8.

187. Ibid., p. 17.

188. Ibid., p. 19.

189. Ibid., pp. 20–21.

190. Ibid.

191. Ibid., p. 18.

192. Ibid.

193. Medley, *1868 Charge*, p. 10.

194. For more on this see Headon, *The Influence of the Oxford Movement*, pp. 121–34.

195. It was Medley's practice on this occasion, and sometimes in the future, to address the clergy separately in a charge before synod.

196. Ibid., p. 40.

197. In fact, Medley was around to see the first episcopal election in the diocese, with the election of his coadjutor, H. T. Kingdon.

198. Medley, *1871 Charge*, p. 5..

199. Ibid., pp. 5–6.

200. Ibid., p. 6.

201. Ibid., pp. 6–7.

202. Ibid., p. 7.

203. Ibid.

204. Ibid.

205. Ibid., p. 18.

206. Medley, *Sermon Before Provincial Synod*, p. 3.

207. Ibid., p. 6.
208. Ibid., p. 15.
209. LPL, Lambeth Conference papers, vol. 2, ff. 8–11.
210. Ibid.
211. See conclusion.
212. LPL, Lambeth Conference papers, vol. 7, f. 77.
213. Ibid.
214. See above, p. 154.
215. These leanings were sharply limited, however. His conception of synods involved strict limitations on their power to legislate on doctrine, for example.
216. LPL, Lambeth Conference papers, vol. 7, f. 140.
217. John Medley, *Other Little Ships* (London: SPG, 1878), p. 6.
218. Ibid.
219. See Liddon, *Life of Pusey*, 4:370, for Pusey's negative reaction to the bill.
220. Medley, *1880 Charge*, pp. 11–17.
221. Medley, *1886 Charge*, p. 3.
222. Medley, *Advantages of Open Seats*, p. 12.
223. Ibid.
224. Ibid.
225. Ibid., p. 13.

Conclusion

1. W. O. Raymond, *John Medley*, p. 121.
2. Ibid., p. 102.
3. Ibid., p. 101.
4. Ketchum, *Life of Medley*, p. 50.
5. Fairweather, *Tractarian Patriarch*, pp. 18–19.
6. Ibid., p. 21.
7. Ibid.
8. Harding, "John, By Divine Permission," p. 76.
9. Ibid.
10. Interestingly, Harding modified the statement in his 1994 book from that of his 1966 article to read, "Medley's theological views were unquestionably typical of the high churchmanship associated with the Tractarians." Harding, *Citizens*, p. 19.
11. Headon, *The Influence of the Oxford Movement*, p. 104.
12. C. F. Headon, "Developments in Canadian Anglican Worship," pp. 27–28.
13. In addition to Finley's thesis and book, quoted previously, see "'Habits of reverence and awe.'"
14. Nockles's *The Oxford Movement in Context*, assembles an enormous body of evidence to refute the received view of the Tractarians as appearing *ex nihilo* to resuscitate a moribund High Church tradition. Frances Knight in *The Nineteenth-Century Church in English Society*, shows the existence of a vibrant Victorian High Church tradition quite separate from the efforts of the Tractarians. Arthur Burns's recent book *The Diocesan Revival in the Church of England 1800–1870*, buttresses Nockles's general arguments by demonstrating the specific error of presuming that the Tractarians alone were responsible for the diocesan revival in the nineteenth century.
15. See Yates, *Anglican Ritualism in Victorian Britain*, for a demonstration of the

existence of such High Church views from the Reformation through to the Victorian period.

16. Burns, *The Diocesan Revival*, makes clear throughout that the old High Church party played a significant role in the diocesan revival movement.

17. The clipping of this letter, which appears to be to a Richibucto, New Brunswick paper is dated April 14, 1881, and included in the vestry books of the Mission Church of Saint John the Baptist, Saint John. PANB, MC223, S5-E-5A.

18. See above, p. 196n. 140.

19. All of these visits are recorded in the *Annals*.

20. See above, p. 143.

21. See *The Nineteenth Century Church and English Society*, p. 210.

22. Nigel Yates makes a similar observation about the difficulties in labeling Churchmen of this period. See *Anglican Ritualism in Victorian Britain*, p. 48.

23. See Harding's conclusion in *Citizens with the Saints*, where he nicely sums up Medley's success in moving his diocese from a Georgian view to a "new conception of Church life," pp. 34–35.

24. Medley, *Two Discourses Preached in the Church of the Advent*, p. 5.

25. See Nockles, *The Oxford Movement in Context*, pp. 80–83, for an account of this Romantic radicalism in the Tractarian R. H. Froude.

26. On this point see W. J. Hankey, "Making Theology Practical."

27. See Hankey, "Making Theology Practical," pp. 90–93, for an account of the Protestant and Catholic limitations of the place of reason and substitution of authority, in reaction to the new "unbelief."

Glossary

The following list of terms is intended as an aid to the nonspecialist reader. Those wishing more detailed definitions should start first by consulting the *Oxford Dictionary of the Christian Church*, 3rd ed. (Oxford: Oxford University Press, 1998). The bibliographies attached to the various entries will provide the next step for those wishing to go further. Since many of the terms on this list have changed from period to period in the history of the church, I have generally defined them in accordance with the meaning that they had during the life of John Medley. I am indebted to the Reverend Doctor Ross Hebb, from the glossary of whose book I have freely borrowed.

archbishop: A senior *bishop* with authority over several *dioceses*. In England there are two archbishops: Canterbury and York. The archbishop of Canterbury initially had authority over all colonial dioceses. Later, as national churches became established, colonial archbishoprics were created.

archdeacon: A *priest* delegated by the *bishop* to have intermediary authority over all or part of a *diocese*.

bishop: The highest of the three ecclesiastical orders of *bishop*, *priest*, and deacon. Bishops generally have authority over a *diocese*. Held by the Church of England to be the successors of the Apostles, bishops are the only order within that church that are allowed to confirm and ordain. Subsequent to the Reformation and prior to Medley's time, bishops were appointed by the Crown. As this study indicates, election to the office became increasingly the norm in the colonies.

canon: Clergy that are appointed to an office attached to a *cathedral*. Residentiary canons are paid and on the active staff. Non-residentiary canons hold largely honorary offices, which may receive no remuneration.

cathedral: That church in a *diocese* where the *bishop* has his throne (*cathedra*) and that serves as the mother church of the diocese.

convocation: Church assemblies of various ranks of clergy established in England during the Middle Ages. Convocation theoretically provided for a degree of self-governance by the church, independent of the state. Convocation was dissolved at the Reformation and only revived during the Restoration period, albeit with limited powers. Dissolved again in the early eighteenth century, it was revived in the mid-nineteenth century as a result of lobbying by both *Tractarians* and *Evangelicals*. Even then, it remained exclusively clerical in membership.

curate: A clergyman who has the care ("cure") of a parish. This term can be applied however to one who was appointed as assistant to the rector or incumbent of the parish. Hence, Medley was referred to as "Cornish's curate" by Keble.

diocese: A geographical area under the authority of a *bishop*. The diocese was generally divided into *parishes*. A group of parishes might comprise one of several archdeaconries in a diocese.

ecclesiologist: A person who had taken an explicit interest in the newly emerging nineteenth-century science of ecclesiology or the study of church architecture. Various "ecclesiological societies" were established around England, generally with the intention of studying and promoting the revival of ancient, primarily Gothic, architectural forms and features. Medley was an active ecclesiologist, belonging to the Exeter Diocesan Architectural Society.

Erastianism: A position which gets it name from the sixteenth-century Swiss Thomas Erastus, who defended the authority of the state over the church, even in ecclesiastical matters. Transferred to the English context, Erastianism was anathema to the Tractarians and the term "Erastian" was often used by them as a pejorative description of any encroachment by the state on the absolute independence of the Church of England.

Evangelical: As one party with the Church of England, Evangelicals are a branch of *Low Churchmen*. In broad terms, Evangelicals stress the subjective aspects of Christian devotion, emphasizing the need for personal conversion and minimizing the importance of external forms and signs. English Evangelicals were politically active, leading the fight for the abolition of the slave trade, for example. In the nineteenth century they divided into an informal spectrum of positions ranging from moderate to extreme. Emphasizing the centrality of the Bible, they opposed the Roman Catholic Church on the one hand and often the Enlightenment on the other. They were fiercely opposed to the Tractarians, who were suspecting of being essentially Roman Catholic wolves in English churchmen's clothing. Ironically, many leading Tractarians (such as J. H. Newman) had begun their lives as Evangelicals before adopting their opposite position in the English ecclesiastical world.

High Church: Another party in the English Church, whose roots go back to the Reformation. The High Church party generally favored the retention of selected ancient forms and theological understandings. For example, High Churchmen would support apostolic succession, baptismal regeneration, the real presence, and the use of some degree of ceremonial in worship. In the nineteenth century the Tractarian movement criticized the older High Churchmen for being lukewarm and favoured a more radical return to Pre-Reformation usages. In common usage any use of ceremonial (religious vestments of any kind, candles on the altar, elaborate church furnishing or decoration, or a host of other things) was justification for their critics to label a cleric as being High Church, if not an outright *Tractarian*.

Lambeth conferences: Conferences held at about ten-year intervals, beginning in 1867. Hosted by the archbishop of Canterbury at Lambeth Palace, they gathered together all of the bishops attached to the Church of England worldwide to discuss various topics.

Lieutenant Governor: The Queen's representative in New Brunswick.

Low Church: The opposite party to the English High Church. In the spectrum of the Church of England, the Low Church inclined further from Roman Catholicism and closer to continental Protestantism. Favoring simple liturgy, devoid of excess ceremonial, suspicious of "Romish" innovations, and generally conservative, they naturally opposed the *Oxford Movement*.

Oxford Movement: A movement of religious reform with the Church of England that began in the 1830s, centered around a group of Oxford clerics and academics. The three great leaders of the movement were John Keble, Edward Bouverie Pusey, and John Henry Newman. Their aim in general was to awaken what they thought to be a moribund church to its ancient "catholic" heritage. Emphasizing traditional *High Church* positions, they published a series of "tracts" arguing for the revival of Pre-Reformation forms and usages. Their more radical tone and later political radicalism distinguished them from the traditional High Churchmen, however. In addition to the triumvirate who informally led the movement, other young priests and scholars were part of this movement. John Medley was one of these.

parish: A smaller geographical unit within a diocese, administered by a *curate*. In England, a parish would be entitled to receive tithes or income of some sort from land or other holdings. In colonial New Brunswick, while the province was divided into civil parishes, and curates were appointed as incumbents of ecclesastical parishes, no system of church tithes was ever devised. While in England every soul within the geographical boundary of the parish could be considered as the spiritual responsibility of the curate, in New Brunswick generally only a minority of residents geographically located with a parish actually claimed membership in the church.

pew: A seat, generally a wooden bench, in a church. Prior to Medley's arrival in New Brunswick, a pew would have usually been constructed with a back, sides, and even included a door, so as to resemble a self-contained box. In order to generate revenue, these pews would be rented or sold at auction. Medley made it one of his first orders of business to abolish pew rents in his new *diocese* and to make all seating in churches "free."

Prebendary: A member of a *cathedral* staff entitled to receive some income from cathedral estates. The Ecclesiastical Commission, formed in 1835, instituted reforms that abolished this income, rendering the office largely ceremonial, similar to that of a *canon*. Medley was a prebendary of Exeter cathedral.

priest: The second rank of the church's three orders. The most numerous of the church's minsters, priests celebrate communion and pronounce absolution, but they cannot ordain or confirm.

Puseyite: A variant on the name of E. B. Pusey, this was a term of insult used by their (generally Low Church or Evangelical) opponents to describe *Tractarians* or members of the *Oxford Movement*. It was also frequently employed to describe anyone holding to *High Church* practices.

Ritualism: A later development of the *Oxford Movement*, which saw the introduction of more and more elaborate ritual into worship. Medieval vestments, incense, hearing confessions, the use of Latin in the liturgy, and other Pre-Reformation usages marked this party. They were highly controversial. As a response parliament passed the Public Worship Regulation Act, by which civil law was employed to oppose their innovations. Several priests were jailed under the provisions of this act. Eventually public opinion, which had been largely hostile to the Ritualists, was altered and many of those customs and practices that had once produced outrage became commonplace in the Church of England.

Sacrament: The catechism of the Church of England contained in the Book of Common Prayer (1662) defined a sacrament as "an outward and visible sign of an inward and spiritual grace given unto us, ordained by Christ himself, as a means whereby we receive the same, and a pledge to assure us thereof." Thus, a sacrament has two parts: the outer sign and the inner spiritual gift. While later *Ritualists* would claim all seven medieval sacraments, since the Reformation the mainstream of the Church of England (*High Church* and *Low Church*) would generally mean by "sacraments": holy communion (the Eucharist or Lord's Supper) and baptism.

SPG: The Society for the Propagation of the Gospel in foreign parts. This was the organization that recruited and, to a greater or lesser extent in the nineteenth century, funded colonial missionaries.

synod: A gathering of church members, under the authority of the bishop, designed to assist in decisions regarding the administration of a diocese. While the early church had held various synods to determine matters of doctrine and discipline, the modern form of synods in the Church of England arose in the nineteenth century, initially in the colonies. Synodical government of colonial churches enabled them to operate more or less independently of the British government in *de facto* or *de jure* disestablished situations. Much debate preceded the establishment of these synods, as we see in the case of New Brunswick. Equally, much variety distinguished their constitutions from place to place. Generally they would include the bishop, clergy of the diocese, and delegates from among the laity.

Tractarian: See the *Oxford Movement* above. Generally, Tractarians were members of the original Oxford Movement. Although, as a term of opprobrium, any person suspected of even High Church inclinations in the mid-nineteenth century might be labeled a Tractarian.

Bibliography

Manuscript Sources

There is still some hope that the largest proportion of the papers and letters of John Medley is stored somewhere and remains to be discovered. References in letters written by his widow, and by one of his sons, after her subsequent death, to the existence of these letters refute the common belief that Mrs. Medley had them destroyed. Having said this, the absence of Medley letters in locations where one might reasonably expect to find them remains a puzzle. For example, there are no Medley letters in the provincial archives of Nova Scotia or Newfoundland, nor in the diocesan archives of Nova Scotia, Newfoundland, Montreal, or Quebec.

The following is a complete list describing those manuscripts pertaining to Medley that have been discovered either by the present author or previous researchers:

New Brunswick Provincial Archives (PANB). These are all cataloged in MC223.
The Annals of the Diocese of Fredericton
Letters of John Medley to Lieutenant Governors
Mission Church Vestry Records
A History of the Mission Church
Christ Church Parish Church Vestry Records
Trinity Church Vestry Records
Christ Church Cathedral Records
Miscellaneous John Medley Certificates
Letters and Notes found in Bishop Medley's Books
The Maritime Advocate
Two Discourses preached in the Church of the Advent, Boston
Newspapers on Microfilm: *The Church Witness* (F8543)
The Gleaner (F12274)
The Headquarters (F12237–42)
The Loyalist (F11046–47)
Also on Microfilm: *Diocese of Fredericton Synod Journals* (F20097)

National Archives of Canada (NAC)
Letters of John Medley to Sir George Parkin
Letters of Margaret Medley to Sir George Parkin
Letters of Edward Medley to Sir George Parkin

University of King's College, Halifax, Nova Scotia (UKC)
Rowley collection of Letters of Canadian Bishops

Lambeth Palace Library (LPL)
Letters of John Medley to Archbishop Longley
Letters of John Medley to Archbishop Tait

Letters of John Medley to Archbishop Benson
Letters of John Medley to the Revd Cecil Wray
British Library (BL)
Letters of John Medley to William Gladstone
Bodleian Library (BodL)
Letters of J. T. Coleridge to John Keble
Rhodes House Library (RH)
Letters of John Medley to the SPG
Misc. SPG archival material pertaining to the Diocese of Fredericton
Pusey House Library (PH)
Letters of John Medley to E. B. Pusey

Primary Sources

The Published Works of John Medley, in Chronological Order:

1833 *Advice to Teachers in Sunday-Schools.* London: John W. Parker.

1835 *The Episcopal Form of Church Government.* London: John W. Parker.

The Duties of Parents and Children. Sermon. E. Heard: Truro, 1835. o.

The Tricentenary of the Reformation. Two sermons. E. Heard: Truro, 1835.

1839 *The Union of the Members in Christ Body.* Sermon. Exeter: P. A. Hannaford.

The Union of the Members in Christ's Body. A Sermon Preached in The Cathedral Church of St. Peter, Exeter, on Thursday, October 10th MDCCCXXXIX, at the Triennial Visitation of the Right Rev. Henry, Lord Bishop of Exeter, by John Medley, M.A., Vicar of St. Thomas. Exeter: P. A. Hannaford.

"Homilies of Saint John Chrysostom" in *The Library of the Fathers.* Oxford & London: J. Henry and J. Parker; Rivington.

1840 *How are the Mighty Fallen.* Sermon. Exeter: P. A. Hannaford; also London: Rivingtons and Longmans; and Oxford: Parker.

A report, containing information obtained during a tour made by the Rev. G. Martin and the Rev. J. Medley, at the desire of the Exeter Diocesan Board of Education. Exeter: W. C. Pollard, 1840.

1841 *Elementary Remarks on Church Architecture.* Exeter: P. A. Hannaford; sold by London: Rivingtons, London; Parker, Oxford, and Stevenson, Oxford.

I believe in the Communion of Saints. Sermon. P. A. Hannaford: Exeter, 1841.

1843 *The Advantage of Open Seats.* Oxford: I. Shrimpton.

The Harvest Field of the World. Sermon. Exeter, 1843.

1845 *Sermons Published at the Request of Mann of his Late Parishioners, 2nd ed.* London: Francis & John Rivington, Exeter: P. A. Hannaford.

1846 *Notes of a Visitation Tour through Parts of the Diocese of Fredericton.* London:SPG.

Two Ordination Sermons preached in Christ Church Cathedral by the Lord Bishop of Fredericton. Fredericton N.B.: J. Simpson.

1847 *The Reformation, its Nature, its Necessity and its Benefits.* Sermon. Fredericton: James P. A. Phillips.

The Staff of Beauty and the Staff of Bands. Sermon. Saint John: W. L. Avery.

A Charge delivered at his primary Visitation held in Christ Church Cathedral, Fredericton, August 24th 1847 by John, Bishop of Fredericton. Fredericton: John Simpson.

1848 *A Statement Respecting the Condition and Wants of his Diocese by the Bishop of Fredericton.* London: J. Masters, 1848.

1850 *A Charge Delivered in the Cathedral of Christ-Church Fredericton to the Clergy of the Diocese Assembled at the Second Triennial Visitation of John, Bishop of Fredericton.* Saint John, N.B.: W. L. Avery.

1851 *Two Discourses Preached in the Church of the Advent, Boston on Sunday, October 19, 1851.* Boston: Charles Stimpson, 1851.

1853 *A Charge to the Clergy of the Diocese, by John Bishop of Fredericton, at his Third Triennial Visitation holden in Christ Church Cathedral, Fredericton.* Fredericton N.B.: J. Simpson 1853.

The Sermon at the Consecration of Thomas Frederick Davis, D.D., and Thomas Atkinson, D.D., to the Episcopate, preached by Appointment in St. John's Chapel, New York, Published by Request of the House of Bishops. New York: Church Depository, Daniel Dana Jr.

1854 *The Canticles Arranged for Chanting, with a Preface.* New Brunswick: J. Simpson.

1855 *Hymns for Public Worship.* Saint John: J. & A. McMillan.

1856 *"Faint, yet Pursuing." An ordination Sermon Preached in the Cathedral of Christ Church, Fredericton, on the Second Sunday in Lent, 1856.* Fredericton: J. Simpson.

A Charge to the clergy of the diocese, by John, Bishop of Fredericton, at his fourth triennial visitation holden in Christ Church Cathedral, Fredericton, 1856. Fredericton: J. Simpson.

The House of God, The Christian's Home—A Sermon Preached at the Consecration of St. Michael's Chapel, Quebec on Tuesday, 18th September, 1856. Quebec: P. J. Lamoureux.

1857 *A Lecture Delivered by the Lord Bishop of Fredericton Before the Church of England Young Men's Society of the City of Saint John at the Hall of the Mechanics' Institute, on Friday Evening, 23rd January, 1857.* Saint John: J. & A. McMillan.

1859 *A charge delivered in the cathedral, Fredericton, on Thursday, September 1, 1859, to the clergy of the diocese, and published at their request.* Saint John: Barnes.

1860 *A Sermon Preached Before His Royal Highness the Prince of Wales on His Visit to Fredericton in Christ Church Cathedral, August 5th, 1860.* Fredericton: John Graham.

1862 *A charge delivered to the clergy assembled in the Cathedral Church, September 3, 1862 and respectfully dedicated to them, and to all the laity of the Church of England in the province of New Brunswick by the Right Rev. John, Bishop of Fredericton.* Saint John: The Dispatch.

1865 *A Charge delivered in Christ Church Cathedral, Fredericton, September 13th, 1865, at the Triennial Visitation by John, Bishop of Fredericton.* Saint John: Wm. M. Wright.

1866 *Address of the Lord Bishop of Fredericton, at a Meeting of Clergy and Lay delegates, Convened by the Unanimous Desire of the Clergy Present at the Late Visitation of this Diocese, and Held at St. John, July 5th, 1866*. n.p.

1867 *The mission of the Comforter, two sermons preached in the Cathedral of Christ Church, Fredericton, New Brunswick, on Whitsunday and Trinity Sunday, 1867 / by John, Bishop of Fredericton.* Fredericton: H. A. Cropley.

1868 *A Charge to the Clergy of the Diocese of Fredericton, Delivered at his eighth Triennial Visitation in the Church of St. Paul's Portland, Saint John, June 30th, 1868.* London: MacMillan and Co.

1871 *A Charge Delivered in Christ Church Cathedral, Fredericton, July 4th, 1871, at the Triennial Visitation by John, Bishop of Fredericton.* Fredericton: H. A. Cropley.

1874 *Charge Delivered by the Right Revd. John, Lord Bishop of Fredericton, at St. Paul's Church, Portland, on Tuesday, June 30th, 1874.* Saint John: Geo. A. Knodell.

1877 *A Sermon preached before the Provincial Synod of Canada in Christ Church Cathedral, Montreal by John, Bishop of Fredericton.* Montreal: Lovell Print. and Pub. Co.

A Charge Delivered to the Clergy of the Diocese of Fredericton, in the Cathedral, on Tuesday, July 3, 1877. Fredericton: H. A. Cropley.

A Sermon Preached in the Cathedral Church, Fredericton, and in St. John's Church, St. John, on the Occasion of the Late Calamitous Fire. Fredericton: H. A. Cropley.

The Book of Job, Translated from the Hebrew Text, with an Introduction, A Summary of Each Chapter, and Brief Notes in Explanation of Obscure Passages. St. John: J. & A. McMillan.

1878 *"Other Little Ships" A Sermon Preached by the Rt. Revd. The Lord Bishop of Fredericton in the Cathedral church of S. Peter, Exeter, on Tuesday, August 13th, 1878, being the Anniversary of the Society of Promoting Christian Knowledge and the Society for the Propagation of the Gospel in Foreign Parts.* London: SPG.

1880 *Charge to the Clergy of the Diocese of Fredericton Delivered at His Visitation held on June 30th, 1880, by John, Lord Bishop of Fredericton, and Metropolitan of Canada.* St. John: Daily News.

1883 *A Charge Delivered to the Clergy of the Diocese of Fredericton.* Saint John.

1886 *A Charge Delivered in Trinity Church, St. John, To the Clergy of the Diocese of Fredericton, by John, Bishop of Fredericton and Metropolitan of Canada, at His Triennial Visitation, St. Peter's Day, 1886.* Saint John: Ellis, Robertson & Co.

1887 *The Sermon Preached in St. Luke's Pro-Cathedral, Halifax, August 12th, 1887, Being the Centenary of the Founding of the Colonial Episcopate.* Halifax: W. Gossip & Son.

Other Primary Sources

The Diaries of John Ruskin. Selected and edited by Joan Evans and John Howard Whitehouss, 3 vols. Oxford: Clarendon Press, 1956–1959.

Life and Letters of Dean Church. London: Macmillan, 1894.

Tracts for the Times. By members of the University of Oxford. London: Rivingtons, 1833–1841.

Binney, Hibbert. *A Charge Delivered to the Clergy of the Diocese of Nova Scotia at the Vitiation Held in the Cathedral Church of St. Paul, Halifax, on the 11th Day of October, 1854.* Halifax: Wm. Gossip, 1854.

Cardwell, E. *A History of Conferences and Other Proceedings Connected with the Revision of the Book of Common Prayer.* Oxford: Oxford University Press, 1849.

Cockshut, A. O. J., ed. *Religious Controversies of the Nineteenth Century: Selected Documents.* London, Methuen, 1966.

Ewing, J. H. *Canada Home: Juliana Horatia Ewing's Fredericton Letters, 1867–1869.* Edited by Margaret Howard Blom, Thomas E. Blom. Vancouver: University of British Columbia, 1983.

Keble, J. *The Christian Year.* Oxford: James Parker, 1866.

Newman, J. H. *Apologia Pro Vita Sua.* New York: W. W. Norton, 1968.

Pusey, E. B. *The Responsibility of the Intellect in Matters of Faith.* Oxford: James Parker, 1873.

Pusey, E. B. *An Historical Enquiry into the Probable Causes of the Rationalist Character Lately Predominant in the Theology of Germany.* London: Rivingtons 1828.

Letters and Diaries of John Henry Newman. Vol. 5. Edited by Thomas Gornall. Oxford: Clarendon Press, 1981; vol. 7, edited by Gerard Tracey. Oxford: Clarendon Press, 1995.

Ruskin, J. *Diaries 1874–1889*. Selected and edited by Joan Evans and John Howard Whitehouse. Oxford: Clarendon Press, 1959.

Secondary Sources

Abrams, M. H. *Natural Supernaturalism: Tradition and Revolution in Romantic Literature.* New York: Norton, 1971.

Acworth, R. *The Philosophy of John Norris of Bemerton.* New York: Georg Olms, 1979.

Addison, A. *Romanticism and the Gothic Revival.* New York: Gordian Press, 1967.

Addleshaw, G. W. O. *The High Church Tradition*. London: Faber & Faber, 1941.

Anson, Peter. In *Fashions in Church Furnishings 1840–1940.* London: Studio Vista, 1965.

Armstrong, A. *The Church of England, the Methodists and Society, 1700–1850.* Aylesbury: Hazell Watson & Viney, 1973.

Avis, P. *Anglicanism and the Christian Church: Theological Resources in Historical Perspective*. Edinburgh: T & T. Clark, 1989.

Bainbridge, S. *Napoleon and English Romanticism.* Cambridge: Cambridge University Press, 1995.

Baker, William J. "Hurrell Froude and the Reformers." *Journal of Ecclesiastical History* 21, no. 3 (July 1970): 243–59.

———. *Beyond Port and Prejudice: Charles Lloyd of Oxford, 1784–1829.* Orono: University of Maine Press, 1981.

Battiscombe, G. *John Keble: A Study in Limitations.* Letchworth: Garden City, 1963.

Bebbington, D. *William Ewart Gladstone: Faith and Politics in Victorian Britain.* Grand Rapids: Eerdmans, 1993.

Beer, J. *Questioning Romanticism.* Baltimore: Johns Hopkins University Press, 1995.

Bell, D. G. "Charles Inglis and the Anglican Clergy of Loyalist Nova Scotia," *Nova Scotia Historical Review* 7, no. 1, 1987.

———. *Early Loyalist Saint John.* Fredericton: New Ireland Press, 1983.

Bell, P. M. H. *Disestablishment in Ireland and Wales.* London: SPCK, 1969.

Bentley, J. *Ritualism and Politics in Victorian Britain: The Attempt to Legislate for Belief.* Oxford: Oxford University Press, 1978.

Boggis, R. J. E., *A History of St. Augustine's College, Canterbury.* Canterbury: Cross & Jackman, 1907.

Bowen, D. *The Idea of the Victorian Church: A Study of the Church of England, 1833–1889.* Montreal: McGill University, 1968.

Bradley, I. *The Call to Seriousness: The Evangelical Impact on the Victorians.* London: Jonathan Cape, 1976.

Brent, R. *Liberal Anglican Politics: Whiggery, Religion, and Reform, 1830–1841.* Oxford: Clarendon Press, 1987.

Brigstocke. *A History of Trinity Church, Saint John, New Brunswick.* Saint John: J & A McMillan, 1892.

Brinton, C. C. *The Political Ideas of the English Romanticists.* New York: Russell & Russell, 1962.

Brooks, C. and J. Cox. "John Bacon Jr and the Medley Memorial." *Bulletin of the International Society for the Study of Church Monuments* 7 (1982): 129–33.

Brooks, M. W. *John Ruskin and Victorian Architecture.* New Brunswick: Rutgers University Press, 1987.

Brown, F. K. *Fathers of the Victorians: The Age of Wilberforce.* Cambridge: Cambridge University Press, 1961.

Brown, M. "Romanticism and Enlightenment." In *The Cambridge Companion to British Romanticism*, edited by Stuart Curran. Cambridge: Cambridge University Press, 1993.

Bull, W. P. *From Strachan to Owen: how the Church of England was planted and tended in British North America.* Toronto: George J. McLeod, 1938.

Burns, Arthur. *The Diocesan Revival in the Church of England c. 1800–1870.* Oxford: Clarendon Press, 1999.

Butler, P. *Gladstone, Church, State, and Tractarianism: A Study of his Religious Ideas and Attitudes, 1809–1859.* Oxford: Clarendon Press, 1982.

———, ed. *Pusey Rediscovered.* London: SPCK, 1983.

Carrington, P. *The Anglican Church in Canada.* Toronto: Collins, 1963.

Cashdollar, C. D. *The Transformation of Theology, 1830–1890: Positivism and Protestant Thought in Britain and America.* Princeton: Princeton University Press, 1989.

Chadwick, O. *The Spirit of the Oxford Movement.* Cambridge: Cambridge University Press, 1995.

———. *The Victorian Church.* 2 vols. London: A & C Black; part 1, 3rd ed., 1971; part 2, 2nd ed., 1972.

Chapman, R. *The Victorian Debate: English Literature and Society 1832–1901.* London: Weidenfeld and Nicolson, 1968.

Cherry, M. "Patronage, the Anglican Church and the Local Architect in Victorian England." In *The Victorian Church: Architecture and Society*, edited by Chris Brooks and Andrew Saint. Manchester: Manchester University Press, 1995.

Clapson, Clive. "John Travers Lewis: An Irish High Churchman in Canada West." *JCCHS* 22 (October 1980): 17–31.

Clarke, C. P. S. *The Oxford Movement and After.* London: Mowbray & Co. 1932.

Clarke, J. C. D. *English Society, 1688–1832: Ideology, Social Structure, and Political Practice During the Ancien Regime.* Cambridge: Cambridge University Press, 1985.

———. *The Language of Liberty, 1660–1832: Political Discourse and Social Dynamics in the Anglo-American World.* Cambridge: Cambridge University Press, 1994.

Coleman, B. *The Church of England in the Mid-nineteenth Century: A Social Geography.* London: The Historical Association, 1980.

Coleridge, J. T. *A Memoir of the Rev. John Keble, M.A.* London: James Parker, 1874.

Cook, D. F. "A Survey of Hymnody in the Church of England in Eastern Canada to 1909." *JCCHS* 8 (September 1965): 36–61.

Coombs, J. *George Anthony Denison, The Firebrand.* London: The Church Literature Association, 1984

Cooper, T. G. "Church Music in Nineteenth Century Canada as Represented by the Choral Compositions of John Medley." Ph.D. diss. University of Georgia, 1989.

Cornish, F. W. *The English Church in the Nineteenth Century.* London: Macmillan, 1910.

Cowling, M. *Religion and Public Doctrine in Modern England.* 2 vols. Cambridge: Cambridge University Press, 1980.

Crouse, R. D. "Christology from Chalcedon to Anselm." In *Who do you say that I am: The Person and Mission of Jesus Christ.* Charlottetown: St. Peter Publications, 1998.

———. "'Deepened by the Study of the Fathers.'" *Dionysius* 7 (December 1983), pp. 137–48.

———. "'Devout Perusal': The Tractarian Revival of Patristic Studies." In *Studia Patristica* 18, edited by E. A. Livingstone, 328–34. (Kalamazoo: 1990), pp. 328–334.

Crowther, M. A. *Church Embattled: Religious Controversy in Mid-Victorian England.* Plymouth: Latimer, 1970.

Crumb, L. N. *The Oxford Movement and its Leaders: A Bibliography of Secondary and Lesser Primary Sources.* Metuchen, N.J.: Scarecrow, 1988.

Curran, S. *The Cambridge Companion to British Romanticism.* Cambridge: Cambridge University Press, 1989.

Daniel, S. H. *John Toland: His Method, Manners and Mind.* Kingston: McGill-Queen's University Press, 1984.

Davies, G. C. B. *Henry Phillpotts, Bishop if Exeter, 1778–1869.* London: SPCK, 1954.

Diffey, T. "The Roots of Imagination: the Philosophical Context." In *The Romantics*, edited by Stephen Prickett. London: Methuen, 1981.

Doll, Peter. "Imperial Anglicanism in North America, 1745–1795." D.Phil. thesis, University of Oxford, 1989.

———. *Revolution, Religion, and National Identity: Imperial Anglicanism in British North America, 1745–1795.* Madison, N.J.: Fairleigh Dickinson University Press, 2000.

Eaves, Morris, "The Sister Arts in British Romanticism." In *The Cambridge Companion to British Romanticism*, edited by Stuart Curran. Cambridge: Cambridge University Press, 1993.

Edgecombe, R. S. *Two Poets of the Oxford Movement: John Keble and John Henry Newman.* Madison, N.J.: Fairleigh Dickinson University Press, 1996.

Edwards, D. L. *Leaders of the Church of England, 1828–1944.* New York: Oxford University Press, 1971.

Ellsworth, L. E. *Charles Lowder and the Ritualist Movement.* London: Darton, Longman and Todd, 1982.

Fairweather, E. R. "John Medley as Defender of 'Ritualism': An Unpublished Correspondence." *Canadian Journal of Theology* 8, no. 3 (1962): 208–11.

———. "John Medley on Irish Church Disestablishment: An Unpublished Letter." *Canadian Journal of Theology* 7, no. 3 (1961): 198–200.

———. *The Oxford Movement.* Oxford: Oxford University Press, 1964.

———. "A Tractarian Patriarch: John Medley of Fredericton." *Canadian Journal of Theology* 6, no. 1 (1960).

Fahey, C. *In His Name: the Anglican Experience in Upper Canada, 1791–1854.* Ottawa: Carleton University, 1991.

Faught, C. Brad. *The Oxford Movement: A Thematic History of the Tractarians and their Times.* University Park: Pennsylvania State University Press, 2003.

Fingard, J. *The Anglican Design in Loyalist Nova Scotia, 1783–1816.* London: SPCK, 1972.

———. "New Brunswick's Gothic Revival: John Medley and the Aesthetics of Anglican Worship." Ph.D. diss. University of New Brunswick, 1989.

———. "The Gothic Revival and the Victorian Church in New Brunswick." *Material History Review* 32 (Fall 1990): 1–16.

———. "'Habits of Reverence and Awe': Bishop John Medley and the Promise of Ecclesiology." *JCCHS* 35 (April 1993): 3–22.

———. "Stained Glass and Stone Tracery: The Gothic Revival and the Shaping of Canadian Sensibilities." *British Journal of Canadian Studies* 5 (1990): 78–98.

Finley, G. and L. Wigginton. *On Earth as it is in Heaven: Gothic Revival Churches of New Brunswick.* Fredericton: Goose Lane, 1995.

Flint, D. *John Strachan: Pastor and Politician.* Toronto: Oxford University Press, 1971.

Forrester, D. *Young Doctor Pusey.* London: Mowbray, 1989.

Frappell, L. "'Science' in the Service of Orthodoxy: The Early Intellectual Development of E. B. Pusey." In *Pusey Rediscovered*, edited by Perry Butler. London: SPCK, 1983.

Galperin, W. H. *The Return of the Visible in British Romanticism.* Baltimore: Johns Hopkins University Press, 1993.

Garrigan, K. O. *Ruskin on Architecture: His Thought and Influence.* Madison: University of Wisconsin Press, 1973.

Geck, A. "The Concept of History in E. B. Pusey's First Enquiry into German Theology and its German Background." *Journal of Theological Studies* 38, no. 2, (1987): 387–408.

Gilley, S. "The Church of England in the Nineteenth Century." In *A History of*

Religion in Britain: Practice and Belief for the Pre-Roman Times to the Present, edited by Sheridan Gilley and W. J. Sheils, 211–33. Oxford: Blackwell, 1994.

———. "The Ecclesiology of the Oxford Movement: A Reconsideration." In *Newman From Oxford to the People*, edited by Paul Vaiss, 60–75. Leominster: Gracewing, 1996.

———. "John Keble and the Victorian Churching of Romanticism." In *An Infinite Complexity: Essays in Romanticism*, edited by J. R. Watson. Edinburgh: Edinburgh University Press, 1983.

———. *Newman and his Age.* London: Darton, Longman and Todd, 1990.

Gilmour, R. *The Victorian Period: The Intellectual and Cultural Context, 1830–1890.* London: Longman, 1993.

Gleckner, R. F. *Romanticism: Points of View.* Englewood Cliffs: Prentice Hall, 1962.

Goslee, D. *Romanticism and the Anglican Newman.* Athens: Ohio University Press, 1996.

Goodenough, S. *The Country Parson.* North Pomfret: David & Charles, 1983.

Griffin, J. R. *The Oxford Movement: A Revision.* Edinburgh: Pentland Press, 1984.

Guy, J. *The Heretic: A Study of the Life of John William Colenso, 1814–1883.* Johannesburg: Ravan Press, 1983.

Haig A. *The Victorian Clergy.* Beckenham: Croomhelm, 1984.

Hammond, P. C. *The Parson and the Victorian Parish.* London: Hodder & Stoughton, 1977.

Hankey, W. J. "Making Theology Practical: Thomas Aquinas and the Nineteenth Century Religious Revival." *Dionysius* 9 (December 1985): 83–126.

———. "The Way Forward in Theology" *150th Anniversary of the Oxford Movement: The Way Forward.* Charlottetown: St. Peter's Publications, 1983.

Härdelin, A. "The Sacraments in the Tractarian Spiritual Universe." In *Tradition Renewed*, edited by Geoffrey Rowell. Allison Park: Pickwick Publications, 1986.

———. *The Tractarian Understanding of the Eucharist.* Uppsala, 1965.

Harding, L. N. *Citizens with the Saints: A Brief History of Anglicanism in New Brunswick.* Fredericton: The Diocesan Synod of Fredericton, 1994.

———. "John, by Divine Permission." *Journal of the Canadian Church Historical Society* 8, no. 4 (December 1966).

Headon, C. N. "Developments in Canadian Anglican Worship in Eastern and Central Canada 1840–1868." *JCCHS* 17, no. 2, (June 1975): 26–36.

———. "The Influence of the Oxford Movement Upon the Church of England in Eastern and Central Canada, 1840–1900." Ph.D. diss., McGill University 1974.

———. "An Unpublished Correspondence between John Medley and E. B. Pusey," *JCCHS* 16, no. 4, (December 1974: 72–74.

Hebb, R. N. *The Church of England in Loyalist New Brunswick, 1783–1825.* Madison, N.J.: Fairleigh Dickinson University Press, 2004.

———. *The Establishment of Synodical Government in Maritime Canada: 1850–1871.* Unpublished paper delivered at the Church History Conference of the Ecclesiastical Province of Canada, Halifax, July 8, 1993.

Hedley, D. "Participation in the Divine Life: Coleridge, the vision of God and the thought of John Henry Newman." In *Newman, From Oxford to the People*, edited by Paul Vaiss, 238–51. Leominster: Gracewing, 1996.

Henderson, J. L. H. *John Strachan: Documents and Opinions*. Toronto: Maclelland and Stewart, 1969.

Hennell, M. *Sons of the Prophets: Evangelical Leaders of the Victorian Church*. London: SPCK, 1979.

Hicks, Bentley. "Synodical Government within Canadian Anglicanism: Retrospective Implications." *JCCHS* 33 (October 1991): 123–40.

Hinchliff, P. *John William Colenso: Bishop of Natal*. London: Nelson, 1964.

House, E. *Edward Feild: The Man and his Legacy*. St. John's: Jesperson Printing, 1987.

Hoyles, J. *The Waning of the Renaissance 1640–1740: Studies in the Thought and Poetry of Henry More, John Norris and Isaac Watts*. The Hague: Nijhoff, 1971.

Hylson-Smith, K. *Evangelicals in the Church of England, 1734–1984*. Edinburgh: T & T Clark, 1988.

———. *High Churchmanship in the Church of England*. Edinburgh: T & T Clark, 1993.

Imberg, R. *In Quest of Authority: The Tracts for the Times and the Development of the Tractarian Leaders 1833–1841*. Lund: Lund University Press, 1987.

Jacob, W. M. *The Making of the Anglican Church Worldwide*. London: SPCK, 1997.

Jagger, P., ed. *Gladstone*. London: The Hambledon Press, 1998.

Jasper D., and T. R. Wright. *The Critical Spirit and the Will to Believe: Essays in Nineteenth-century Literature and Religion*. Basingstoke: Macmillan, 1989.

Jones, F. "Bishop Feild: A Study in Politics and Religion in Nineteenth Century Newfoundland." D.Phil Thesis, University of Cambridge, 1971.

———. "The Early Opposition to Bishop Feild of Newfoundland." *JCCHS* 16 (June 1974): 30–40.

———. *Edward Feild, Bishop of Newfoundland, 1844–1876*. St. John's: Newfoundland Historical Society, 1976.

———. "The Making of a Colonial Bishop: Feild of Newfoundland." *JCCHS* 15 (March 1973): 2–12.

Jupp, R. "'Nurseries of a learned clergy': Pusey and the Defence of Cathedrals." In *Pusey Rediscovered*, edited by Perry Butler. London: SPCK, 1983.

Kent, G. "The Right Reverend Hibbert Binney, Colonial Tractarian Bishop of Nova Scotia 1851–1887." M.A. thesis, University of New Brunswick, 1969.

Ketchum, W. Q. *The Life and Work of the Most Reverend John Medley*, D.D. Saint John: McMillan, 1893.

Knight, F. "The Influence of the Oxford Movement in the Parishes: A Reassessment." In *Newman From Oxford to the People*, eidted by Paul Vaiss, 127–40. Leominster: Gracewing, 1996.

———. *The Nineteenth-Century Church and English Society*. Cambridge: Cambridge University Press, 1995.

Knox, R. B. *James Ussher, Archbishop of Armagh*. Cardiff: University of Wales Press, 1967.

Kroll R., et al. *Philosophy, Science, and Religion in England, 1640–1700*. Cambridge: Cambridge University Press, 1992.

Latourette, K. S. *The Nineteenth Century in Europe: The Protestant and Eastern Churches*. Grand Rapids: Zondervan, 1959.

Lear, E. J. "Edward Feild (1801–1876) Ecclesiastic and Educator: His Influence on the Development of Denominational Education in Newfoundland." M.Ed. thesis, Bishop's University, 1986.

Lee, G. H. *An Historical Sketch of the First Fifty Years of the Church of England in the Province of New Brunswick.* Saint John: Sun, 1880.

Liddon, H. P. *Life of Edward Bouverie Pusey.* 4 vols. London: Longmans, 1893.

Low, L. and A. Harding. *Milton, the Metaphysicals, and Romanticism.* Cambridge: Cambridge University Press, 1994.

Machin, G. I. T. *Politics and the Churches in Great Britain, 1832–1868.* Oxford: Clarendon Press, 1977.

MacNutt, W. S. *New Brunswick: A History 1784–1867.* Toronto: Macmillan, 1963.

Marsh, P. T. *The Victorian Church in Decline: Archbishop Tait and the Church of England, 1868–1882.* Pittsburgh: University of Pittsburgh Press, 1969.

Matthew, H. C. G. *Gladstone, 1875–1898.* Oxford: Clarendon Press, 1995.

McClelland, V. A. "Gladstone and Manning: a Question of Authority." In *Gladstone, Politics and Religion*, edited by Peter J. Jagger. London: Macmillan, 1985.

Meacham, S. *Lord Bishop: The life of Samuel Wilberforce, 1805–1873.* Cambridge: Harvard University Press, 1970.

Mills, F. V. *Bishops by Ballot: an Eighteenth Century Ecclesiastical Revolution.* New York: Oxford University Press, 1978.

———. "The Colonial Anglican Episcopate: A Historiographical Review." *Anglican and Episcopal History* 61 (September 1992): 325–46.

Millman, T. R. "Beginnings of the Synodical Movement in Colonial Anglican Churches with special reference to Canada." *JCCHS* 21 (1979): 3–19.

———. *Jacob Mountain, First Lord Bishop of Quebec, a Study in Church and State, 1793–1825.* Toronto: University of Toronto Press, 1947.

———. "A Sketch of the Life of Francis Fulford." *JCCHS* 17 (December 1975): 82–93.

Millman, T. R. and R. Kelley. *Atlantic Canada to 1900: A History of the Anglican Church.* Toronto: Anglican Book Centre, 1983.

Mockridge, C. H. *The Bishops of the Church of England in Canada and Newfoundland.* Toronto: Brown, 1896.

Morley, J. *The Life of William Ewart Gladstone.* 3 vols. Toronto: George N. Morang, 1903.

Mossner, E. C. *Bishop Butler and the Age of Reason: A Study in the History of Thought.* New York, Macmillan, 1936.

Mountain A. W. *A Memoir of George Jehoshaphat Mountain, D.D., D.C.L., late Bishop of Quebec.* Montreal: J. Lovell; London: S. Low, Son & Marston, 1866.

Mozley, T. *Reminiscences: Chiefly of Oriel College and the Oxford Movement.* London: Longmans, Green, 1882.

Newsome, D. *The Parting of Friends: A Study of the Wilberforces and Henry Manning.* London: John Murray, 1966.

———. *Two Classes of Men; Platonism and English Romantic Thought.* London: John Murray, 1974.

Nias, J. C. S. *Gorham and the Bishop of Exeter.* London: SPCK, 1951.

Nockles, P., "Church and King: Tractarian Politics Reappraised." In *Newman From Oxford to the People.* Leominster: Gracewing, 1996, pp. 93–126.

———. *The Oxford Movement in Context.* Cambridge: Cambridge University Press, 1994.

———. "Pusey and the Question of Church and State." In *Pusey Rediscovered*, edited by Perry Butler. London: SPCK, 1983.

O'Donnell, G. "The Spirituality of E. B. Pusey." In *Pusey Rediscovered*, edited by Perry Butler, 231–54. London: SPCK, 1983.

Osmond, O. R. "The Churchmanship of John Strachan." *JCCHS* 16 (September 1974): 46–59.

Overton, J. H. *The Anglican Revival.* London: Blackie & Son, 1897.

Parsons, Gerald. "Rethinking the Missionary Position: Bishop Colenso of Natal." In *Religion in Victorian Britain, Vol. 5 Culture & Empire*, edited by John Wolffe. Manchester: Manchester University Press, 1997.

Potter, J. L. "The Episcopate of Hollingworth Tully Kingdon, Second Lord Bishop of Fredericton." M.A. thesis, University of New Brunswick, 1970.

Prickett, S. *England and the French Revolution.* Houndmills: Macmillan, 1989.

———. *Romanticism and Religion: The Tradition of Coleridge and Wordsworth in the Victorian Church.* Cambridge: Cambridge University Press, 1976.

———. *The Romantics.* London: Methuen, 1981.

Purdy, J. D. "The Church of England in New Brunswick During the Colonial Era 1783–1860." M.A. thesis, University of New Brunswick, 1954.

Raymond. W. O. "John Medley." In *Leaders of the Canadian Church*, edited by Bertal Heeney. Toronto: Musson, 1918.

Reardon, B. M. G. *From Coleridge to Gore: A Century of Religious Thought in Britain.* London: Longman, 1971.

———. *Religious Thought in the Nineteenth Century.* Cambridge: Cambridge University Press, 1966.

Reed, J. S. *Glorious Battle: the Cultural Politics of Victorian Anglo-Catholicism.* Nashville: Vanderbilt University Press, 1996.

Richardson, D. S. "Christ Church Cathedral, Fredericton, New Brunswick." M.A. thesis, Yale University, 1966.

Rivers, I. *Reason, Grace, and Sentiment: a Study of the Language of Religion and Ethics in England, 1660–1780.* Cambridge: Cambridge University Press, 1991.

Roberts, M. "Coleridge as a Background to the Oxford Movement." In *Pusey Rediscovered*, edited by Perry Butler. London: SPCK, 1983.

Roper, H. "The Anglican Episcopate in Canada: An Historical Perspective." *Anglican and Episcopal History* 57 (September 1988): 255–71.

Ross, M. *The Impossible Sum of our Traditions: Reflections on Canadian Literature.* Toronto: McClelland & Stewart, 1986.

Rowell, G. " 'Church Principles' and 'Protestant Kempism,' Some Theological forerunners of the Tractarians." In *Newman From Oxford to the People*, edited by Paul Vaiss. Leominster: Gracewing, 1996.

———., ed. *Tradition Renewed.* Allison Park: Pickwick Publications, 1986.

———.*The Vision Glorious: Themes and Personalities of the Catholic Revival in Anglicanism.* Oxford: Oxford University Press, 1983.

Rowlands, J. H. L. *Church State and Society: The Attitudes of John Keble, Richard Hurrell Froude and John Henry Newman 1827–1845.* Worthing: Churchman Publishing, 1989.

See, Scott W. *Riots in New Brunswick: Orange Nativism and Social Violence in the 1840's.* Toronto: University of Toronto Press, 1993.

Shearman, H. *How the Church of Ireland was Disestablished.* The Church of Ireland Disestablishment Centenary Committee, 1970.

Soloway, R. A. *Prelates and People: Ecclesiastical Social Thought in England, 1783–1852.* London: Routledge and Kegan Paul, 1969.

Spray, W. *David's Kingdom: A History of the Anglican Church in the Parish of Chatham, New Brunswick.* Chatham: St. Paul's Church Corporation, 1979.

Stanton, P. *The Gothic Revival & American Church Architecture: An Episode in Taste, 1840–1856.* Baltimore: Johns Hopkins University Press, 1968.

Stephenson, A. M. G.,*The First Lambeth Conference, 1867.* London: SPCK, 1967.

Strong, R. *Alexander Forbes of Brechin: The First Tractarian Bishop.* Oxford: Clarendon Press, 1995.

Sullivan, R. E. *John Toland and the Deist Controversy: A Study in Adaptations.* Cambridge: Harvard University Press, 1982.

Sykes, S. W. *The Integrity of Anglicanism.* New York: Seabury Press, 1978.

Taylor, F. *The Last Three Bishops Appointed by the Crown for the Anglican Church in Canada.* Montreal: J. Lovell, 1870.

Teale, R. "Dr. Pusey and the Church Overseas." In *Pusey Rediscovered*, edited by Perry Butler. London: SPCK, 1983.

Thompson, P. *William Butterfield.* London: Routledge and Kegan Paul, 1971.

Toner, P. M. *New Ireland Remembered: Historical Essays on the Irish in New Brunswick.* 2nd ed. Fredericton: New Ireland Press, 1989.

Toon, P. *Evangelical Theology, 1833–1856: A Response to Tractarianism.* Atlanta: John Know Press, 1979.

Trench, M. *Charles Lowder: A Biography.* London: Kegan Paul, Trench & Co., 1881.

Tucker, H. W. *Memoir of the Life and Episcopate of Edward Feild, D.D., Bishop of Newfoundland, 1844–1876.* London: W.W. Gardner, 1879.

Vaiss, P. *Newman From Oxford to the People.* Leominster: Gracewing, 1996.

Warre-Cornish, F. *The English Church: The Nineteenth Century*. Vol. 8, part 1. New York: A. M. S. Press, 1910.

Watson, J. R. *An Infinite Complexity: Essays in Romanticism.* Edinburgh: Edinburgh University Press, 1983.

Watson, R. *Christ Church Cathedral: A History.* Fredericton: The Bishop & Chapter of Christ Church Cathedral, 1984.

———. *Christ Church (Parish) Church, Fredericton: A History.* Fredericton: 1984.

Wheeler, M. "Gladstone and Ruskin." In *Gladstone*, edited Peter J. Jagger. London: The Hambledon Press, 1998.

White, J. F. *The Cambridge Movement: The Ecclesiologists and the Gothic Revival.* Cambridge: Cambridge University Press, 1962.

Wolffe, J. *The Protestant Crusade in Great Britain, 1829–1860.* Oxford: Clarendon Press, 1981.

———. *Religion in Victorian Britain, Vol. V, Culture and Empire.* Manchester: Manchester University Press, 1997.

Woolverton, J. F. *Colonial Anglicanism in North America.* Detroit: Wayne State University Press, 1984.

Wright, E. C. *The Loyalists of New Brunswick.* Fredericton: 1955.

Yates, N. *Anglican Ritualism in Victorian Britain 1830–1910.* Oxford: Oxford University Press, 1999.

———. *Buildings, Faith and Worship: The Liturgical Arrangement of Anglican Churches 1600–1900.* Oxford: Clarendon Press, 1991.

———. *The Oxford Movement and Anglican Ritualism.* London: The Historical Association, 1983.

Index